LENSEN

The Russo-Chinese War

OTHER BOOKS BY GEORGE ALEXANDER LENSEN

Report from Hokkaido:
The Remains of Russian Culture in Northern Japan

Russia's Japan Expedition of 1852 to 1855

The Meaning of Yalta:
Big Three Diplomacy and the New Balance of Power
WITH JOHN L. SNELL (ED.), CHARLES F. DELZELL,
AND FORREST C. POGUE

The Russian Push Toward Japan;
Russo-Japanese Relations, 1697–1875

The World Beyond Europe:
An Introduction to the History of Africa, India,
Southeast Asia, and the Far East

Russia's Eastward Expansion (edited)

Revelations of a Russian Diplomat: the Memoirs of
Dmitrii I. Abrikossow (edited)

Korea and Manchuria Between Russia and Japan 1895–1904:
The Observations of Sir Ernest Satow, British Minister
to Japan (1895–1900) and China (1900–1906) (edited)

The Soviet Union: An Introduction

The d'Anethan Dispatches from Japan, 1894–1910
The Observations of Baron Albert d'Anethan, Belgian
Minister Plenipotentiary and Dean of the Diplomatic Corps
(translated and edited)

THE
RUSSO-CHINESE
WAR

by George Alexander Lensen

SOPHIA UNIVERSITY·TOKYO
IN COOPERATION WITH
THE DIPLOMATIC PRESS
TALLAHASSEE·FLORIDA

PUBLISHED BY

SOPHIA UNIVERSITY

7, KIOI-CHŌ, CHIYODA-KU, TOKYO

IN COOPERATION WITH

THE DIPLOMATIC PRESS, INCORPORATED

2305 AMELIA CIRCLE, TALLAHASSEE, FLORIDA

Library of Congress Catalog Card No. 67–26314

To

Professor L. CARRINGTON GOODRICH

for whom I wrote
my first paper on Russo-Chinese relations
twenty years ago

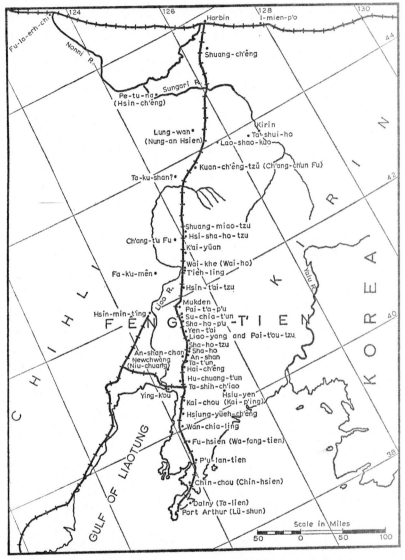

THE SOUTH MANCHURIAN RAILWAY
Compiled by George A. Lensen; drawn by Bonnie Paige.

Contents

Russia is China's nearest neighbor
And thus her nearest foe as well. . . .
Long are the borders, and the neighbor
As numerous as the flocks of birds
That fly abroad in spring. . . .
If Europe halts its war with China
Russia will be left to hold the field. . . .
Surrounded on all sides,
She could burn on the flanks
And burn in the rear
Until completely consumed by fire.

—From the long narrative verse
*Voina Kitaia s khristianskimi narodami
1900 goda* (The war of China with the
Christian peoples of 1900) by F. B.

Prologue

IN JUNE OF 1900, the eyes of the world were focussed on Peking. Foreign diplomats and residents were besieged in the capital city by fanatic insurgents and imperial troops. Throughout China native Christians and Western missionaries were being put to the sword, while here and there pockets of survivors struggled against overwhelming odds.

The Boxer uprising, as the great upheaval is known in history, the siege of Peking, and the subsequent liberation of the diplomats have been the subject of many a book and of at least one Hollywood technicolor spectacular. In the preoccupation with China proper, however, sight has been lost of events in Manchuria. The Russo-Chinese War which developed here is virtually unknown in the West, although it forms a standard subject heading in Soviet card catalogues.

The causes of the rebellion in China and of its successful deflection by the Manchu Government from itself against the foreigners were manifold. Yet they were dominated by one factor: mounting hatred of the "ocean devils" who had come to China's shores and for two generations had ridden roughshod over Chinese rights and feelings.

More than once I had to look into the eyes of death and many times had to relive and reconsider the

1

meaning of all the events that had preceded the outbreak of the anti-European movement [V. V. Korsakov, a Russian survivor of the Peking ordeal, recalled]. My conclusion was always the same: European Christian civilization had brought into the midst of the Chinese people, who though heathen had a culture of their own, such hypocrisy and falsehood, that the Europeans could not have expected any outcome other than hatred and mistrust on the part of all who loved their native land. The manifestation of this general hatred was merely a question of time and circumstance.

Having lived for more than five years in Peking and having seen everything there is to see, I shall say only one thing: never in my life have I come across persons who were so heartless and wooden in feeling and thought as those [Westerners] whom I met in Peking.

Should one be surprised after this that not only the most peaceloving man, if he be constantly oppressed and unjustly wronged, can reach [a stage of] wrath, but that also a people, driven to desperation, will rise against their oppressors?

A number of secret societies agitated against the foreigners. The Society of Harmonious Fists, popularly known as the Boxers, was most notorious. Its anti-Christian propaganda was a clever mixture of truth and vilification. Its appeal was enhanced through magic formulas and acrobatic exercises, which allegedly bullet-proofed its adherents. Not taken seriously at first by many Chinese officials, the Boxer movement gained momentum until it could no longer be stopped on the local level. When the Imperial Court issued orders to the

Tartar Generals to support the Boxers, hostilities between China and the West began in earnest.

Russia made common cause with the Western Powers and Japan in liberating the foreigners who were besieged in Peking, Tientsin, and elsewhere. Indeed, in view of her proximity to China and because of the large garrison which she had on hand in Port Arthur, she was able to rush more troops to the scene than any Western Power. Yet she refrained from seeking supreme command of the allied forces and shortly after the capture of Peking withdrew her men from China proper.

Russia felt that the Boxer movement had not been directed against her. Officially she regarded it as an internal uprising against the throne, and intervened to save the Manchu Dynasty from revolution. Privately she believed that the conflict had been the result of Western economic and missionary penetration of China, something in which few of her subjects were involved. In fact, Russian bureaucrats and military men were hostile to capitalists and regarded Western missionaries as "spiritual businessmen, who come to play the role of wolves in sheep's clothing." Unlike the other Westerners, whom the Chinese called "ocean devils," the Russians had not come from across the seas. They were direct neighbors of the Chinese and valued the special relationship which had existed between their countries for centuries. But while Russia acted with greater restraint than the other European Powers in Peking and spoke of Russo-Chinese friendship, believed in Russo-Chinese friendship and tried to further Russo-Chinese friendship, her withdrawal from China proper went hand in glove with a deepening commitment in the Three Eastern Provinces, as the Chinese called Manchuria.

Russian encroachment on Chinese territory was not unique. France, England and Germany had carved out spheres of influence in the south, center, and north of China respectively. Her justification in terms of national need appeared greater from a Russian point of view. She shared with China the longest frontier in the world. Siberia was underpopulated and exposed to Chinese infiltration. The creation of buffer zones in Manchuria and Mongolia would lay to rest the specter of a "Yellow Siberia." Furthermore, Manchuria jutted into the path of Russian communication.

The Trans-Siberian railway, construction of which was begun in 1891 for strategic and economic reasons, was to form an iron link between Europe and Asia. The world's longest railroad, it originally was to wind along the Amur River up to Khabarovsk, and thence run southward to Vladivostok. But the terrain proved so difficult and the route so circuitous, that a shortcut through Manchuria suggested itself. In 1896, Russia obtained the necessary concession from China, and in 1897 began construction from a station on the Transbaikal section of the Siberian railway. The following year Russia acquired a lease on Port Arthur and Talienwan (Dalny) at the southern tip of the Liaotung Peninsula in south Manchuria, and began building a connecting branch to the main line of the Manchurian railway. With construction proceeding from both ends simultaneously at a pace of 1¾ miles per day, Vladivostok and Port Arthur were to be joined by rail by the end of July, 1900. Before long the Trans-Siberian railway with its Manchurian extension, the Chinese Eastern Railway, would bridge the land mass from the Baltic Sea to the Pacific Ocean and give Russia the iron sinews of world power.

The line through Manchuria was laid ostensibly by a private corporation, the Chinese Eastern Railway Company. The controlling interest was Russian, and the sums invested by the Imperial Government in this enormous enterprise were staggering, but the government remained in the background and special military forces, recruited by the Company, rather than regular army units guarded Russian property and lives in the foreign land. The engineers and skilled workers were Russian, but the bulk of the labor force consisted of Chinese coolies, almost 100,000 of them. The project was Russian, but its execution depended on Chinese collaboration. The withdrawal of Chinese laborers, not to mention sabotage and destruction of the long line in the vast strange region, could disrupt Russian plans at any time and reduce the sinews of power to tapes of paper. This is what happened for a while in the long, hot summer of 1900.

The conflict which ensued in Manchuria differed basically from the struggle in China proper. The Boxer movement spread only gradually into the Three Eastern Provinces. When it did, it was not so much a popular uprising as an anti-Russian effort, instigated by outside agitators. Regular Chinese armies played a more important role in hostilities in Manchuria than in China proper. Not only were two thirds of the Manchurian railway destroyed and scattered, Russian colonies of railway employees and their families and railway guards attacked, but Blagoveshchensk, a city on the Russian side of the Amur, was bombarded and the invasion of Russia by Chinese forces seemed imminent. When Russian armies poured into Manchuria, a brief but regular war between Russia and China developed. This is the story of the Russo-Chinese War.[1]

---

[1]The diplomatic negotiations between Russia, China, and the other powers concerning the evacuation of Manchuria, which have been described repeatedly, were an aftermath of the Russo-Chinese War and do not form part of this book. Nor are Russian operations with the allied powers in China proper, also covered elsewhere, included. Please turn to the Bibliography for acknowledgements and some comments on the method of transliteration and the sources used. In 1900, China was still under the Manchu Dynasty. Western observers generally made no distinction between "Chinese" and "Manchu" and the terms are here used interchangeably.

The Ordeal at Liao-yang

KONSTANTIN KUSHAKOV was troubled. A captain of the railway guard, he had been in South Manchuria now for two and a half years and was familiar with local conditions. The seemingly unprovoked shooting of a Russian captain and two Cossacks by Chinese soldiers in April 1900, and the posting of anonymous proclamations on the walls of temples and inns in the town of Hsiung-yüeh-ch'êng in mid-May, exhorting the populace to rise and exterminate the foreigners, had alerted him to the spread of the Boxer movement to Manchuria. He did not trust the assurances of the local Chinese commander that the placards were merely the work of "pranksters."

The call to arms had been followed by clandestine night gatherings outside the town walls, at which strange orators harrangued the crowd. One evening Kushakov, who had heard about the meetings from Chinese interpreters and servants in the Russian employ, chanced upon one himself. Two speakers towered over the Chinese audience. From afar Kushakov could notice that they wore yellow sashes and headbands and had their sleeves rolled up. As he drew nearer he saw also that their cheeks, lips and eyebrows were painted. One of them was doing gymnastic exercises with his arms while shouting furiously. He may have had hypnotic powers,

7

for bystanders said he could put people to sleep and waken them again at will. One of the Cossacks accompanying Kushakov remarked that these were definitely Boxers. When the interpreter conveyed this to the Chinese standing nearby, they protested that there were no Boxers in this part of the country and made no hostile move toward the Russians. Yet in the morning the same agitators were back and instructed the youth in gymnastics and the use of cold steel.

The merchants quickly sold out whatever arms they had in stock and blacksmiths were kept busy forging new knives, swords and spears. Sabotage became common. The Russian telegraph lines were cut repeatedly and attempts were made to derail trains by disconnecting the rails or by piling up ties on the tracks. The working relationship between Russians and Chinese was poisoned. Many interpreters and servants quit, fearful of remaining in the Russian service. Laborers were more inclined to continue, but those who remained no longer had the confidence of their masters. The "braided devils" were up to something, the Russians sensed. The supervisors and foremen who but recently had lashed the workers with tongue and knout no longer dared to do so, and walked along silently, armed to the teeth.

Yet Russian misgivings were not universal. Only railway agents of lower rank and common railway guards, who were in direct contact with the mass of Chinese inhabitants and workers, felt the change in attitude toward them. They noticed the sudden insubordination of Chinese laborers, frequent strikes, the rude conduct of the villagers and even of tradesmen, and the appearance of parties of soldiers where there had been none before. They had friends among the populace, and listened with mounting alarm to their warnings. But their superiors, to whom they reported their misgivings, were not impressed. They continued to regard the Chinese as a submissive and inoffensive people.

As the situation deteriorated, the need for more railway guards increased, but the territory involved was enormous and the number of men at hand, infinitesimal. Kushakov had only 240 men to guard a sector of about 172 miles. To strengthen one post would mean to weaken another. There was no way of predicting where trouble would break out next. Indeed, the waves of unrest could inundate all guard posts at once, the Russians being no more than a drop of restraint in a raging sea of discontent.

Military men sensed the danger and clamoured for reinforcements. But the civilians who directed the railway construction deeply mistrusted the military. They viewed them as an economic drain and even wanted to use the proud Cossacks and soldiers as common laborers. "Who do you think you are?" a bureaucrat had scolded a Cossack captain. "Indeed what is a cavalry captain and what is an engineer?" Kushakov later mused bitterly. "The former has already laid down his honest head in battle. . ., leaving his wife and children barely provided for, while the latter to this day successfully disburses over tens of millions, receives an enormous salary, makes liberal use of it, and in the future, of course, will be a capitalist." Some engineers felt that the presence of Russian troops irritated the populace and hired Chinese guards, who, however, lorded over their own countrymen worse than any foreigner.

Trusting the assurances of Chinese officials more than the warnings of their railway guards or their junior agents, the administrators met the crisis by arming their civilian employees and promising them financial compensation for property losses, even for their lives.

Troops were on hand in the Kwantung region on the southern tip of the Liaotung Peninsula, which had been leased to Russia by China in the spring of 1898. But the requests of Colonel Mishchenko, commander of the railway guards along the Port Arthur line, to Vice Admiral Evgenii Alekseev, commander-in-chief of the Russian land forces in the Kwantung region and the Russian naval forces in the Far East, to replace or bolster the weak railway guards with regular army troops, were undercut by a circular from Chief Engineer Iugovich, dated July 2, asserting that the Chinese were in complete agreement and peace with the Russians.

Earlier, on June 28, Finance Minister Sergei Witte had written to Minister of War Lieutenant General Aleksei Kuropatkin that Iugovich still believed that the sending of troops to the northern portion of the Chinese Eastern Railway could have the most adverse effect on its construction. Witte urged, therefore, that no troops be dispatched to Manchuria until he himself so requested. A small detachment had been sent to the south, where Iugovich had reported some disturbances. Witte did not demand its withdrawal, but he asked that no additional troops be sent there until absolutely necessary. Like Iugovich, he was concerned lest the sending of regular troops worsen the situation by damaging the still seemingly good relations between the railway authorities and the Chinese administration and thereby strengthen the Boxer cause.

By the time the Chief Engineer, who lived some 600 miles away, in Harbin, comprehended the seriousness of the situation, it was too late. "In view of the fact that an echelon could be transported from Vladivostok to [Port] Arthur by sea in five days, such a situation can be explained only by a complete lack of confidence in the reports of the commander of the railway guard, thanks to the assurances of the 'China experts,' " Kushakov reflected in disgust.[2]

On May 23, a mob had attacked three Cossacks whom Kushakov had sent into Hsiung-yüeh-ch'êng to purchase supplies for the kitchen, and they escaped only by sabering down several Chinese. Unable to restrain the populace, the Tartar General asked Kushakov to keep his men out of the city. The impotence of the authorities elsewhere became increasingly apparent in June. Boxer agitators came into the open and inveighed against the officialdom as well as against the foreigners. Where officials refused to collaborate they were run out of town by the aroused populace, the soldiery siding with the people. The Boxers grasped control and began recruiting a militia of their own.

It is an old Chinese maxim that a sage does not stand under a tottering wall. As the Boxer uprising was beginning to shake the foundations of the state, the provincial officials pondered whether to side with the

[2]Witte requested military aid on July 9, in a dispatch to Nicholas II, who was then at Belostok. "In a telegram received today," Witte wrote, "the Chief Engineer of the Chinese Eastern Railway reports that an edict of the Chinese Emperor, ordering the troops to join the Boxers to drive the Russians away from the Chinese Eastern Railway, has been intercepted in T'ieh-ling. In view of this state of affairs, I consider it essential to send a detachment from Khabarovsk to Harbin as quickly as possible and at least with one battalion to occupy the [railway] line from the border of the Ussuri region to the Mu-tan River, as otherwise the railway, the guard and the employees can be placed in a hopeless position." The Minister of War supported Witte's request in a report to the Emperor the same day.

rebels or with the established order. Their hesitation gave the insurgents free rein and the outbreak of hostilities was inevitable. No one listened to the orders of a new Tartar General, brought in by the Boxers in Mukden, to lie low until regular Chinese troops had been assembled for a general attack on the Russians. Aroused to a fever pitch, the mobs waxed impatient.

On July 2, Mishchenko telegraphed to Kushakov that the northern posts were in serious danger and ordered him to hasten to Liao-yang with all the guards that could be spared from the southern posts. The detachment thus assembled was small. It consisted of 56 foot-soldiers and 20 cavalrymen. When the chief of railway traffic did not supply him with transportation, Kushakov decided to make use of the locomotive with which Mishchenko had sent him instructions. The locomotive engineer and the station master had no orders and refused to comply. Kushakov placed them under arrest and coupled a number of flatcars to the locomotive. But when the train rolled out of the station, the switchman, a Chinese, released the switch and the engine ran off the track. Night had fallen before Kushakov and his men could resume their journey. Slowly, very slowly, the train felt its way, mindful of possible sabotage.

Stopping at the various guard posts, Kushakov learned that mounted Chinese detachments rode along the line every day, ordering the villagers to move away from the railway and to assist in its destruction. At one station a mob of banner-bearing Boxers passed by the train. Many officials and townspeople had tried to stem the Boxer tide, but had been beaten and robbed.

Kushakov ordered the posts to prepare for a Chinese attack. All construction was to be discontinued and the employees withdrawn to the guard posts. He told the men that reinforcements would soon arrive from the south, but they were overconfident and retorted they did not need any. Contrary to orders from Port Arthur, they had kept their women and children, pay money and accounts with them, and boasted that they would teach the Boxer riff-raff how to fight. Kushakov was not worried about the guard posts consisting of 15 to 20 men. He was sure they would be able to withdraw honorably and with small losses in the event of a Chinese attack. Not so the smaller posts, manned only by 5 or 6 guards. "I kept thinking, what will they die for?" Kushakov recalled. "It is too dear a sacrifice to the stubbornness of three, four high [railway] agents. To die for the Tsar, to die for the glory of the fatherland, that is an enviable death; but to let honorable and selfless soldiers perish for the sake of stubbornness or mistake would be regrettable indeed. . . ." He removed the tiny posts and joined them to the larger, more important ones.

Between Sha-ho and Liao-yang, the Russians saw no Chinese women and children. Some of the villages along the railway line were completely abandoned. No longer did Chinese urchins meet the train, and adults who could be seen here and there merely hastened past. But the welcome Kushakov and the detachment of 76 men received from their compatriots as they pulled into Liao-yang Station on the afternoon of July 3, was that much warmer. With a gay Russian song on their lips they marched to the nearby village of Pai-t'ou-tzu,[3] where the headquarters of the 2nd Company was and where Mishchenko was staying at the moment.

The city of Liao-yang, in whose shadow Pai-t'ou-tzu

[3]The Chinese name is not certain. The Russians spelled it "Baitosy."

lay, was one of Manchuria's oldest. Formerly the capital of the Liao Dynasty, it had remained an administrative center. Surrounded by a sturdy stone wall, it housed a population of about 70,000, and was renowned among other things for its manufacture of coffins.

While dinner was being prepared, Kushakov learned from the officers of the 2nd Company that hostilities had already begun in this part of Manchuria. On June 27, malefactors had set fire to a railroad bridge and barracks near Liao-yang. *Poruchik*[4] Shchekin and his men had chased them away with gunfire and a number of Cossacks of the 8th Don Cossack Sotnia had ridden in pursuit. At the city of Liao-yang regular Chinese troops had fired at the Cossacks, killing one of them and 2 horses. The permanent way of the railroad, the bridges and the telegraph lines were damaged constantly and fire had been set that very day to the coal mines at Yen-t'ai, where *Podesaul*[5] Denisov had been dispatched with 50 Don Cossacks of the 8th Sotnia in pursuit of the culprits. Mishchenko was complaining bitterly that Port Arthur sent no reinforcements, did not even acknowledge his requests, and was berating the railway authorities for their lack of cooperation, when a Cossack messenger came galloping with the report that 400 Chinese infantrymen and 100 cavalrymen with mountain guns had engaged the 50 Cossacks, and that Denisov, though he had already suffered casualties, had decided to hold his ground until receipt of instructions. Without waiting for the dinner that was being cooked for them, Mishchenko took 56 railway guards of the 6th Company under

[4]First Lieutenant.

[5]The Cossacks had special names for their units and ranks. A Cossack sotnia was roughly equivalent to a cavalry squadron. A *podesaul* was the assistant of an *ataman* or Cossack headman.

the command of Kushakov and 25 men of the 2nd Company under Shchekin, boarded a train and hastened to Denisov's aid.

As the train arrived at the scene of battle, the Chinese were moving around Denisov on the eastern side, trying to cut him off from Liao-yang and push him into the path of their main force of 3,000 men, which, it developed later, was approaching from Mukden. When Kushakov and his men jumped off the train and advanced against the right flank of the enemy, however, the Chinese desisted from their maneuver and taking up position at a local village directed their fire at the newcomers. The Russian lines advanced quickly and when they were about 300 paces from the enemy, Shchekin and his men took the train directly to the village and leaping off, charged with their bayonets. Their comrades took up the cry of "ura!" and stormed the Chinese position. The Chinese turned heel, and fled in disorder, the cavalry galloping away toward Mukden, the infantry hiding in a nearby grove.

The Chinese had been thrown into particular confusion by the appearance of Russian soldiers in their rear. These turned out to be Noncommissioned Officer Karpenko and 27 railway guards from Yen-t'ai. After the Chinese had set fire to the coal mines at Yen-t'ai, Karpenko and his men had set out to join Mishchenko. They had been fighting their way through enemy lines when they had chanced upon the battle and plunged right into it.

Many Chinese were killed in hand-to-hand combat and by volleys fired after them as they fled. The Russians counted more than 200 Chinese corpses. Their own casualties numbered 4 dead and 5 wounded, Karpenko being hit in the shoulder. Dr. Khmara-Borshchevskii, a civilian physician who had agreed to accompany the guard detachment when the railway doctors evacuated to safety, bandaged the injured under fire.

As the victorious Russians with their wounded and dead returned by train to Liao-yang, they reflected that the Chinese attacks had shown that regular troops were making common cause with the Boxers. A force of 3,000 Chinese with artillery was reported to be en route from Mukden to Liao-yang, there to join ten newly formed battalions. What could they do in the face of such superior manpower?

At dawn on July 4, Shchekin and 15 railway guards rode on a locomotive and tender to inspect the bridge across the Sha River, about 12 miles south of Liao-yang. Although this bridge and others en route were intact when the Russians arrived, on their way back, at about 5 A.M., they found that one temporary bridge had been set ablaze by the Boxers. They put out the fire and vainly searched the neighborhood for Boxers. At 10 A.M. they left Liao-yang again to pick up a detachment of guards at another station. But as their locomotive approached the station, the switchman, who was a Chinese, let two sets of wheels of the tender go on one track, then moved the switch, sending the other two sets of wheels and the locomotive on the other track. Fortunately the locomotive was going very slowly and the engineer had time to apply the brakes, and only two sets of wheels of the tender were derailed. Whether the derailment was due to an accident or to sabotage was not certain, but the fact that the Chinese switchman disappeared pointed to the latter. It took about 45 minutes to get the train moving again.

Shchekin reached the station without further mishap and took aboard some 81 railway guards. The train started back after midnight. At about 8 A.M. it was at the burned bridge, where a temporary but not yet fully completed detour was in the making. With the help of the guards the train got through, and at 11 A.M. returned to Liao-yang.

On the afternoon of July 5, Engineer Girshman, the chief of railway construction on the southern section, passed through Liao-yang. Mishchenko was concerned about the fate of the other posts, north of Liao-yang. It was likely that they had been attacked at the same time as the post at Yen-t'ai. Mishchenko wanted to go north and join forces with the posts at Mukden and T'ieh-ling, but for this his detachment was not large enough. He asked Girshman, therefore, to inform the authorities in Port Arthur about the clashes that had occurred and to request reinforcements. But Girshman, who stopped only briefly, insisted that there was no cause for alarm. He asserted that the Tartar General of Liao-yang, to whom he had made a present of 5,000 taels of silver, was favorably disposed toward them. Girshman ordered the railway employees not to leave their places and exhorted them to continue construction with vigor and courage. As a gesture of his own bravery—as he scurried off to the safety of Port Arthur—he handed his revolver to one of the worried employees.

Girshman's train was the last train from Liao-yang. By morning (July 6) the bridge south of the station had been destroyed, and a train with wounded could not get through. Soon the bridge north of the station was destroyed also. The Russians at Liao-yang were cut off. Left behind by Girshman were 104 civilian employees with their families and belongings, 11 steam engines and much rolling stock, railway funds (a large quantity of silver bullion) and all construction papers. The Chinese offered Mishchenko free passage for all Russians, all engines and the rolling stock, if he withdrew from Liao-yang Station to the south, but Mishchenko refused to leave. He ordered *Shtabs-kapitan*[6] Sakharov with the 3rd Sotnia to join him, and renewed his plea to Port Arthur for reinforcements. He sent three Cossacks to try to reach the various northern posts, inform them of the happenings, and order them to make their way to him, and if this was no longer possible, to withdraw to Harbin, the headquarters of railway construction.

Mishchenko decided to hold out in the wooden, iron-roof isolation barracks[7] not far from the Russian colony at Pai-t'ou-tzu. His detachment numbered only 204 officers and men. Fatigued as they were already from constant patrolling of the vast region and from daily guard duty, he now put them to work on fortifying the barracks area. The place was enclosed by a seven foot earth wall, to which the Russians with Chinese labor hastily added a breastwork. The only real shelter was offered by the ice-house, where the families of the employees were told to take cover. Their belongings and those of the soldiers, as well as the money and files were taken from Pai-t'ou-tzu to the barracks. The Russians labored around the clock. When they did lie down, their nerves were so tense from constant strain and exertion, that they found little rest.

Meanwhile the Chinese forces made preparations of

[6]Captain Junior Grade.

[7]Special "plague barracks" had been built near every station to contain the spread of possible epidemics.

their own. They dug entrenchments on three nearby hills (in the north, south, and east) and set up light pieces of ordnance on the city wall. The Russians could see from afar what the Chinese were doing. The Chinese did better than that. They had some of their country-men inspect the layout of the Russian fortifications from within. While Russian noncoms were measuring off the distances in all directions, Chinese strode freely be-tween the Russian redoubt, the city, and their own en-trenchments, for Chinese laborers assisted in building the Russian fortifications. Chinese participated also in moving Russian belongings from Pai-t'ou-tzu to the bar-racks. When the last item, the upright piano of the rail-way engineer, had been carried out of the Russian colony, a Chinese asked whether this was all, and when the Russians said yes, a mob of Chinese promptly rushed into the buildings and set them afire.

Meanwhile Chinese troops poured into the villages north and south of Liao-yang. Everywhere everything Russian was put to the torch, and up and down the railway line, as far as the Russians could see, fires lit up the sky. The Chinese were not content with driving out the foreigners. Russians captured at isolated posts were ridiculed and tortured, then beheaded and their corpses thrown to the pigs. So deep was the passion aroused in the Chinese that they did not stop with the living. They dug up the graves and desecrated the remains. Nor were they satisfied with taking vengeance on the hated in-truder. No trace of him was to remain. Instead of ap-propriating his possessions, the Chinese wantonly de-stroyed them. They burned barracks and stations and stores of wood and coal. They demolished the rolling stock and ran the expensive engines off the destroyed bridges. They dismantled the tracks, burning what could be burned and tossing the rest into the river.

Mishchenko was furious that no reinforcements were forthcoming from Port Arthur. His detachment was surrounded by a forty-fold host, while the civilian employees and their families hung around his neck like a millstone. He could not hold indefinitely, nor could he cut his way through. But where could he turn? All day, on July 6, Don and Kuban Cossack scouts poked around in every direction. The north and south proved teeming with Chinese troops; the east was barred by the walled city of Liao-yang, bristling with infantry and artillery. The west was open only to a point, the Liao River forming a cul-de-sac.

While the Cossacks deftly scouted the surroundings, an endless flow of Chinese poured into Liao-yang. Chinese cavalry detachments scurried from village to village and from hill to hill, as Chinese troops peppered the Russians from the city walls, the villages and the mountain entrenchments. Enervating as the fire was, it came from too great a distance to be effective, and the Russians responded only sporadically, saving their precious ammunition. The Chinese did not advance, preoccupied as they were with plundering and destroying what the Russians had left behind at Pai-t'ou-tzu, and by evening they stopped shooting. But silence did not descend upon the land. A frightful din emanated from behind the city walls, where whooping Chinese shot off firecrackers in celebration of the arrival of troops from Mukden, while the soldiers in inns and opium dens, provided by Boxer leaders, drank and smoked themselves into a state of patriotic ecstasy. The colorful paper lanterns that people carried, the illuminated multicolored paper dragon that wound its way through the streets, and especially the glow of the burning railway colony and the Christian mission added to the macabre atmosphere.

That night Kushakov was in command of the listening posts. Making the rounds, he talked to the interpreter of the Chinese Eastern Railway Company, who had heard that the Chinese would attack in the morning. The information was correct, and Kushakov, relieved at dawn on July 7, had barely fallen asleep, when the Chinese opened their bombardment. Mishchenko peered through his binoculars from the breastwork. "They have begun their advance," he told Kushakov, who had rushed out. "Forbid the men to shoot needlessly. Instead, begin to fire platoon volleys at those cannons there. They have already adjusted their fire well, and must be silenced."

Just then several grenades burst into the inner courtyard ripping open the belly of one of the horses and wounding several others. A soldier, carrying water to the breastwork, collapsed. When a comrade ran up to him, the soldier jumped up and exclaimed with a laugh: "It frightened me." He did not feel the blood flowing from his back.

The crackle of rifle fire from Pai-t'ou-tzu and the nearest hills increased. "Unseen bumble bees started to hum, to whistle, and we began to bow to them, not out of fear, of course, but out of politeness," Kushakov recalled. "You laugh at the soldiers, and in spite of yourself duck. If only it were in time, for the bullet has already bored into the distant barrack wall, and all you do is bow to it."

Shchekin and *Sotnik*[8] Mamonov directed the defense of the eastern face of the Russian position; Denisov was

[8]Cossack First Lieutenant.

in charge of the northern face; Kushakov of the southern face. Mishchenko was in overall command. He spent the entire day on the faces, calmly pointed out the targets, and gave orders. He walked about encouraging the faint of heart and praising the brave. Twice he was near death. One grenade fell a few steps from him, but burst in the barrack nearby. Another grenade hit just below him as he sat on the breastwork and even lifted him up somewhat, but failed to explode.

Kushakov stood at the breastwork and directed the fire against the Chinese guns. After half a dozen well directed volleys the Chinese gunners moved their weapons to a more distant hill. Suddenly one of the watches on the breastwork yelled, "Sir! The Chinese are crawling already from the railway embankment nearby!" and collapsed in mortal convulsions. Indeed, the Chinese, advancing from three sides, were within 400 paces. "Fire!" Mishchenko commanded, and the battle was joined.

It became almost comfortable [Kushakov reflected]. Hereafter you did not hear the whistling of bullets and the hissing and explosion of shells, not even the moans of the wounded neighbor. You look where your own bullets fly, you do not glance to the sides, you do not look into your soul. You want to jump from the breastwork and dash after the bullets, to stab the insolent fellows to death. You do not think of your own death, but are possessed by the desire to kill as quickly and as fiercely as possible.

Nothing is worse than when your own side does not fire, and when you stand around without anything to do. . . . Your hearing is strained to capacity. The whistling and snapping of the bullets, the rumble and crackle of the shells, the slightest moan, even the smacking of the bullet into the body of your neighbor, you can hear it all, and then you yourself are dying almost every minute. It is good if you do not let yourself go, if you catch the coward in you in time, begin to give orders, to talk, to joke. In short, the nerves are calmer when there is more activity and movement.

It is far better when you attack. Then you run along the line, give orders, think about your little maneuver, indicate targets. The enemy makes more changes, and not a minute passes without a new situation and a new decision. You are fully occupied with all this and think less frequently of death. You hear and see everything ahead of you and do not feel death near you and in you. But here you have been driven into a little courtyard, are bombarded from all sides with rifle and artillery fire and, what's more, are not allowed to shoot back, but are to wait until the enemy comes up practically to the breastwork. In attacking, the wounded and dead remain on the spot, while you advance forward. Here, however, they are underfoot and call you in a soul-rending voice. You step on them; they grab you by the legs, weep and convey their last wish. . . .

And the smell of blood, the moans, the convulsions, all this is before the eyes of the defender, right beside him. No, only unto an enemy can one wish to defend oneself.

The well-aimed rapid fire of the Russians drove back the attackers, but only temporarily. At 10 A.M. they advanced again on foot and on horseback, this time under the cover of the station buildings and rolling stock, some cars being only 400 paces from the left flank of the defenders. Their attack was supported by a heavy barrage of rifle and cannon fire. Two Chinese guns blasted the Russian right, one the Russian front. Fourteen Russians were killed, 5 wounded. The breastwork offered little protection and had the Chinese been better shots, they would have decimated the little force. Their high angle fire from a distance was quite effective, but when they brought their artillery closer, the shells burst into the embankment or overshot their mark.

As the cannonade subsided, riflemen crawled toward the Russians. Watching intently, the Russians fired at the soldiers the moment they appeared, for unless they were stopped dead in their tracks wave after wave would follow and overwhelm them by sheer numbers. The area the Russians defended was small; about 350 square feet. They could see, they could smell every death. Spattered with blood, nauseated from the stench, the hunger, the heat and the exertion, they fought back doggedly. The effectiveness of their fire during the first assault gave them heart, and aiming most carefully, they forced the Chinese to withdraw again.

The Russians had not eaten all day, and the men were ordered to take turns going to the barracks for dinner. But the moment the Chinese noticed that the Russian fire had decreased, they attacked for a third time, depriving the Russians of nourishment again. The Russians had knocked the gut out of the Chinese offensive, however. Having suffered heavy casualties, the Chinese advanced cautiously and reluctantly, here and there in small numbers, and soon turned back again. In disorder they withdrew from Pai-t'ou-tzu to Liao-yang, not knowing how close to collapse the Russians were. The ammunition of the latter had shrunk to 20 cartridges per man, and the soldiers were so exhausted from the lengthy ordeal that they kept falling asleep right during the engagement. Two thirds of the horses had been killed and the whole yard was littered with cadavers. The ground was soaked with human and animal blood.

Retreat to Ta-shih-ch'iao

THE RUSSIAN POSITION in the barracks near Pai-t'ou-tzu was critical. The men lacked the strength and ammunition to withstand another sustained Chinese attack, and there was no assurance that reinforcements were forthcoming from Port Arthur. At a council of the officers, the doctor and the engineers, called together by Colonel Mishchenko, the Russians decided, therefore, to try to fight their way south, toward the Kuban Cossack sotnia of *Shtabs-kapitan* Strakhov, then battling its way toward them. That evening they buried nine comrades who had been killed during the day and made an opening in the western face in preparation for their departure. The costly steam engines, the rolling stock, the machine shops, even 20,000 in silver and all their personal belongings had to be left behind, the boxes with coins being dumped into the well.

As the Russians were getting ready, the Chinese took advantage of the halt in fire to attack for the fourth time. The Russians flew back to the faces and shot several volleys, but it was too dark for effective aim. Besides, many ran out of ammunition. Their bayonets, permanently fixed on the rifles, could hardly keep at bay the numerous attackers.

They were saved by a daring ruse. Instead of waiting for the human wave to close over them, Mishchenko feigned an attack. As the 2nd Company under Malinov and Shchekin charged with loud hurrahs in the cloak of darkness, the Chinese, knowing of the approach of other forces, were tricked into believing that reinforcements had already arrived, and hastened back to Liaoyang to defend the city. Meanwhile the railway employees, preceded by a vanguard of Kushakov's men, had slipped away with the first shots of the "counterattack." Now that the Chinese were gone, the 2nd Company also stole away, covering the retreat.

Several days in the ice-house with constant thought of death had completely disheartened many of the civilian employees and their families. As they were ordered to follow the detachment, some of them panicked and scattered blindly. One husband abandoned his wife and child and galloped away on horseback. Cossacks had to be sent after the fugitives to flush them out of hiding in the fields and drag them back to the column, where they were surrounded by soldiers and guarded until they calmed down. Many Cossacks dismounted to give their horses to the wounded, to women, old men and the ill. Nevertheless, the hike was exhausting for the civilians and the detachment had to halt almost every half-hour to allow stragglers to catch up.

The Russians did not follow the permanent way of the railroad, but travelled some two miles to the west to avoid detection. Taking to the fields they went around villages in which there were soldiers. Only twice were shots fired in their direction, but they did not respond and slipped away. On the morning of July 8, after a night march of 12 hours, they reached the Sha River, a dozen miles from Liao-yang. The railway bridge across the river, and the station buildings and barracks at Sha-ho-tzu had been burned, scattered Chinese corpses and empty cartridge cases telling a tale of resistance.

Only two days before, the local guard post of 12 men under Noncommissioned Officer Padalka and several railway employees had been besieged by some 200 Chinese. Locked in their stone-walled barrack, they had kept the enemy at bay until out of ammunition. Then Boxers had been able to run up with sheafs of kaoliang, a tall grain which was used for roofing and heating of houses, and igniting them had set fire to the doors, windows and roof of the building. At the very moment when everything had seemed lost, a train had sped up to the burning barrack, blowing its shrill whistle and spewing bullets from the carriages. Padalka and his men had burst out in a desperate bayonet charge and the bewildered Chinese had taken to their heels, pursued by the shots of the timely reinforcements which, it developed, consisted of only seven full-throated soldiers and one technician (Didenko). By the time the Chinese had bethought themselves, the handful of Russians—some seriously wounded, some with light burns—had been whisked away by the train to An-shan-chan.

No train appeared to carry off the motley procession that now had reached the Sha River. But they were no less cheered, as they lay resting their weary bones, by the sudden appearance of Strakhov with 70 Kuban Cossacks of the 3rd Sotnia and 40 infantrymen of the 2nd Company. Strakhov had fought his way from Ying-k'ou[9] to Liao-yang Station only to find Mishchenko gone. They had missed each other en route, because Strakhov had followed the track, while Mishchenko had gone

---

[9] Also spelled Yingkow. It was the port of Newchwang. Ying-k'ou was sometimes called (New) Newchwang.

around the Chinese positions in the west, returning to the railroad only at Sha-ho-tzu in the morning. At Liao-yang, which Strakhov had reached at dawn on July 8, he had seen the Chinese advancing against the Russian barracks with unfurled banners. Hearing no fire returned from the barracks, he had peered through his binoculars and seen that Mishchenko's detachment had escaped. Native Christians had confided to Strakhov that Mishchenko had set out for the Sha River, with Chinese pursuers mistakenly headed toward the Liao, and he had hastened back to join forces. The combined strength of the two groups numbered 307 railway guards and 102 civilians,[10] some of whom were armed and fought side by side with the guards. Their chances for survival were greatly improved, for small Chinese detachments, not knowing that they were short of ammunition, no longer dared to molest them.

As Mishchenko's detachment looked at the remains of the little post, crowds of armed Chinese could be seen on the hills in the east. But they undertook no action and after a brief rest, Mishchenko and his caravan continued from Sha-ho-tzu along the railway track to An-shan-chan. The permanent way had been ruined only in a number of places, but everywhere the railway buildings had been burned and the telegraph lines cut. At An-shan-chan too the bridge and pump-house had been destroyed. But from here to Port Arthur the railway and the telegraph were still intact. To keep them so Mishchenko stopped in an excellent mountain position, and dispatched an officer to Port Arthur to transmit a detailed report and to purchase ammunition.

The wounded, the sick and the railway employees and

[10]Two employees had been killed at Liao-yang.

29

their families, meanwhile, were escorted by the 8th Don Cossack Sotnia to Ta-shih-ch'iao, where Colonel Dombrovskii's detachment was.[11] The railway line split at Ta-shih-ch'iao, running northward to Mukden and westward to Ying-k'ou. Ta-shih-ch'iao thus constituted the strategic key of the army corps operating in Southern Manchuria.[12] The track between An-shan-chan and Ta-shih-ch'iao had not been damaged, and the peasants continued to work the fields peacefully. Yet in no village on the way to Ta-shih-ch'iao could the Russians buy eggs or vegetables. The inhabitants firmly refused to sell anything. From Hai-ch'êng the Russians put through a telephone call to Ta-shih-ch'iao, and a train was sent to pick them up.

On July 11, over 100 men from the southern railway posts under the command of *Poruchiks* Gulevich and Rozhalin joined Mishchenko, boosting the strength of his detachment to 450, half of them on horseback. Thus reinforced and no longer tied to the defense of civilians, occupying the An-shan-chan gateway to the broad northern plain, and connected by rail and telegraph with Russian forces in the south, Mishchenko was prepared to play the role of a forward detachment, executing army orders. But the authorities in Port Arthur had no instructions about the use of railway guards. They would not consider Mishchenko's detachment as a regular army

[11]Dombrovskii's detachment consisted of 6 companies of the 11th East Siberian Rifle Regiment, the 1st Battalion of the 8th East Siberian Rifle Regiment, 2 sotnias of Cossacks and 1 section of sappers, plus 6 guns and 1½ sotnias. It had arrived in Ta-shih-ch'iao from Port Arthur by rail on July 9.

[12]Upon mobilization the 1st and 7th Rifle Regiments, which had come to Kwantung from the Southern Ussuri region, and the 11th East Siberian Regiment of the 3rd Rifle Brigade had occupied the railway line from Port Arthur to Ta-shih-ch'iao.

force, would not supply him with artillery or a single soldier for offensive action and ordered him to withdraw to Ta-shih-ch'iao, within army protection.

On July 12, a native Christian reported that a column of about 200 Chinese troops was approaching approximately 2 miles to the east. Chinese mounted patrols appeared in front of the Russian position and Russian scouts located several hundred Chinese in the rear. Short of provisions and clothing and without tents, the Russians did not wish to be besieged. Furthermore, the chief of Hai-ch'êng Station reported that 2,000 Chinese soldiers threatened his station and the railway line. It seemed senseless to hold out at An-shan-chan, where the railroad had already been destroyed. Better hasten to Hai-ch'êng and save it from a similar fate.

At 7 P.M., when the detachment was about ready to depart, a Cossack galloped up and reported that his patrol had come upon a large enemy detachment with artillery near the eastern heights and had been engaged. Mishchenko at once dispatched Rozhalin with a half-sotnia to the eastern heights to distract the attention of the Chinese. As Rozhalin and his men opened fire on the bewildered Chinese, who did not expect an attack at this point, the Russian detachment deployed along the permanent way of the railroad and headed for Hai-ch'êng.

It was a cool evening, and men and horses moved along briskly. At about 10 P.M., a brief but violent thunder storm suddenly forced them to the ground, and transformed the terrain into a sea of mud. Henceforth the progress was slow and painful, the drenched guards stepping from tie to tie, the animals sinking knee-deep in slush. It was dawn when the detachment reached

Hai-ch'êng Station, thoroughly exhausted. Friendly inhabitants had urged Mishchenko to avoid Hai-ch'êng in view of the presence of a strong Chinese force, but conscious of the respect and support that his earlier victories against great odds had earned him among the populace, Mishchenko ventured there, requesting military support from Colonel Dombrovskii. The 7th Company of the 7th East Siberian Rifle Regiment, which Dombrovskii sent from Ta-shih-ch'iao by train, came within an hour of Mishchenko's arrival, and another train was formed for the evacuation of Mishchenko's detachment and of the tiny force of Berezov, the valient station master who with 24 men, in defiance of orders from his superiors, had kept Hai-ch'êng Station open to provide Mishchenko with railway transportation.

The western height, overlooking the railroad track near the city of Hai-ch'êng, was occupied by Chinese troops who had to be cleared out before the train could proceed in safety. With the 7th Rifle Company in reserve, and the Kuban and Don Cossack Sotnias riding to cut off retreat to the city, the 2nd and 6th Companies of the guard advanced against the Chinese. Taking cover behind the railway embankment, the Russians quickly went up to the height, shooting from time to time at the ridge. Then, without further exchanging fire because the Chinese were too well covered, the Russians charged up the mountain and hitting the right flank of the Chinese turned them to flight. As the Chinese scattered into the kaoliang fields, pursued by the Cossacks of the 3rd and 8th Sotnias, the 7th Company was recalled to protect the train against a possible assault from the city; but the Chinese did not like to reinforce defeated troops, and no attack followed. Toward the end of the engagement

Dombrovskii himself sped up on a train with half a company of his own 11th East Siberian Rifle Regiment. To punish the Chinese for their hostility and to dissuade them from molesting Ta-shih-ch'iao, where Russian forces were still vulnerable, Dombrovskii went back after reinforcements. Meanwhile four gun emplacements and trenches were dug on the height which the Russians had taken overlooking the city, only a mile away.

At 9 A.M. on July 14, Dombrovskii returned from Ta-shih-ch'iao by train with an entire company of his regiment and a half-battery. The company was under Captain Ivanov, the artillery under *Shtabs-kapitan* Petrenko, with Colonel Nikolai Desenko in command of the whole detachment. The Chinese military knew of the impending attack, for early in the morning Mishchenko had sent Chinese laborers into Hai-ch'êng to warn unarmed civilians to leave town. Before the Russians had time to unload the guns, Chinese troops sallied from the city and swiftly struck their flanks. The 7th Company of the 7th Regiment stayed to defend the guns, while the company of the 11th Regiment took up position on the right flank, the 2nd and 6th Companies of the guard on the left flank. Under the cover of rifle volleys the guns were unloaded, and quickly went into action. Petrenko was a brilliant artillery officer and so effectively sprayed the attackers with shrapnel, that they began to retreat along the entire front. The Russians pressed after them, the 2nd Company of the guard and a company of the 11th Regiment taking the offensive. As the Russian troops advanced and as rifle volleys from the companies on the height and artillery salvoes from Petrenko's guns bombarded the city, the Chinese combatants rushed out of the east gate and headed for the hills. Hai-ch'êng was at the mercy of the Russians, but as Dombrovskii had strict orders not to engage in an offensive, they did not follow up their victory and occupy the city, but withdrew also.

The half-battery and the company of the 11th Regiment departed by train for Ta-shih-ch'iao and half an hour later the companies of the railway guard and the company of the 7th Regiment began loading another train. As soon as the Chinese saw that the Russians had boarded the train, they came swooping back and set fire to all station buildings, the pump-house and the railway bridge. Their cavalry even threatened the train, until turned away by a number of volleys from the last flatcar. Four Russian guards were wounded in this engagement, one of them mortally.

Slowly the trains moved southward, preceded and flanked by Cossack patrols. About 6 miles from Ta-shih-ch'iao, Chinese militiamen and Boxers with antiquated weapons attacked the first train. Jumping off the flatcars and taking cover behind the railway embankment, the Russians scattered the attackers with a series of volleys. Rozhalin and his Kuban Cossack squadron dashed in pursuit and brought back a silken banner with the Chinese inscription "For Fatherland and Truth."

At 8 P.M. Mishchenko and his men finally reached Ta-shih-ch'iao. The South Manchurian detachment, which had a regiment, a company, a Cossack sotnia and a field battery at Ta-shih-ch'iao, embraced by this time also a like unit at Hsiung-yüeh-ch'êng, three rifle regiments with formidable batteries at Port Arthur, 86 fortress guns at Chin-chou, and units of the Cossack Regiment along the railway line. Yet Mishchenko and his comrades were not pleased to learn of this military strength. Angrily they wondered why no troops had been sent to their aid, and why they had been charged exhorbitant prices for ammunition that they had to buy from the army.

Nor were the railway guards welcomed as heroes. They were criticized for having caught Chinese chickens and pigs and for wearing Chinese jackets and Manchu trousers. Having had no other means of supply, the railway guards resented the reprimands as grossly unfair, and remained aloof from the regular armed forces until a new commander with a different outlook arrived in the fall.

The 170 odd miles of railroad north of Ta-shih-ch'iao had been "surrendered to the Chinese for exploitation," as the saying went. The Chinese, of course, did not "exploit" the railway. They destroyed it. In places they plowed it under for cultivation. The loss in property thus incurred by Russia amounted to some 18 million rubles on the southern line alone, according to Kushakov's estimate. In human terms, Mishchenko had lost 62 men killed in combat, 2 dead from emaciation after release from captivity, and 12 "missing" (captured and tortured to death). Fifty-three of his men were wounded, and one quarter of the entire detachment was disabled from exhaustion after the grueling marches.

Shadow Boxing At Hsiung-yüeh-ch'êng

WHEN KUSHAKOV SPED from Hsiung-yüeh-ch'êng to the aid of the northern posts on July 2, the city was without leadership. The aged Tartar General, unable to cope with Boxer subversion, had departed for Kai-chou[13] followed by part of his troops. Some of the garrison had gone over to the insurgents; others had left for Ying-k'ou. Here was an opportunity for a mature Russian officer to step in and by the bloodless pacification of the region to gain the sympathy, if not support, of the common people.

Cornet Basilevich, who with his Verkhneudinsk Cossacks and riflemen took over the protection of the nearby railway station after Kushakov's departure, showed more zeal than reflection. He searched the neighboring villages for firearms and confiscated even the oldest and most useless weapons. He added to the public ire when he began chopping down Chinese telegraph posts. The Chinese at that time had not yet cut the Russian lines, and the action was the more foolish, because Kushakov had already interrupted Chinese communication by grounding the Chinese lines in several places inconspicuously with thin wire. After felling the Chinese telegraph posts, Basilevich and his men approached Hsiung-yüeh-ch'êng. Excited Chinese on the walls, waving flags

[13]Known also as Kai-p'ing.

and hats, shouted and motioned them to go away. But Basilevich ordered *"pravoe plecho!"* (column left!) and headed for the city gates. Finding the inner gates locked, he ordered them forced. The Chinese opened fire, killing one of the Russians and wounding another. The Russians carried off the latter, but left behind their slain comrade. The Chinese promptly decapitated the corpse and triumphantly displayed the head on the wall. The destruction of the Chinese telegraph and the seeming attempt of Basilevich to take possession of the city had united Boxers and non-Boxers against the "foreign devils." Yet the Chinese did not pursue the Russians, and the latter remained physically unmolested at the railway station. For the time being, Chinese hostility was confined to indecent gestures and shouted insults from the city walls.

On July 13 and 19, Russian reinforcements arrived from Port Arthur by train and bivouacked behind the railroad embankment about a mile east of Hsiung-yüeh-ch'êng. Through their binoculars the officers looked at the distant walls and vainly tried to espy the head of the slain rifleman.

The reinforcements, commanded by Colonel Khorunzhenkov, consisted of the 1st East Siberian Rifle Regiment, the 2nd Light Battery of the 1st Brigade, a half-sotnia of the Verkhneudinsk Cossack Regiment, and a platoon of the 7th East Siberian Rifle Regiment. Pitching their tents on sand, so as not to ruin the crops and thereby anger the populace, feeding their horses with fodder brought from Vladivostok, and restricting their troops to camp, the Russians bivouacked passively. They were warm, stuffy and dusty, as they sat in their dark tents day after day with nothing to do but eat their tasteless meals and drink hot tea. Peasants from neighboring villages came with chickens and fruit for sale, but there was no contact with the city. Bored and restless, the officers rode up to the wall of the Chinese fortress, the regimental photographer, V. A. Dobrazhenskii, taking pictures from as close as 800 paces. Chinese failure to take notice of them merely added to the frustration of the officers. They had orders to proceed to Ta-shih-ch'iao, but could not leave the fortress with a hostile garrison in their back; yet they also had orders not to take the fortress until the Chinese opened hostilities. As Captain I. E. Ivanov, commander of the 2nd Company of the 1st East Siberian Rifle Regiment, put it, all they could do was to "sit at the sea and wait for the weather."

On July 24, Lieutenant Colonel Desino, Dombrovskii's chief of staff, telegraphed from Ta-shih-ch'iao, that the Chinese were bombarding the Russian bivouac there. Later, after telegraphic communication with Ta-shih-ch'iao had been cut, word was received that the Chinese were also attacking Kai-chou, half way between Hsiung-yüeh-ch'êng and Ta-shih-ch'iao. A company set out by train for Kai-chou, but did not get through. The railway bridge south of the station had been destroyed and the station itself was aflame. That night signal lights could be seen in the city and on nearby mountains.

The size of the Russian reinforcements had spread panic among the inhabitants of Hsiung-yüeh-ch'êng. The Boxers tried to prevent their evacuation, and massacred those who fled. But some of the townspeople killed the Boxer sentinels and made good their escape. Dissension broke out among the regular troops and the Boxers. The former felt that they did not have sufficient strength to cross swords with the Russians and wanted to withdraw to Kai-chou; the latter insisted that the Russians could and should be wiped out. In view of the Boxers' claim that they were invulnerable, a logical compromise was reached. The bulletproof Boxers could charge the Russians while the Chinese army fired at them from a safe distance. After the Russians had been put to flight, the army would relieve the tired Boxers and pursue the beaten enemy.

At noon on July 25, the Russian officers assembled in the mess before dinner to listen to a telegram from Nicholas II, giving his blessings, and expressing his confidence in the valor and zeal of their troops. The hurrah with which the officers responded to the Imperial message had not died down when shots rang out on the left flank of the Russian forces. The Chinese had launched a surprise attack. Undetected they had moved to within half a mile from the bivouac, had occupied a village and the right bank of the river, and now opened fire on Russians who had taken the horses to water, on the bivouac and on the station, where the railway employees sought cover. The Russian troops ran to their arms and were ready for combat, when a horde of banner-waving Boxers stormed up from a village to the south. A volley from the 6th Company of the 1st Regiment spun around many Boxers, but others continued onward into the bayonets of the 5th Company, which punctured their invulnerability. The 2nd Company meanwhile advanced against rifle fire on the right flank, firing volley after volley. For many of the junior officers and men this was their first engagement, their first "smell of powder." Pale but alert and serious, they had taken off their caps and crossed themselves before going into action. Now and then one of the soldiers would duck as a bullet whizzed past, but a comrade would shout, "Why do you bow, do you know her?" and the soldier would keep his head up straight. When the Chinese riflemen, whose aimless shooting had done little more than alert the Russians, saw the butchery of the Boxers, some 200 of whom lay strewn about the battlefield, they fled to the gulf or into the mountains.

The city of Hsiung-yüeh-ch'êng was practically deserted. There remained only a few dozen marauders who had stayed to plunder the houses of the rich, several Boxers in hiding, and a number of peaceful townspeople who saw no reason for a Russian attack, now that the Boxers were crushed and the troops gone. But the high walls of the city hid the situation from the Russians. At 4 P.M., after a preliminary bombardment, the 1st and 2nd Battalions assaulted the city from the north and east with textbook precision. They put their scaling ladders against the walls (in one place they clambered up a rockslide), and in a moment plunged into the city, wreaking destruction everywhere. Marauders and trusting inhabitants alike were cut down. As Kushakov bemoaned: "War is cruel and does not sort out victims."

The Chinese troops and the Boxers who survived the Hsiung-yüeh-ch'êng engagement fled toward Kai-chou. They had lost some 300 men, as against 5 Russians wounded. On the way, they met a Chinese detachment of 150 soldiers and urged its commander to assume leadership of the fight against the Russians. The shrewd officer, who disliked Boxers and Russians alike, agreed to engage in guerilla warfare—to destroy the railway and fall upon Russians here and there, but to avoid giving battle. His ranks swelled to 500, the officer swooped down upon the railroad.

The Tartar General of Kai-chou was appalled when he saw the Russian station and bridge aflame, and sent an interpreter to Ta-shih-ch'iao to assure the Russians that he had had nothing to do with the sabotage. Yet he made no effort to cope with the Boxers and in order to avoid responsibility left town. The Tartar General's assistant, a merchant and former contractor on the railway construction without military experience, feigned illness, and command of the Kai-chou garrison passed into the hands of the individual officers. The garrison numbered between 1,200 and 1,500 Chinese, including many ill-armed militiamen. Except for a few antiquated cannons it had no artillery. But Khorunzhenkov's detachment was short of cavalry "eyes," and not aware of the weakness of the Kai-chou forces.

The misuse of Cossacks for garrison duty in the Kwantung region at the outbreak of hostilities led to a general overestimation of Chinese strength, for the infantry could not probe enemy positions effectively, and the actual composition of large concentrations of Chinese could not be determined from afar. Not until they were upon them, did the Russians usually know whether they faced regular troops, sword-wielding Boxers or shovel-swinging peasants.

On July 27, Khorunzhenkov sent Lieutenant Colonel Dubel't with the 2nd Company of the 1st Regiment, parts of the 2nd Company of the 7th Regiment, and a group of telegraph and railway workers on a train toward Kai-chou to put a halt to the destruction of the railroad and make whatever repairs possible. He himself followed with the bulk of the detachment, partly by train and partly on foot and horseback, to punish the Chinese for having burned down the railway station and bridge. By the following evening his detachment bivouacked near the city and remained encamped for the next three days.

Chinese artillery, which had greatly improved since the Sino-Japanese War of 1894-95, kept Khorunzhenkov at a distance, and Chinese sorties, albeit ineffectual, deprived the Russians of rest, for at night almost half of them manned the guard lines fearing an enemy attack. It was easier to see someone in the dark by looking up, and the soldiers were posted in low lying places. These were flooded by rains, and the men often stood knee-deep in water, the more fatigued for being wet. Stealing through the high kaoliang after dark to within 500 paces of the camp, two or three dozen Chinese would suddenly open fire and arouse everyone. Wild as their blind shots went, they kept the Russians on edge and strained their nerves. It was fortunate for the Russians that the Chinese never launched a full scale night attack, for in the darkness numerical superiority could not have been nullified by better marksmanship.

Although Khorunzhenkov had set out to punish Kaichou and, furthermore, had to take the fortress to secure his rear before proceeding to Ta-shih-ch'iao, where he was to join forces with Dombrovskii, he hesitated. Seeing the mountains teeming with thousands of Chinese and not realizing that they were largely ill-armed villagers, Khorunzhenkov lingered, requesting reinforcements from Dombrovskii at Ta-shih-ch'iao and from General Fleisher, commander of the 1st East Siberian Rifle Brigade, then at Ying-k'ou. Only a small unit could be spared by Dombrovskii, but Fleisher himself set out with a mixed detachment of one infantry battalion, two guns and two Cossack squadrons of the railway guards.

Instead of speeding to Kai-chou by train, Fleisher tried to gain the element of surprise by approaching round about on foot. With time the ancient roads of Manchuria had worn several feet below the general level of the land. Heavy rains transformed the roads into streams, and the surrounding countryside into a sea of mud. As the riflemen and horses slushed through the plowed fields in the dark of night, wearily lifting their feet, falling down, and pushing and pulling the artillery pieces which constantly got stuck, they drained all their strength.

Knowing only of the approach of the reinforcements, not of their utter exhaustion, Khorunzhenkov went to the attack on August 1. His strike force consisted of 5 companies of infantry with eight guns and 3 or 4 dozen Cossacks—a maximum of 1,000 men—two companies remaining behind to garrison Hsiung-yüeh-ch'êng and one to guard the baggage and railway trains.

It was a very hot day, and the soldiers marched without their packs, burdened only with cartridges and biscuits. They halted at the river, not far from the half destroyed railway bridge. From here they could see the gray walls of Kai-chou, across the river, about a mile upstream. Directly ahead on the other side, half a mile from the bridge, loomed the charred station buildings, embedded in a semi-circular height, one end of which hinged on the gulf, the other end of which went up to the fortress-city. Beyond Kai-chou there was another ridge. The two rows of mountains had been turned into a formidable cannon-studded two-tier defense line, manned by 3,000 well equipped, European-style trained troops and

43

by 500 Boxers, some of whom came down to meet the Russians, shooting from villages near the station and from the river bank.

When the Russian battery began bombarding the fortress and the mountain emplacements, Chinese guns responded in kind, and the scattered Chinese units harrassed the Russian gunners from different directions. To drive the Chinese riflemen out of the villages and to secure their flank, which would be exposed to fire from the mountain position when they attacked Kai-chou, the Russians sent across the battered bridge a raiding and scouting party, followed by the 2nd and then the 7th, and eventually the 3rd and 4th companies. Halfway through the operation they received orders from General Fleisher not to engage in a serious battle till he arrived with reinforcements, but by then it was too risky to withdraw or to stay put like sitting ducks, and they pushed on. Enemy fire was heavy and cover inadequate, but Ivanov with his 2nd Company managed to clamber up a rocky mountain. He found himself quite unexpectedly on the right flank of the Chinese main position, only 500 paces from their exposed trenches. Swooping down on the surprised Chinese, Ivanov captured the key to the entire defense work. By now Fleisher's vanguard appeared on the horizon, while his mounted patrols poked the right flank of the Chinese, and the Don and Kuban Cossack squadrons of the railway guard raced to cut off their retreat. The defenders fell back all along the line.

From the heights Ivanov looked down on the city-fortress as if it were in the palm of his hand. Seeing that the walls were being cleared and the garrison was withdrawing, he stormed the walls from two sides, penetrating through a breach he had espied from above. Though the appearance of Fleisher's force had hastened the Chinese departure, Kai-chou was actually taken by a single company. Yet once again the enemy slipped through Russian fingers. Had Khorunzhenkov given Fleisher time to close in on the flanks of the Chinese, he might have succeeded in punishing them. As it worked out, all that the Russians captured was an empty city and the shadow of the enemy. On the other hand, so shaken were the Chinese by the defeat, that they molested no further the strategic railroad from Port Arthur to Kai-chou and Ta-shih-ch'iao, the lifeline of Russian operations against Mukden.

A relatively wealthy place, with silk combings and silk materials as its main industry and article of trade, Kai-chou was like any South Manchurian city—dark, dirty and malodorous, with earthen houses, unpaved roads and open sewers. Most of its 25,000 residents had fled. As Ivanov accompanied Fleisher through the empty streets the day after its capture, past corpses of soldiers and civilians—a naked man, a pregnant woman, someone with a gaping grenade hole in the stomach—he heard the desperate shrieks of a woman. They rushed into the house from where the shouts came and thwarting the attacker calmed the frightened Chinese. In the words of Ivanov:

Isolated instances of plunder and violence unfortunately are an unavoidable evil in war time. However disciplined a unit may be, there will always be in every company of 200 men some 5 or 10 scoundrels, who hold nothing on earth sacred. As the saying goes, *"v sem'e ne bez uroda"* [every family has its black sheep].

Under certain military circumstances, for example during the conquest of inhabited places, when the bloody business has unbridled the soldier's animal instincts and enflamed his passions, such men slip away from under the surveillance of the commanders, who are busy with the attainment of specific military objectives, such as pursuing the enemy, safeguarding the units after fighting, and posting guards.

Fleisher made every effort to prevent such acts and no individual soldiers were permitted in the city, the officers of the companies that garrisoned Kai-chou personally patrolling the streets to insure tranquillity. Within a week order had been restored sufficiently for some of the townspeople to come into the open and resume their normal occupation.

As Ivanov had occasion to explore the city more thoroughly, he penetrated beyond its outer drabness. Entering a Buddhist temple he was deeply impressed by the artistic beauty and emotional magnetism of a statue of Buddha, which radiated goodwill and humaneness. For a long time Ivanov stood lost in thought. When he left the temple he did so with a new feeling of respect for the Chinese people, who valued and so effectively expressed the ideals of love, forgiveness and mercy.

Escape to Korea

THE TARTAR GENERAL of Fêng-t'ien Province, who resided in Mukden, was against war. Intelligent and well informed, he realized that China was not yet able to drive out the foreigners, and that any attempt to do so would only add to China's plight. He impressed this on the military and civilian authorities of his province and with the support of the merchants and officials worked to restrain the restless populace. Every day tens of revolutionaries were executed.

To discredit the Boxers once and for all the military governor decided to expose their professed invulnerability. His experiment was eminently practical. He had over 400 of them arrested, and ordered them lined up at a temple outside the city and shot. But he had not counted on Boxer infiltration of his own ranks. The general whom he entrusted with the execution was a Boxer, who had the firing squads secretly remove the bullets from the cartridges. At the appointed time, when the crowds had gathered for the grim spectacle and the military governor had arrived in a sedan chair, the general commanded several volleys to be fired at the prisoners who dramatically remained unharmed. He himself went up to one of the condemned and six times discharged his revolver pointblank, but the Boxer did not drop dead, and stood there bowing politely. The crowd was beside itself with delight and the Boxer cause was greatly enhanced instead of discredited.

The Tartar General's continued opposition to the Boxers aroused public dissatisfaction and military insubordination. In despair he reported everything to the central government in Peking and giving up control of the local forces washed his hands of responsibility for their actions.

The railway station, located about ten miles from the city of Mukden, was guarded by the 2nd Transcaspian Rifle Battalion. When *Poruchik* Valevskii, its commanding officer, learned on July 5, that Chinese troops with artillery support had arrived from the city and were digging in near the station, he withdrew the guards and civilian employees to the isolation barracks and, ordering the neighboring guard posts to join him at once, made defense preparations.

On the morning of July 6, Chinese artillery began to bombard the barracks. According to Russian estimates the Chinese force then numbered 3,000 infantry and cavalry (5,000 by evening), and the Russians could not make any sorties. The flat, bare terrain near the barracks enabled the 70 Russian marksmen to keep the Chinese at rifle shot distance, but they had to watch helplessly as the Chinese cut the telegraph lines, burned the bridges and set fire to the station buildings and the home of Engineer Verkhovskii. The bombardment continued throughout the day and into the night.

At about 1 A.M. a gay Russian song suddenly drifted from the north. The defenders understood at once why the 14 men from a little northern post thus announced their arrival, and shifting their fire provided them with cover as they bayonetted their way through. Meanwhile reinforcements from Mukden tightened the ring around them.

Word from Chinese Christians that all other Russian posts had been attacked that day, dispelled any hope of outside help. Indeed it was up to the battalion to come to the rescue of smaller posts. During the night of July 6 to 7, the entire detachment and the civilians managed to make their way to Mukden Station, the Chinese plundering the property they left behind, instead of pursuing them. They continued southward to the beleagured station of Su-chia-t'un. Here a rift developed between Valevskii and the civilians. Some of the latter wished to go around the station and avoid another conflict with the Chinese. But Valevskii with the support of Engineer Verkhovskii persuaded the civilians, including some ladies, that the liberation of 12 railway guards of the 2nd Company and 5 technicians bottled up in Su-chia-t'un was a sacred duty and a practical necessity.

The Chinese force proved only 300 strong and Valevskii's detachment easily put them to flight. But the rescuers had come too late. The station, the railroad, the telegraph posts and the barracks had already been destroyed on the 6th. Near the burned barracks lay several beheaded and completely disfigured Russian corpses, with chopped off extremities, cut open bellies and with crosses carved on their chests. Maddened, the Cossacks tracked down the fleeing Chinese and dispatched them with vengeance.

Only three Cossacks and two civilian employees of the hapless post had managed to escape, snatching horses from under killed Chinese attackers and galloping to the Liao River, where they hid in the water. Downstream, toward Ying-k'ou, they had proceeded at night for 21 bitter days, feeding on frogs, shells and whatever else they could find. With festering, worm-eaten wounds and swollen, ulcerous legs, naked but armed, they had reached their destination, and had been rushed to a hospital, where one of the guards had expired shortly.

After plundering what the Russians had left behind, the Mukden forces belatedly set out in pursuit of Valevskii's detachment, and caught up with it en route to Yen-t'ai. Fifteen Russians were killed or wounded, but the Chinese cavalry, bravely though it fought, could not overcome the well aimed volleys of the Russians, and withdrew with heavy casualties. At Yen-t'ai Station the Russians met Chinese troops, sent from the opposite direction, from Liao-yang, and in two engagements defeated them. They advanced to the T'ai-tzu River and at night, on July 9, approached Liao-yang. Hiding in the bushes, they sent out four scouts and Engineer Verkhovskii, who was thoroughly familiar with the surroundings, to reconnoiter the enemy positions and to locate Colonel Mishchenko, who from here had ordered them to come to his support.

Verkhovskii and his four companions succeeded in getting past Liao-yang and all the Chinese outposts undetected to the village of Pai-t'ou-tzu, where the Russian colony had been. Finding it destroyed, they made their way to the barracks, where Mishchenko's detachment had defended itself. A grisly scene greeted their eyes. The charred remnants of the barracks stood in a sea of carnage, a large number of horse cadavers and the desecrated, headless corpses of their countrymen, who had been exterred, lying strewn all over the place. The only movement came from a pack of satiated dogs and pigs, that had feasted on the ghastly remains. Gagged by the nauseating sight and the unbearable stench and overcome by the thought that Mishchenko's detachment had been wiped out, the five scouts started back. On the way they managed to capture a Chinese soldier and from him learned that the bulk of Mishchenko's detachment had gotten away, but with heavy losses and pursued by the Chinese. They had missed Mishchenko by only two days! Chinese Christians, fleeing to the mountains, told them that everywhere Christian missions had been destroyed and the missionaries killed and that the Russian railway posts had been withdrawn or annihilated.

It seemed futile to try to catch up with Mishchenko, especially since the railway appeared to have been destroyed already and no help was forthcoming from Port Arthur, which itself was said to be in grave danger. There was likely to be less opposition away from the railroad. Calling everyone together, Valevskii announced, therefore, that he had decided to turn eastward, to Korea. Verkhovskii demurred; Korea seemed too far away. Ying-k'ou, the treaty port of Newchwang, was closer and was bound to be protected by English and Russian vessels. He felt that they should go there, breaking up into little groups and traveling at night, down the bushlined course of the Liao River.

The rift between civilian and military thinking lay not so much in the direction as in the manner of withdrawal. Believing that the much larger detachment of Mishchenko had been wiped out by the pursuing Chinese and that any military engagement would be catastrophic for their smaller number, weighted down as they were with women and wounded, Verkhovskii felt that they must avoid detection at all cost, and that this was possible only if they broke up. Valevskii would not hear of it. He argued that little groups would be more vulnerable and inclined to panic. Morale was a survival factor, and could be maintained only if the unit stayed together and retreated with discipline and honor.

The next afternoon, as they followed eastward, along the T'ai-tzu River, they ran into Chinese forces. In the exchange of fire that developed, Valevskii was felled by a large caliber bullet in the chest. Entrusting his money and his last words to his mother to Sargeant Borodich, he gave his final orders to the men who had gathered at his side, and taking out his revolver tried to end his agony. A Cossack wrested the weapon from his hand. Seconds later he expired. Weeping openly, without tools to dig a grave, the bereaved comrades covered his body with stones and prayed for his soul. At the graveside the noncom Pilipenko, who took over command, announced that they would proceed to Korea, as decided by Valevskii. When he asked Verkhovskii to select the best route, the engineer replied: "The route is easy here—directly along the river, and all the time east. But you will have to go a long time."

During the night one of the Cossacks awakened Pilipenko and told him that some of the civilians and soldiers were whispering about splitting off, now that the officerless detachment was incapable of defending itself. To cut short the discussion that was developing, Pilipenko gave orders to move out at once. Walking under the cover of bushes and crossing the river back and forth to mislead would-be pursuers, the men were only loosely in touch with each other. When Pilipenko counted heads at the first break, Verkhovskii, the majority of the employees and 14 guards had disappeared.

Undaunted the outfit continued as a unit. Here and there it had to fight, now retreating, now advancing, suffering casualties, but retaining its morale, since it was strong enough to demand and obtain food, clothing and transportation for the ill and wounded. Thus Pilipenko led the men to Korea, where they were well received and whence the Russian Consul, Aleksandr Pavlov, sent them on a steamer to Port Arthur.[14]

The fate of those who had deserted the detachment was less fortunate. One relatively large group consisting of a technician, a telegrapher and his wife, the wife of a machinist, some 6 guards and several foremen also made their way to Korea. But without the strength to demand what they needed, they suffered far greater hardships, for days went without food, carried their wounded on their backs and finally escaped across the border only due to the kindness and courage of a Chinese family, that took pity on the wretched refugees, hid them in its home, fed them, and secretly ferried them across the Yalu River to Korea, rejecting payment for its mission of mercy. The ordeal left lasting scars on the minds of the survivors. Abandoning his wounded wife to the Chinese rabble, the telegrapher had saved his life only to be haunted by his conscience for the rest of his years.

The others who had followed Verkhovskii's advice and split into small groups were hunted down by the Chinese and with but few exceptions tortured to death. Verkhov-

[14]According to *Die Kämpfe der russischen Truppen in der Mandschurei im Jahre 1900* (The battles of the Russian troops in Manchuria in 1900), a German summary of official Russian General Staff reports, the Russian railway officials and guards withdrew from Mukden to Ta-shih-ch'iao, whither Colonel Dombrovskii had been sent from Port Arthur with the 11th East Siberian Rifle Regiment, and arrived there after repeated engagements on July 14. Sixty-five men of the guard under Valevskii and Pilipenko had become separated, according to this version.

skii himself fared worst of all. Kushakov saw his head displayed in a cage on the wall of Liao-yang. There was no mistaking it. It was the whole head, with skin and teeth and the familiar beard. The skull bore marks of three fatal blows; two front teeth had been knocked out from the roots and bent. One eye had been torn out and dried-up dangled from the face.[15]

[15]Informed before the attack that Verkhovskii was being held prisoner in Liao-yang, the Russians offered a reward for his liberation and promised to spare the city if he were released. On September 15, the Emperor had authorized exchanging a senior Chinese official, captured by the Russians, for Verkhovskii. Later, after his head was discovered, orders were given to find the remainder of the corpse. The Chinese produced a coffin which allegedly contained the body, but when the Russians opened it, they found a manekin instead.

The Struggle for Ying-k'ou

THE WAR IN MANCHURIA differed from the conflict in China proper in that it was basically bilateral rather than international. Operations at Ying-k'ou, the port of Newchwang on the Gulf of Liaotung, were an exception. They too involved the military confrontation of Russia and China, but Ying-k'ou, a city of about 80,000 inhabitants at the mouth of the Liao River, was a treaty port, with an international settlement and rival foreign interests. Here there were foreign consulates and European stores, a Roman Catholic mission, a Russo-Chinese bank, a Customs House, a club and even a boulevard on which its English, German, Belgian and Russian residents promenaded.

Situated west of the South Manchurian railway line (yet connected to it), Ying-k'ou was closer to the Sino-Western conflict that had erupted at Ta-ku and Tien-tsin[16] than other South Manchurian cities and thus was quick to experience Boxer agitation. First, agents had plastered the city with anti-Christian posters and proclamations, while small groups of adolescents at street corners had aroused the populace with magic formulas and exercises. Then, adult Boxers, pouring into Manchuria at different points, had held mass meetings in the city, haranguing against the Westerners, and forcing

[16]Known also as T'ien-ching.

the local merchants to display flags in their honor. Un-molested, if not encouraged, by the Intendant of Circuit,[17] the ill equipped and disorganized but fanatical Boxers began building barricades and bridged the narrow streets with roof-top passageways.

In mid-June Vice Admiral Alekseev telegraphed to the Minister of War that the Russian consul in Newchwang had requested the strengthening of the guards. Alekseev asked permission to send one company and a half-sotnia of Cossacks should this become necessary. The Minister of War forwarded the telegram to the Minister of Foreign Affairs with the recommendation that Alekseev be given authority to take whatever measures he deemed necessary to prevent the outbreak of hostile disturbances near territory occupied by Russia and to protect the railway construction. Foreign Minister Count Mikhail Murav'ev agreed, but in his reply expressed the desire that Russian forces not go far beyond the Kwantung region, lest they encounter numerically superior units of insurgents, who, as it now seemed obvious, had the support of government troops. Reading the report of the Minister of War and his recommendation that Alekseev be given the requested authorization, Emperor Nicholas II commented in his own hand: "It is extremely important for us not to scatter our forces."

Upon the outbreak of hostilities at Tientsin and the destruction of the railway line in Manchuria, Colonel Dombrovskii had been sent from Port Arthur to Tashih-ch'iao with the 11th East Siberian Rifle Regiment and a battery and sotnia of Cossacks. After the arrival of reinforcements from the Ussuri region, Colonel Khorunzhenkov had followed with his detachment from Port

[17]*Tao-t'ai.*

Arthur to Ta-shih-ch'iao by train, while units of the 7th and 8th East Siberian Rifle Regiments had proceeded to Ying-k'ou and Ta-shih-ch'iao by sea. In July the land forces at Ying-k'ou had been augmented by Mishchenko's guards, who had retreated to the Russian settlement from the southern sector of the railway. Moreover, as Ying-k'ou was a treaty port, Russian gunboats were on hand when unrest swept the country.

When large Chinese forces massed at Newchwang, which lay some distance north of Ying-k'ou, the intendant sent his assistant to the Chinese commander, General Shou, to inform him of the presence of Russian gunboats which, he warned, would level Ying-k'ou to the ground, should the Russian settlement be attacked. General Shou angrily retorted that the intendant should defend himself with the 15,000 men he had and move into the Russians' rear, should they bypass the port city. The intendant demurred, but promised to bridle the Russian action by diplomatic means. In this he succeeded until August 4. Guided by the reassurances of the intendant as well as of the foreign merchants that all was calm and well, the Russian Consul, Andrei Timchenko-Ostroverkhov, asked Colonel Mishchenko and General Fleisher (who had arrived on July 29) not to disrupt the peace with military action.

Meanwhile General Chin Ch'ang, the commander of the Chinese armies in Fêng-t'ien Province, decided to counteract Russian occupation of key points on the Liaotung Peninsula by moving major forces to Newchwang and An-shan-chan, keeping a general reserve at Sha-ho-tzu. At the same time he requested Peking to send 20 battalions to the Gulf of Liaotung to operate behind Russian lines and destroy the railway. Small detachments were to fight delaying actions, and gradually fall back on Newchwang. It was the Chinese plan to lure the Russians to An-shan, then strike them with overwhelming numbers from three sides—from Newchwang, Sha-ho-tzu and the Ch'ien-shan mountains—the Ying-K'ou detachment and Peking forces cutting off any escape. Heretofore Chinese action had been uncoordinated and ineffective. Now large forces—some 50,000 troops with 60 guns—under one commander-in-chief threatened to give a completely new dimension to the war.

While the Chinese were making preparations for a large battle, a small engagement rocked Ying-k'ou on July 26. Learning that some of the troops, driven by Khorunzhenkov from Hsiung-yüeh-ch'êng, were fleeing toward Ying-k'ou, Mishchenko went out to meet them with two and a half companies and 2 guns. As he rounded the city from the northeast, past the eastern fort, the Chinese raised a flag and rushed to their positions. Unwilling to expose his back to the guns of the fort, Mishchenko gave the Chinese one hour to remove their forces from the walls. Defiantly the Chinese poured Mauser-armed riflemen onto the faces of the fort and onto the walls of the city. Commanders with flags appeared and messengers galloped into the city. Fifteen minutes before the expiration of the ultimatum the Russians began to deploy their forces. Kushakov and Mamonov led their companies of railway guards toward the northern and eastern faces; Troitskii and Prokopenko with the riflemen of the 7th East Siberian Company guarded the right flank against a sortie from the city. The moment the hour was up, the Russians opened fire, and although the Chinese replied, the accuracy and rapidity of the Russian salvoes and volleys quickly emptied the faces. Within fifteen minutes the Russians scaled the wall. The enemy poured out of the fort on the opposite side and fled to the city, while two squadrons of Cossacks, sabers raised, sped toward them from behind a village.

As the Russians stepped out of the fort, they were fired upon from the city wall. They returned the fire and began to advance against the city, when a special messenger from the Consul halted the attack. The fleeing troops from Hsiung-yüeh-ch'êng, whom Mishchenko tried to cut off, were forewarned by the fighting and scattered among the neighboring villages, melting into the population. Mishchenko proceeded to the little Russian settlement and remained there until August 4, without further offensive action.[18]

Mounted patrols, sent out by Mishchenko, kept close track of enemy movements. They ascertained that Chinese forces were heading toward Newchwang and Ta-shih-ch'iao. From Newchwang to Ying-k'ou large numbers of troops could be floated downstream in a day, and the threat to the Russian settlement, already endangered by the forces in the nearby city, was real. A certain nervousness was the result, especially on the part of newly arrived troops.

One night a soldier staggered into his barracks, shouting that the Boxers were attacking. Awakened, his

---

[18]Westerners were deeply suspicious of Russian designs. Even before the outbreak of the Boxer uprising John Fowler, the American consul at Chefoo, had predicted that Russia would seize the port of Newchwang. Now he reported that Mishchenko had "attacked suddenly without any reason" and that the Consular Body, including the Russian consul, had protested the "unjustifiable action of [the] Russian military authorities" and had received "verbal assurance not to repeat such an action."

comrades sprang to their feet and began firing out of the windows into the dark, oblivious of the barracks vis-à-vis. As bullets whistled through the other building, its occupants likewise rushed to the windows and shot back. Several soldiers were wounded. Hearing the gunfire the sentinels called out the guards and utter pandemonium broke out. Kushakov, who like the other officers had been lying in bed, rushed out saber and pistol in one hand, his clothing in the other. His soldiers did not recognize him out of uniform and it took him and his undressed fellow-officers some time to restore order. Boats were sighted on the river and fire was opened at them, although, as it developed later, these were merely frightened Chinese civilians trying to get away from the shooting. Upon closer investigation it was learned that the soldier whose shouts had triggered the melee had stepped into the night and squatted down to relieve himself. When he had finished and straightened up, someone had hit him over the head. Whether it was a Boxer who had stolen into camp or a fellow Russian who was frightened by the sudden apparition from below was never determined.

Meanwhile Boxer influence had risen in the Chinese city, which was cut off from the foreign settlement by barricades, erected by the European residents, and manned by English and German volunteers, a small Japanese and a small Russian landing force and a company of the 7th East Siberian Regiment. The authority of the intendant, who had profited from his association with the foreigners and tried to preserve the *status quo,* was undercut by an officer from Newchwang who joined the Boxers in advocating the extermination of the white men, especially the Russians. Fearing for his own life and property, the intendant fled onto barges. Boxers tried to prevent his escape and plunder his fortune, but they were no match for his well armed escort and many were killed.

That day, on August 4, as rumor of the intendant's flight spread through Ying-k'ou and people speculated that he had sought refuge with the Russians, mobs headed for the European barricades. A volley from the defenders killed nine Boxers and the rest withdrew, but the officer from Newchwang began to distribute fire-arms and ammunition to all who wanted them. The peaceful townspeople fled in every direction until the gates were closed and guards posted to prevent their departure. The propertyless minority that remained, looted the houses of the refugees.

One company of the 7th East Siberian Regiment had helped man the barricades since the end of July. Now, with the outbreak of disorders and confirmation from the Russian Consul that regular Chinese troops had participated in the attack, Fleisher ordered Mishchenko to advance on the city from the southwest with two companies and two Cossack sotnias of the guard and a gun, while two companies of the 7th East Siberian Regiment were sent to occupy the European settlement. The gunboat *Gremiashchii* was directed to bombard the fort at the mouth of the river, the *Otvazhnyi* the city.

At 3 P.M. Mishchenko approached the fort he had taken on July 26. It had been reoccupied by the Chinese. As the Cossack sotnias opened fire from the brick works and the 6th Company advanced in combat line, the Chinese garrison hastily withdrew to the city. A signal flare was shot into the air and the *Otvazhnyi* began the naval bombardment. Almost at once hobbling women with bound feet, clutching infants in their arms, and other peaceful residents, young and old, laden with hastily gathered belongings, rushed out toward the river and jumping into boats sought safety mid-stream. Chinese troops meanwhile poured out of the southern gates to meet the guard companies in the outskirts, but the Russians hit them before they took up their positions and threw them back into the city. As the Chinese fled back through the gates they suffered heavy casualties from Russian gunfire. Within the city they found themselves pounded by Russian artillery from land and from the river as well as by volleys from the barricades. Dropping their weapons some soldiers fled to the boats on the river; the majority ran out of the gates again and stampeded toward the 6th Company. Throwing the 2nd Company, which he had kept in reserve, into the battle line too, Mishchenko butchered the onrushing Chinese, who in their flight were trying to break through the Russian lines. An attempt by the officer from Newchwang and a disorderly horde of soldiers to take the eastern fort was foiled by a platoon of the 6th Company and a platoon of artillery. The officer was wounded in hand-to-hand combat, and he and his detachment scattered into the high kaoliang. The Russians lacked men to close the ring around the Chinese and many fled past their flanks. The other Russian units could not be shifted quickly enough for effective pursuit and one even opened fire on the fort which the Russians had taken, so that they had to take cover in a water-filled ditch to escape the bullets of their comrades.

In the city the Russians captured the arsenal and military stores and many banners and flags. Leaving behind half a company to guard the entrances to the city, they started back for the little Russian settlement, three miles away. They were soaking wet and caked with mud. They had had to cross the fortress moat with water to their necks, and now the very heavens had opened up and threatened to wash them away. The driving rain converted the roads to rivulets and the rivulets to streams. Every place was covered with water and underneath the mud clung to their tired feet. The horses refused to pull the gun, and the exhausted soldiers, crawling on all fours across the slippery hillocks, ravines and ditches had to drag it by hand. When they reached the settlement at last at 1 A.M., officers and common soldiers alike flopped down without undressing, dirty and drenched to the bone, and fell asleep at once.

The following day, on August 5, Vice Admiral Evgenii Alekseev, arrived in Ying-k'ou on the cruiser *Zabiiaka*. With him came his chief of staff, Colonel Flug, and his diplomatic commissar, Ivan Korostovets, who had served as Second Secretary of the Russian Legation in Peking from 1891 to 1894 and in later years was to become Russian Minister to China (1909-12). Alekseev was a man of 55, short and stocky, with a large head and a slightly hooked nose and penetrating black eyes. He wore a small beard, which had begun to gray. Full of energy and drive, he demanded action from his subordinates. Usually polite, he became sharp in his speech when his wishes were not understood or carried out halfheartedly. "In spite of his Russian name I would not have called him Russian," Korostovets recalled. "It is said that his mother was Armenian. He had a practical, lively mind, with little inclination, as is often the case among Russians, for metaphysical generalization and chimeras. I consider his major shortcomings [to have

63

been] indecision, susceptibility to flattery, and intolerance of the opinions of others."[19]

The next day, on August 6, Alekseev addressed the following letter to the American Vice Consul, who represented the interests of a number of countries.

> The hostile behaviour of the Chinese Authorities, who had first encouraged the rebellion and then declared that they could not maintain order ended in an open attack on our forces placed in the city in accordance to the wish of the Consular Body.
>
> During the said attack the Chinese Authorities had fled leaving the town to its fate.
>
> To avoid disorder and looting by the Chinese Mob and with the object of protecting the commerce of the Port and the property of the foreigners the Russian Military Authority found it necessary to place the town under the guard of the Imperial Russian troops.
>
> It may be added that the perfidious destruction of the Chinese Eastern Railway by the insurgents and soldiers also necessitated our placing in Yinkou a force of troops to protect the same.

[19]A somewhat different picture of Alekseev was given by the German naval attaché in St. Petersburg, *Korvetten-Kapitän* Hintze. In a confidential dispatch he described Alekseev's reputation in the Russian capital: "The Russian officers . . . are *unanimous* in their praise of Admiral Alekseev . . . . They mention as his traits of character primarily the following: determination underneath outward smoothness, tenacity underneath apparent complaisance, a man who lives and lets live, big-hearted, sensible, and very knowledgeable about East Asia. . . . Alekseev applies his screw where he needs it, and turns it very softly and imperceptibly, but always continues to turn it, more slowly or more rapidly, depending on the circumstances, till he has tightened it. . . . Alekseev has no enemies, but he does have many people whom he has won over through material [benefits] or through kindness and obligingness. He has offended only those people whom he definitely needs no longer."

Nevertheless the Imperial Government tried to avoid this extreme measure, Yinkow being a Treaty Port. It is to be understood that the temporary administration that is to be established in the interest of the Russians as well as the foreigners and Chinese will not infringe the rights and privileges which they have enjoyed previously in Yinkow.

The foreign Community has to note that the sole object of the provisional Russian Administration is to maintain peace and order and restore trade, and I hope in these endeavors to have the sincere support of the foreign representatives.

The temporary administration of which Alekseev spoke was to be civilian. But the problem of setting up any Russian administration that would not conflict with the established foreign interests in this active, international port was great, if not insurmountable. While one Russian writer asserted that "in three days the question was settled to everybody's satisfaction, both of the European residents and of the native population," in point of fact the Westerners were displeased and even questioned the need of the Russian occupation. Although Alekseev's letter noted that the Russian forces that had been attacked in the city had been placed there "in accordance to the wish of the Consular Body" and although Korostovets wrote that Timchenko-Ostroverkhov, at the request of the foreign consuls, had asked Alekseev for reinforcements, assuring him that the foreigners would not object if the Russians occupied Ying-k'ou, indeed that they would turn to the Japanese, who had two gunboats and a transport there, if the Russians did not do so, English and American representatives reported that the Russians had moved in under the pretext of an "alleged attack." They denounced the shelling of the city by the *Otvazhnyi* and when informed that the army threatened to bombard the Chinese sector if all arms were not surrendered objected to such "barbarity."

Alekseev was pleased with the occupation of Ying-k'ou, which had occurred with little bloodshed and, he believed, in accordance with the wishes of the foreign consuls. "Now the bird has been killed and the hunters look who will succeed in picking it up," he told Korostovets. "We must not miss this opportunity." On August 9, he announced that the civil administration would consist of Timchenko-Ostroverkhov, the Russian consul, who was well acquainted with local conditions, as administrator, Secretary Khristofor Kristi as Acting Consul, Clapier de Collongue as commandant of Newchwang and Shmit (Schmidt) of the Russo-Chinese Bank as deputy commissioner of Customs.

The British objected to the raising of the Russian flag over the Customs House, which was registered in the name of Sir Robert Hart, a British subject, and thus extraterritorial in status, but they eventually accepted Russian assurances that this was not a reflection on English rights and Cecil Bowra, the English Commissioner of Customs, consented to remain in his job, with the understanding that Shmit would not interfere in the internal functioning of his office and staff. The English also did not like but reluctantly went along with the deposit of the customs revenue in a special account of the Russo-Chinese Bank rather than its surrender to the temporary administration of the city. (The Chinese Customs Bank, where the money had been deposited customarily, had been closed when the Chinese left Ying-k'ou).

On August 19, regulations were issued for the provisional government. As civil administrator, Timchenko-Ostroverkhov was advised by a council, composed of the military commandant, the customs commissioner, the sanitary inspector, the chief of police, the treasurer and the city judge as well as of representatives of the Consular Body, foreign commercial firms and Chinese merchants. The civil administrator had the right to issue byelaws, levy taxes and duties on the Chinese, dispose of Chinese government property and confirm administrative expenditures. The city judge had jurisdiction over cases involving foreigners lacking consular representation, and was to try all cases brought to him by the police as well as cases between Russians and Chinese.

The Amur Incident

O N THE LEFT bank of the Amur River, at its juncture with the Zeia, stood Blagoveshchensk. Founded in 1856 as a military post, it had been named originally Ust'-Zeisk (Mouth of the Zeia Place). In 1858, in view of its strategic location and commercial significance, it became the military, civil and judicial center of the newly established Amur Province and the seat of the military governor. It was renamed Blagoveshchensk (Good News Place) in commemoration of Governor General Nikolai Murav'ev-Amurskii's announcement here of the annexation of the Amur region. Part of the Cossack population was moved about 4½ miles up the Amur River to form the new Cossack village (stanitsa) of Verkhne-Blagoveshchensk (Upper Blagoveshchensk); part went to Ignat'evskaia Stanitsa.

The newly founded city of Blagoveshchensk grew rapidly. By 1900 it had nearly 38,000 inhabitants with 3,700 houses, mostly of wooden construction. Its streets were wide and straight, running parallel with the Amur River and intersecting at right angles. An American traveler found the wide streets of Blagoveshchensk "as fine for its leading banks and stores as Portland, Maine or Portland, Oregon could show, or any smaller city of the Union." As for the wooden structures, he remarked:

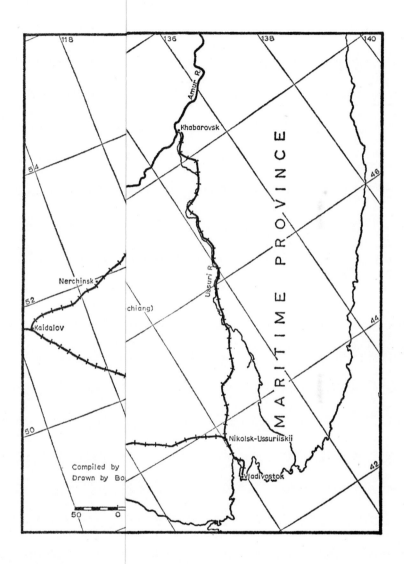

118   136   138   140

Amur R.

Khabarovsk

54

48

MARITIME PROVINCE

Nerchinsk

52

Ussuri R.

chiang)

Kaidalov

44

50

Nikolsk-Ussuriiskii

Compiled by
Drawn by Bo

Vladivostok

42

50   0

"I never had believed that a log-house city could be so picturesque and substantial in appearance. Upon the churches the people have lavished their chief wealth. At least three of them are beautiful and costly buildings that would do honor to any European capital, and a fourth that is building will, when completed surpass them all." Blagoveshchensk possessed schools, a public library, a theatre, and a telephone service. "In short, so far as outward civilization went," a highly critical Social Democratic exile observed, "Blagoveshchensk stood in no way behind European towns of the same size, and was even in some ways more advanced."

The Amur River formed the boundary line between Russia and China for hundreds of miles. On the right bank opposite Blagoveshchensk, lay the Manchu town of Sakhalian.[20] It had been opened to foreign trade in 1858, and during the Manchurian gold rush in the 1880's had mushroomed in size to a population of about 50,000. The inhabitants of both sides of the Amur freely went back and forth between Blagoveshchensk and Sakhalian by boats and junks in summer or directly across the ice in winter, the Manchurians and Chinese being the main suppliers of meat and vegetables for the Russian city.

Reports of unrest in China began reaching Blagoveshchensk in May of 1900, but they aroused little concern, for unrest and disorder were all too common in that country, and all eyes were turned on the Boer War in

[20]This is the Russian appellation, adopted in this book to avoid confusion with Sakhalin Island. The Manchus called it Sakhalian or Sakhalian Ula; it became known also by the Chinese name of Ta-hei-ho or Ta-hei-ho-tun, later Hei-ho or Hei-ho-tun. In 1949, when the county seat was transferred from (old) Aigun, twenty miles south, the city adopted the name of (new) Aigun or Ai-hun, as it is called in Chinese.

Africa. That the people of Manchuria would resent foreign activity in their heartland and agitate for the withdrawal of the Russians from the interior, treaty rights notwithstanding, was understandable enough to the residents of the border city. But for decades relations between Russia and China had been good, friendlier than between China and the other foreign powers, foreign diplomats complaining that pro-Russians dominated the court, and their enormous common frontier had remained unguarded. No thought was given to a sudden strike by China against Russian shipping on the Amur or against Russian territory beyond. When it came, it appeared to the Russian residents of Blagoveshchensk as "truly Asiatic" in deception.

The Chinese were successful in hiding their large-scale preparations from the Russians. This is the more remarkable because the Chinese inhabitants of Blagoveshchensk seem to have been informed of the pending attack, and on July 8, began crossing the Amur with their belongings. Others could not liquidate their business and leave in time; others yet deemed it safer to stay than move their possessions within reach of the Chinese soldiery. But whether or not they had pledged their support to Boxer agents, as rumors alleged, they withheld what they knew from the Russians, and the latter regarded them as more than mere bystanders.

Toward the end of May the strains of martial music drifted across the Amur River from Sakhalian, and Russians who had gone to purchase cattle from the Chinese reported seeing some 7,000 troops in the mountains beyond Sakhalian. But Chinese activity was dismissed as routine maneuvers. Reports from China proper about the outbreak and course of hostilities gradually brought home the seriousness of the Far Eastern situation, yet not fully, since government dispatches tied up the wires, and telegrams from the Russian news agency arrived irregularly.

On June 24, word was received of the allied capture of the Ta-ku forts and the same day posters ordering the mobilization of the Priamur region were plastered all over Blagoveshchensk. But although reservists began pouring into the city from the neighboring villages and settlements during the night and although ships were sent out on the Zeia River to bring in more, the selection of horses proceeded so quietly and discriminately as to strengthen the feeling that the mobilization was merely tentative. Nor was it sure at whom it was directed. Japan, against whom Russia had a defensive alliance with China, was acting jointly with the Western powers, while the idea of China, the Sick Man of the Far East, taking on the rest of the world singlehandedly seemed inconceivable. Here and there fanatical Boxers might cause trouble, but as A. V. Kirkhner, who lived in Blagoveshchensk, wrote: "So accustomed had everyone become to looking on China and the Chinese with utter disdain, and so familiar had their cowardice become to all inhabitants along the border, that there was hardly anyone who expected a serious war with China."

Yet if they did not fear the Chinese, the reservists were embittered against them for being the cause of their having been torn from their homes and livelihood at great personal loss. Drowning their sorrows in vodka, they beat up peaceful Chinese. "It's your fault, you dogs, that we're taken from our work and our families and sent to our deaths!" they muttered. Russian workmen who found their wages pulled down by cheap

71

Oriental labor, also vented their wrath on the hapless Chinese, who bore the pain and indignity with silent hostility. Forewarned by Boxers or frightened by the drunken attacks of the Russian soldiers and frequently driven out of the neighboring villages by Russian peasants, Chinese and Manchus streamed across the river to the Chinese side. While practically no one thought war imminent, many believed a clash with China over control of both sides of the Amur River unavoidable sooner or later, and looked forward, indeed prepared for it.

Telegrams received in Blagoveshchensk on June 28, conveying the government's declaration of June 24, that it was not at war with China, the troops it had dispatched to Ta-ku and Tientsin going there merely to help the friendly government of China crush the insurgents who were destroying the railroad, added to the existing confusion. To calm the populace the governor closed down all drinking places and formally warned that anyone spreading false and alarming rumors or in any way molesting the Chinese inhabitants would be punished to the full extent of the law. Meanwhile the city council and the local military authorities took measures to protect Blagoveshchensk from internal disorder or bandit raids. Old rifles were ordered repaired and distributed among the Russian subjects, four steamers were armed and armored to patrol the Amur River, Cossacks were sent out to protect the telegraph line, three Cossack sotnias were assigned to duty along the Amur, and border units were instructed how to guard against inroads of bandits and vagrants. There was no question, however, of warding off a full-scale military attack by China.

Rumors cannot be decreed away, however, and alarm mounted. Chinese and Russian homes were robbed and suspicion fell on those of the "opposite" nationality. Angered by their maltreatment, Chinese residents shed their passivity and threatened that China would go to war with Russia. Whether or not they believed their own threats, they began to transfer their money to banks in China and to exchange paper currency for gold. Chinese servants and cooks actually said that they wanted their pay because there would soon be war, but the Russians merely reassured them that they would be safe in the event of war. In an editorial, dated June 29, the Blagoveshchensk newspaper *Amurskii Krai* reminded its readers that their proximity to the Manchurian border entailed not only certain risks and sacrifices on their part, but also certain responsibilities.

The proximity of Manchuria imposes on us residents of Blagoveshchensk certain obligations, which are further increased by the circumstance that within the precincts of our city there are not a few emigrants from China, who, in the great majority of cases, live orderly, and by their work and peaceful activity assist the historical course of our cultural mission. These inhabitants of our city, who carry on their shoulders a considerable part of the city's unskilled labor, supplying us with a countless array of necessary provisions, who even help our house-keeping with their distinctive organization of the distribution of these products through the whole city, these our inhabitants must themselves be glad that the difficult historical moment through which they are living happened to catch them on our territory, where they must be sure that their life will go on just as peacefully and quietly as in the past.

The editorial pointed to the need of preserving a "sober view" of current events and not giving oneself over to artificially created feelings of hostility. While the uneducated Chinese masses could readily be fanned up against the Russians, the Russians, as more educated and intelligent, should lean backwards to preserve the good relations between the peoples of the two countries. It warned that mistreatment of Chinese residents might embitter the entire Chinese populace and lead to serious consequences.

If the local Chinese residents merely threatened the Russians with war, Chinese merchants in nearby Aigun warned members of the Upper Amur Company, with whom they had considerable business dealings, that military hostilities were definitely in the offing and that they had better evacuate their residences opposite the city. They reported that all Chinese residents along the Zeia River had withdrawn with their families to the Chinese side, their place being taken by Manchu soldiers in disguise. They alleged also that Chinese soldiers in civilian garb had traveled on Russian steamers to Mo-ho, and that rapid fire cannons had been received in Aigun during the winter.

Many residents did leave Blagoveshchensk, and headed for the gold mines, their country houses, or back to Russia, frequently to be stranded along the way as it was hot and dry and the Amur and Zeia Rivers were going down. Other townspeople turned their houses into fortresses and fired their rifles and revolvers into the night to ward off would-be intruders. Yet in the absence of war, girls who wanted to become nurses were turned away and reservists were sent on to other places. Word of the assassination of the German Minister in

Peking had been received on July 12, and the outbreak of disorders at Harbin and along the railway line was reported shortly. But this only confirmed the belief of the majority that troubles were confined to the capital and the interior of Manchuria and that Blagoveshchensk would be beyond the pale of fighting. There is no more striking illustration of this than that on July 12, the bulk of the garrison left the city for Khabarovsk.

The loading of the garrison with its horses, fodder and military supplies onto six steamers and nine barges took all day.[21] It was a festive affair, marked by religious services, a military review, patriotic speeches and exhilarating march music. When the vessels finally pulled out in the evening, the Russian side of the river was lined with civilian well-wishers and the remaining handful of troops. Galloping along the bank, Cossacks accompanied the departing garrison, while gun salutes from the 2nd Battery, which had stayed in Blagoveshchensk, thundered above the hurrahs shouted from both land and water. No less a gathering of people stood on the Chinese side of the river and watched with fascination the cheerful exit from Blagoveshchensk of its defenders. When the Cossacks, who accompanied the vessels, galloped onto a shallow bank off shore, the Chinese withdrew at once to Sakhalian, fearful of a Russian crossing.

A day and a half later, on the morning of July 14, an incident occurred downstream. The private steamer *Mikhail*, en route from Khabarovsk to Blagoveshchensk with five barges (the first one laden with guns and shells, the others empty), was passing the Chinese village of

---

[21]The steamer *Pavel* with two barges, *Semen Dezhnev* with three barges, *Molly* with two barges, *Khanka* (?), *Shilka* with two barges and *Lidiia* with two barges.

Aigun, when the Chinese signalled with flags for her to dock. As the Russians failed to note or understand the flags, the Chinese fired several rounds and the *Mikhail*, manned only by *Shtabs-kapitan* Krivtsev and several Cossacks who accompanied the cargo, halted. Seeing the military supplies, the Chinese officials who came aboard to inspect the cargo declared that the ship was under arrest. When Krivtsev and his orderly went ashore to discuss the matter, they were grabbed and taken away to Aigun.

A couple of hours later, the government steamer *Selenga* appeared from downstream and, on a whistle from the *Mikhail*, pulled up alongside. The Chinese shouted from shore that Colonel V. B. Kol'shmit commander of the Amur border region, land at once, but Kol'shmit demanded that the senior Chinese official come aboard instead. In view of the military preparations that were evident all along the bank of the river at Aigun and upstream, Kol'shmit could dally no further and ordered both ships to continue full steam ahead. As soon as the ships got under way, the Chinese opened fire. The fairway of the river did not allow the Russians to hug their own shore all the time, and repeatedly they had to run the gauntlet of the Chinese batteries within murderous range. The cannons overshot their mark and the shells flew over the vessels harmlessly, but the shower of rifle bullets that rained upon the vessels took its toll, felling the colonel, 4 Cossacks and 2 sailors. The steersman remained behind the wheel on his knees after his legs were shot through. Critically wounded, Kol'shmit briefly stopped at Cossack Post No. 1 to take aboard a new commander (Cornet Vertoprakhov), leave behind the four empty barges, and have word of the Chinese attack relayed all along shore. At 6 P.M. the vessels reached Blagoveshchensk riddled with bullets, and began to disgorge the wounded and dead.

News of the incident electrified Blagoveshchensk. Russian belief that the attack had been a deliberate act of war was strengthened by the testimony of Krivtsev. Detained by the Chinese at Aigun, he had been whisked overland to Sakhalian and from there had been sent across the river on a boat at about the same time that the ships arrived. He bore a communication from the district chief[22] of Aigun to the effect that he had acted on orders from the military governor of Tsitsihar (Hei-lung-chiang), not to let a single ship pass.

That night, on July 14, two companies of the 2nd East Siberian Line Battalion, 6 guns of the 2nd Battery of the 2nd East Siberian Artillery Brigade and a sotnia of the Amur Cossack Regiment crossed the Zeia and headed for Cossack Post No. 1 to protect the barges, left there by the *Mikhail*, and to prevent a repetition of the Chinese attack at Aigun. The following day, on July 15, a special meeting of the city council deliberated on measures necessary for the defense of Blagoveshchensk itself, notably the organization of a volunteer defense force. The river bank was divided into six guard sectors, headed by officers and civilians named by the city council, with Lieutenant Colonel Orfenov, commandant of the city, above them. The internal security of Blagoveshchensk was left in the hands of Chief of Police Batarevich, Lieutenant General K. N. Gribskii, Military Governor of the Amur Region, assuming overall command of the entire defense of Blagoveshchensk and vicinity. Messengers from the cavalry reserve and the telephone,

22*Amban.*

where available, were to connect the different sectors with the city guard house, from where Orfenov was to direct the defense of the river bank.

Gribskii assured the city council of his full support and provided military instructors for the volunteers. "I am confident," he declared, "that in view of such energetic measures and the attitude with which the citizens have met their obligations at this difficult moment, the Lord will help us preserve our city from all hostile action on the part of our treacherous neighbors." When someone asked Gribskii whether anything should be done with the many Chinese who lived in and around Blagoveshchensk, he said, no. Special measures were neither necessary nor advisable, for no war had been declared between Russia and China. Gribskii added that he had reassured a delegation of Chinese subjects that no harm would come to peaceful foreigners on Russian soil. Gribskii told the councilmen that he foresaw no danger for the city, and read to them a telegram from the Governor General, announcing the arrival soon of special forces to protect Blagoveshchensk and keep open navigation on the Amur River. After overseeing the distribution of surplus weapons to transport drivers and to the newly formed 2nd Company of the 1st Blagoveshchensk Reserve Battalion and after issuing instructions about the guarding of the camps and other areas, therefore, Gribskii deemed his presence no longer needed. Preceded by a half-sotnia of Cossacks, he departed to join the forces that had headed for Cossack Post No. 1, from where he planned to move against the Boxers at Aigun to secure navigation on the Amur River.

Blagoveshchensk and the river bank, stretching over 6 miles from the military camps to the mouth of the

Zeia, were left defended by one company of the 2nd East Siberian Line Battalion, the local garrison and two units of the Blagoveshchensk Reserve Battalion (one of them, the 2nd Company of the Reserve Battalion as yet unarmed), one sotnia of the Nerchinsk Cossack Regiment, and two guns. The citizens of Blagoveshchensk realized that the number of troops that remained was small, but few knew any exact figures. The Chinese, it may be added, were probably better informed, for not only were Chinese in the employ of many of the commanders and of the townspeople, but that day an unusual number of Chinese poked into every place, including the camps, offering radishes for sale. The citizens of Blagoveshchensk had heard that there were Chinese troops and guns across the river at Sakhalian and they were alarmed enough by everything to volunteer their services, yet at the same time they dismissed the Amur incident, Krivtsev's message notwithstanding, as an accidental breakdown in Chinese discipline, and went along with the opinion of Gribskii that Blagoveshchensk itself was not in danger.

Panic at Blagoveshchensk

THE 15TH OF July was a clear and warm Sunday, too beautiful to think of war and death. The commanders of the various defense sectors did plan to get together to coordinate strategy and work out the organization of the defense force, but they had not done so yet. Most residents were out for their afternoon stroll along the quay, watching the mail steamer *Sergei Vitte*, which was running behind schedule, the loading of other vessels, and the departure of the steamer *Burlak*. Taking advantage of the calm that had settled over the city following the excitement of the night before, Chinese and Manchus had ventured back to Blagoveshchensk in the morning to fetch some of their belongings. A steam cutter patrolled the shore, and the police searched the Chinese and Manchus who came and went across the Amur, but all this was done calmly and without foreboding.

It was too lovely a day for the reservists who had not yet been issued rifles and had no duties to stay cooped up in the barracks, and a thousand or so dashed to the stream for a refreshing swim. Suddenly the Chinese opened fire from across the river. Whether they had mistaken the onrush of the bathers for an attack or merely found the swarm of naked bodies an attractive target, whether they tried to stop the *Burlak*, or whether they had planned an offensive at this time aware that the Russian frontier was denuded of the regular forces is not known. One thing is certain, the rifle fire and the ensuing cannonade caught the Russians completely by surprise.

Panic stricken, the residents who had strolled along the quay in their Sunday fineries ran down the streets leading away from the Amur, pursued by Chinese bullets. From the houses along the waterfront frightened families rushed into the open dressed as they were, while those aboard the steamers stampeded ashore, crowding and shoving each other, so that some fell into the river.

The signing up of volunteers had been in progress still in the city council building when the cannonade commenced, and those who had already registered or were about to do so grabbed the nearest rifle and cartridges. There were not enough weapons to go around and as the men fought over them many were injured. Buildings and stores believed to contain guns and ammunition were forced open, few residents having had the foresight to purchase their own. But even here there were not enough, the Chinese as the crowd believed, having bought up rifles and revolvers recently.

As those who succeeded in arming themselves dashed toward the river bank, they collided with the fleeing multitude. The confusion was compounded by the rumor that the Manchus had effected a landing on shore, and many turned to defend their own homes. Some packed up and left the city. The two companies of troops had not had time to assemble at the designated place, the order of the governor having only just been proclaimed and many of the soldiers being off duty on Sunday. No emplacement had yet been prepared for the two guns, and as they began to return fire, they did so from an open place at the soldiers' bathhouse.

Had the Manchus really crossed the river, they could have overrun the city without difficulty. Indeed, the few thousand Chinese and Manchus who were still in Blagoveshchensk could easily have set fire to the wooden city and destroyed it, especially because there was a strong wind. Seeing a group of Manchus, about to cross to the Chinese side when the bombardment began, the volunteers near the river attacked them (thereby giving rise, perhaps, to the rumor of a Manchu landing) and might well have exterminated them had they not been scattered, Russians and Manchus alike, by artillery fire from Sakhalian.

The steamer *Burlak*, which had left just before the bombardment (indeed whose departure, as noted already, may have triggered it), tried to turn back, but ran aground and remained disabled for the duration of the attack on Blagoveshchensk. The steamers *Grazhdanin* and *Neronov* sought cover on the Zeia River. It would have been quite easy, therefore, for the Chinese to have crossed the Amur. The Russians marvelled that they did not do so. In the words of A. V. Kirkhner, one of the eye-witnesses, "God saved the city of Blagoveshchensk."

Chinese grenades exploded in the streets, wounding several persons. A woman and her daughter were killed, the infant in the mother's arms escaping injury. There were other casualties among the bathers, in the barracks, and elsewhere, but no one stopped to investigate, and the inhabitants, in a long, gypsy-like caravan poured out of the city to the new slaughter-house and to the village of Astrakhanovka. Most horses had been taken by the military upon mobilization, and the people found it difficult to cart away their belongings. Many walked laden down with their most precious possessions; others carried nothing, not even food. By about 9 P.M. the Chinese guns fell silent, and the volunteers who had stood fast began digging trenches along the water front.

Meanwhile the detachment which Gribskii had joined had advanced on the left bank of the Amur River in the direction of Aigun. The steamers *Mikhail* and *Selenga* had proceeded alongside. As they came upon Chinese forces, fire was exchanged, the two guns of the *Selenga* being of particular help. When the rumble of artillery was heard from Blagoveshchensk and word of the attack followed, however, Gribskii halted his advance on Aigun and during the night hastened back with the troops.[23] He had established that a strong force of Chinese was holding the right bank of the Amur and was building ramparts along the river bank.

At Post No. 1 Gribskii left one company and 2 guns to join with armed Russian peasants in thwarting a Chinese landing at that point. The steamer *Selenga*, which had exchanged fire with Chinese shore batteries, returned to the mouth of the Zeia; the *Mikhail* remained opposite Aigun. The *Selenga* brought the crewmen of another vessel, the steamer *Telegraf*, which oblivious of the hostilities had approached Aigun from Harbin,

[23]Upon his return to Blagoveshchensk Gribskii had at his disposal for the defense of the city 2½ battalions of troops, 14 guns, 5 sotnias and one local detachment (the 2nd East Siberian Line Battalion of 4 companies); 5 companies of the 1st Battalions of the Stretensk and Chita Regiments; the 2nd Battery of the 2nd East Artillery Brigade (8 guns), ½ battery of the Transbaikal Artillery Division (4 guns), the 2 guns of the *Selenga*, 3 sotnias of the 2nd levy of the Amur Cossack Regiment and 2 sotnias of the 1st Nerchinsk Cossack Regiment, as well as 1 Reserve Company, 480 rural militiamen and 670 urban militiamen.

towing a barge of Chinese cargo. Caught in a sudden barrage of fire, the *Telegraf* had managed to escape to the Russian side but had run aground near Post No. 2, her crew saving itself aboard the *Selenga*.

On July 16, the Chinese resumed the bombardment on a much heavier scale. It was perhaps the most dangerous day for the city, the cannonade being extremely fierce and the residents not yet accustomed to it, fearful, as they had been all through the night, that a Chinese landing was in the offing. Homes and stores were locked and shutters closed. The streets were deserted except for occasional carts and refugees who traveled now in this direction now in that seeking to outguess the Chinese grenades. At street corners, protected by the walls of houses, men stood in animated groups and speculated about the future. They did not fire back at the Chinese.

While the men talked action, Anastasia Iudina, a twenty-nine year old mother and housewife, whose husband was away seeking gold and whose brother-in-law was ill at home, stepped into the forefront of the defense. Born and raised in a little village in the province of Tomsk, she had been married to a peasant at the age of 16 and had eventually moved to Blagoveshchensk, where like other Siberian women she worked in the fields, went hunting and handled boats. One day her husband had discovered gold and overnight Iudina had become rich. But underneath her fineries there beat the heart of a sturdy *Sibiriachka* (Siberian woman).

Unperturbed by the bombardment on the 15th, she had left her children and nephews at home with the housekeeper and had stepped into the bullet-spattered street to find medicine for her ailing brother-in-law. On the way to the apothecary a woman walking in front of her was hit in the leg by a bullet. Iudina stopped to apply a bandage, then continued to the apothecary, obtained the medicine and started back. Just then a group of Chinese came running her way. Thinking that the invasion had occurred, she fell to her knees and prayed. Fortunately the Chinese were Blagoveshchensk Chinese and meant no harm. She got up and hastened home, narrowly missed by grenades and bullets from across the river.

Before going out, Iudina had told her housekeeper to make a suit of men's clothing out of her apparel. Now she changed into a jacket, a shirt and wide trousers, and fastening a revolver and a dagger, picked up a rifle and went to the quay. There foxholes were being dug, and taking a shovel she carved one out of the stony ground for herself. Except for a brief visit to her house to change her white cap to one of a safer color and to peep at her sleeping children, she spent the night on guard, unrecognized as a woman in the dark.

When she ventured out again on the 16th, dressed like a lady, and stepping up to a crowd of people who had taken cover asked about the latest news, her nonchalance aroused ridicule. "Well look at that, Madame Iudina has come out to the war!" someone jeered. "If it will be necessary, I shall be able to stand up for Holy Russia," Iudina retorted calmly. Just then police officer Zaletaev of the 2nd sector rode up and asked whether someone would volunteer to take all boats from the shore to the commissary dock. No one responded. Nor did the crowd heed a similar plea on the part of Zinov'ev, a volunteer commander, who followed Zaletaev. Wishing to inspire the people, Iudina, who stood next to Zinov'ev, asked that he tell them where and for what purpose the boats were needed, so that they would know for what to die. But all he replied was, "Go away, we do not need any women here!" Enraged she responded: "How so? When the men do not go, I, a lady, can set out, and shall be able to die for Russia." Seeing that she would not give way, Zinov'ev explained that the boats were needed to take the troops over to the Chinese side, and that they had to be readied by nightfall, so that the soldiers could cross without heavy losses.

Starting out for the boats, which the official had indicated, Iudina turned back to the crowd and called upon her countrymen to join her so that all of them, acting together, could move the boats quickly. Only one man, a Pole, went with her. "Let us go, *Pani* [Lady]," he said. "You are fearless. With you it will be fun even to die!" As she started out for the boats, forgetting about her children and everything but the task ahead, abuse followed her. "There a skirt went to deliver the boats! She will wreck them! There's a bitch!" the crowd taunted.

With the aid of the Pole and her housekeeper, Evdokeia ("Dunia") Katysheva, who had accompanied her, Iudina attached two boats to the sides of a third, and climbing into that one, took the three boats to the designated place. Katysheva's legs hurt very much and sending her back home, Iudina and the Pole continued their heroic effort, enveloped by Chinese bullets. They conveyed the thirteen boats that had been pointed out to them originally, as well as some others which had to be moved elsewhere, rowing and poling with the last ounce of their strength. Two bullets flew through her skirt and at one point Iudina fell into the water, but the Pole pulled her back into the boat. This time when she reached shore she collapsed in a faint. Her companion poured water over her and revived her, kissed her hand, and disappeared. Slowly she walked back up hill to the entrenchments. A bullet grazed her hair and hit a volunteer nearby. Exhausted though she was, she stopped to bandage him.

When Iudina reached the entrenchments the officers, Cossacks and volunteers cheered her. "Long live our Siberia with our strong Russian women!" someone shouted, and a lusty three-fold hurrah thundered from the throats of the men. One of the officers came up to shake Iudina's hand and to congratulate her, and another three-fold cheer followed. The heroism of Iudina was greater than that of Joan of Arc, the author of a popular booklet wrote enthusiastically, for Joan had been inspired by divine voices and sustained by the support of her countrymen, while Iudina, facing stark reality, had been her own sole support.

Walking back home she passed the crowd that had abused her and they abused her again, making fun of her exhaustion. Undaunted she staggered on to see that her children were all right, then change back into her male attire and return to the entrenchment. But when she reached her house, she found it besieged by a mob, trying to break down the gate. People shouted that there were Chinese inside and threatened to kill all occupants and her. Offering to open the gate, Iudina calmed the crowd, and at a pre-arranged bell signal the shaken housekeeper appeared. The mob would not accept her word that there were no Chinese in the house, however, and storming in, proceeded to loot until Iudina, who had made her way inside, stepped out onto the perron and firing her pistol into the air threatened to kill all trespassers. Though there were some who wanted her bayonetted, the crowd withdrew and with frightened anger set out to look for Chinese.

The Massacre

ON THE MORNING of July 16, Boxer proclamations had been found posted in the Chinese quarter of the city. Few Russians could read them and paid no heed to them at first. But then they were translated and it was discovered—or so at least the story went among the Russian residents—that they gave notice of a Manchu landing that very night and called on the Chinese living in the city to join in the hostilities. On the basis of this information—whether actually gleaned from the posters, obtained from another source, or merely the figment of somebody's fears—Chief of Police Batarevich reported to the military governor, that it was necessary to remove at once all Chinese from the city and the region to the other side of the Amur. Gribskii so ordered.

There began a general round-up of all Chinese at police headquarters. The reservists who joined the police in this task and assembled and escorted the Chinese and Manchus to the police were a motley crew, for there were neither weapons nor uniforms to go around. Dressed in a mixture of civilian and military clothing they shouldered long American axes as they herded their charges along.

The Chinese quarter was searched. Migrants whose barracks were near the quarter and other self-appointed vigilantes went through stores in search of weapons and hiding Chinese. Beating up the latter, particularly if they tried to run away or resist arrest, they emptied the stores not only of weapons, if they found any, but of food stuffs, Russian stores being shut tight.

The undeclared opening of war, the absence of a substantial military defense force (the return of some of the companies and guns not being generally known), the presence of a multitude of Orientals whose language was strange and whose loyalty uncertain, and concern for the lives of their own families, intensified by wild rumors, preyed on the minds of the residents, who were worn from the strain of sleepless, harried nights and days, until a mixture of fear and desperation gripped Blagoveshchensk. Such was the mood of the city, when a massive column of people was sighted on the horizon at about 5 P.M. Nervously the residents, many of whom had not been able to secure arms, fretted about the identity of the approaching multitude, as it disappeared in a valley. It was too soon to be the relief force, expected from Stretensk. Had the enemy crossed the Amur upstream and was advancing now to deal the death blow?

The crowd, when it came into view again at closer range, did consist primarily of Chinese and Manchus. They were not an invasion host, however, but individuals who had fled from the city or lived within a radius of about 30 miles. Ferretted out from the surrounding countryside, they were being forcibly driven back to police headquarters by whiplashing Cossacks. The more reluctant ones were stabbed to death, as the few dozen weary horsemen prodded on a mass of 1500, some of them armed.

While Russians who spoke up in defense of the Chinese and Manchu residents of Blagoveshchensk were labelled traitors by their compatriots, the corraling of

Chinese and Manchu residents at the police station was intended partly for their own protection, calmer heads realizing what could happen to them in the turmoil of an enemy crossing or the outbreak of fire. In many instances Chinese themselves sought the security of the police station and asked that their shops be guarded. Few men could be spared for this at the moment of crisis, however, and those who were assigned occasionally broke into the stores themselves.

The new arrivals swelled to several thousand the number of Chinese and Manchus apprehended. There was not room for such a mass of people at police headquarters and they were moved that evening to the courtyard of a lumber mill at the Zeia River. Here they were guarded by only 80 recruits, armed with axes. Yet they spent the night quietly, and made no attempt to escape. The following day, on July 17, the first party of Chinese, numbering probably about 3,000 to 3,500 people,[24] was herded to Verkhne-Blagoveshchensk station for deportation to the other shore. That there was no legal right for such action is obvious, for according to international law Chinese residents could not have been expelled from Russian territory even in time of war, and no war had been declared. But the bombarded and threatened inhabitants of the border city thought only of self-preservation, and the removal of the large foreign element from among their midst seemed a vital safety factor.

The Chinese were escorted by the 80 recruits and by some 20 Cossacks and volunteers under the over-all command of police officer Sh.[25] It was a hot day and the

[24]Estimates vary from 400 to 6,000.

[25]Neither his name nor those of other participants in the massacre are given in full in any of the sources available.

distance was over six miles. Driven along at a rapid pace some of the Chinese, especially old men, became terribly tired. They discarded their knapsacks and pieces of clothing, yet still could not keep up with the others, falling behind or collapsing by the wayside. Police officer Sh. ordered that stragglers be axed to death, and several dozen were slain, some shot by the Cossacks. When their fateful path was retraced ten months later, Chinese clothing of all sorts was found scattered along the road, as well as Chinese queues, human skulls, some with traces of flesh and brains, scattered bones and whole skeletons. It was learned that the escorts had gone through the discarded clothing for valuables, indeed in a number of instances had searched and robbed the Chinese directly.

A number of armed Cossacks rode out from Verkhne-Blagoveshchensk to meet the caravan and help convey the Chinese across the river. Inhabitants of the settlement also flocked to the scene. What happened next was the subject of much controversy.

As to how they were conveyed across, there are the most diverse rumors [Kirkhner wrote at the time]. It is true only, that there were no boats or steamers on hand to take them over and that there was no possibility to bring them from below, as any boat or steamer that showed itself on the Amur was fired upon from Sakhalian. One could not send such a mass beyond the Zeia, as the Manchus were attacking Post No. 1 this very night, and there were too few troops beyond the Zeia. There was no place and no one to keep, guard and feed 3,000 Manchus in the city and besides there was no time to bother with them. Such was the situation of July 4[17] from a purely factual point of view. We shall not begin to discuss how one should have acted in this case, because now, when the danger has passed, it is difficult to look impartially upon something that occurred during one of the most critical moments of the siege, particularly as an investigation about this is underway.[26]

The findings of the investigation to which Kirkhner referred were not made public. Only ten years later did an article in the highly reputable Russian journal *Vestnik Evropy* reconstruct the story on the basis of the official court archives. According to this article, whose author signed himself merely as "V," a place was selected for the crossing above Verkhne-Blagoveshchensk, at the most narrow point of the river.

Nevertheless [V. wrote] the width of the river at this place was over 100 sagenes [i.e. over 700 feet], while the depth reached over 2 sagenes [i.e. over 14 feet]. The current was very strong here, and furthermore a considerable wind was blowing. Having chosen the place, it was decided that this was enough, that nothing further was needed for the crossing. The Chinese were simply driven into the water and ordered to swim. Part of those in front went into the water. Some swam, but soon began to drown. The remainder did not dare to go into the water. Then the Cossacks began to urge them on with *nagaikas* [thick, twisted whips] and all

[26]The Blagoveshchensk massacre is sometimes pictured as typically Russian. G. Frederick Wright disputed this at the time: "This work of devastation has not been ordered by those high in authority. It is rather the result of mob violence such as instigates the promoters of lynch law in the Southern States, or, more nearly, such as has from time immemorial animated the pioneers in America against the Indians."

who had rifles—Cossacks, settlers, old men and children
—opened fire. The shooting lasted about half an hour,
after which a considerable number of Chinese corpses
piled up on shore. Then, after the shooting, the commander of the detachment decided to resort to ordi-
nary arms as well. The Cossacks chopped with their
sabers, while the recruits were ordered to kill the
"disobedient" Chinese with their axes. When some of
the recruits lacked fortitude for this, the Cossacks
threatened "to decapitate them as traitors." The Chinese cried; some crossed themselves with the "Ortho-
dox cross," pleading that they not be killed, but
nothing helped.

Before the completion of the crossing a mounted
party of Cossacks from one of the Amur Cossack regiments also participated in the shooting at the Chinese.
The commander of the mounted party at first had not
wanted to fire, but upon the demand of Sh., ordered
his men to fire five rounds each, and then continued
on his way, in spite of the request of *Ataman* N. [who
headed the Cossacks that had come out from the settlement to meet the caravan], to remain with his detachment and "shoot a while longer," as the Cossacks of
the settlement had run out of ammunition. He agreed
only to take a note from N. to the squadron commander about the sending of help; but this request
remained unfulfilled. During the crossing of the first
party of Chinese, it was found, the majority had
perished: some had drowned, others had been slain.
Not more than a hundred Chinese had swum to the
other shore and saved themselves.

"The sum total of depositions of eyewitnesses of the
crossing," an official note states, "lead to the belief that

this was actually not a crossing but an extermination and drowning of the Chinese." So also was the crossing understood by the recruits, one of whom testified during the investigation that he was ordered to "drown the Chinese," another that "I drowned the first party." Only one participant in this bloody business, the recruit Iakov Iavlev, showed a feeling of love for man in regard to one Chinese boy, 10 or 11 years old, before whose eyes his mother was killed in the water and who himself was wounded in the left elbow and the head. Noticing the boy standing in the water, when there were already no Chinese alive on shore, Iavlev, with the permission of Sh., dragged the wounded [boy] out of the water and took him to the office of the Military Commander of the Amur, which placed the unfortunate child into the lazaret. . . .

No better was the fate of the second party of Chinese, sent from the city of Blagoveshchensk. This party was small: the investigation determined exactly that it consisted of 84 persons, escorted by 10 men. Setting out, the senior escort had asked the chief of police what to do with the Chinese at the designated place. The chief of police had replied enigmatically: "You will find out yourself there what must be done." In Verkhne-Blagoveshchensk another giver of orders for the "crossing," N., had been more sincere: he referred directly to what had been done several hours before and proposed that it be repeated. Without protest the senior escort of the second party, Cossack sargeant B., ordered that his party too be driven into the water with whips, and then opened fire at it. The official documents calmly state, that "almost the entire party perished."

Nor were they satisfied with these two massacres. On July 6 [19] and 8 [21] there were sent two more parties (the 3rd and 4th) of Chinese, of 170 and 66 persons, to the settlement. Fifty recruits with axes, under the command of *Shtabs-kapitan* R., were assigned to escort the third party. Dispatching this party, the chief of police informed R. that *Ataman* N. was in charge of the crossing, and dissimulatingly asked that he reaffirm to the latter that one should not shoot at those who are crossing. There are few depositions how this party was conveyed across and they are onesided, being the testimony of persons in charge. Of 170 persons there saved themselves at most 20, who succeeded in swimming across the Amur.

On the 8th [21st] the last (4th) party of Chinese set out for the place where their compatriots had perished, escorted by 36 men under the command of *Poruchik* A. When the Chinese left the city, they were followed by a huge "audience." This "audience" fell upon things discarded by the Chinese on the way, and began to fight over them. There is less information yet how this fourth crossing took place. A. testified during the investigation that upon bringing the party to the river, he let the police take charge of the crossing, and they executed it in the previous fashion. This method of "swimming" across, the witness regarded as determined by higher authorities, "as it had been practiced before, was known to everyone and was not cancelled by anyone." How the crossing had actually taken place, *Poruchik* A. did not know: "He rode away to the side, so as not to see the painful sight." Another witness, a policeman, gave some details. Assuming that they would be shot, the Chinese of the 4th party, as they reached the settlement, fell on their knees and begged that they not be killed. At the crossing point, however, "they plunged into the water of their own accord and having moved away some 60 paces began to shout that they thanked the Russians very much for not killing them." The first Chinese to swim across to the opposite shore, pushed off from there a boat and a board and thereby made it possible for most of their comrades to save themselves. Somewhat less than half the party drowned. . . .

The persons responsible for the bloody crossing did not hide their actions, though their reports to their superiors asserted that the majority of the Chinese had succeeded in swimming across and that "stern measures" had been necessary, the Chinese refusing to obey orders. Upon receipt of the reports the military governor of the Amur Region ordered an inquiry made, but did not himself report the matter to the Governor General even after the investigation disclosed that a criminal act had been committed. As a result General Gribskii himself was indicted. In his defense he argued that he had acted in accordance with the law in ordering, for the preservation of peace, the round-up and deportation of all Chinese who were suspicious or did not want to remain in the city. He asserted that he had left it to the chief of police to determine who should be taken away and insisted that he had made it clear to the latter that boats must be obtained in the settlement for the crossing. He had taken no interest in the details of the operation.

During the investigation the chief of police pointed the finger at Colonel V., chairman of the Amur military government, as responsible for the massacre. When he had instructed two of his subordinates to request his cooperation in getting the Chinese across the Amur, he had replied over the telephone: "You are bothering me with the Chinese; it will be no tragedy, if they will all be drowned and killed."

Private sources bear out the official testimony about the massacre. They add some interesting sidelights. Several days before the bombardment, a number of rich Chinese merchants had sought the advice of the Director of the Russo-Chinese Bank, whether to leave Blagoveshchensk or not. The Director had sent them to General Gribskii, who had assured them that they were fully protected by Russian laws and need fear nothing, much less leave town. When the day after the bombardment orders were issued for the arrest of all Chinese without exception, many Russians tried to keep the Chinese working for them, even offered to post bail, but the police would not allow this. Only a large firm and several influential individuals succeeded in defying the police and in retaining their Chinese employees. A number of wealthy Chinese also managed to bribe their way to freedom from the police. One wealthy Chinese who had hidden with a retired Russian colonel was ordered to pay 1,000 rubles, when the police discovered his whereabouts. He paid 800, but when he refused to pay the remainder following the massacre of his countrymen, was thrown into jail.

The investigation delved also into atrocities committed elsewhere in the Amur region. It established that upon receipt of a report from the *ataman* of Poiarkovskaia village, concerning the detention of 85 Chinese and a Chinese colonel, Colonel V. had telegraphed: "Send Chinese river or annihilate if they resist." When the *ataman* had sought to clarify whether he was to send the Chinese "into" the river or "across" it, the colonel had retorted in a dispatch on July 20: "One must be crazy and foolish to ask what to do with the Chinese. When one is told to do away with them, one should do so without deliberation. The Chinese colonel is not to be kept in a separate place, but in a cell on the same level as the others. Everything in his possession should be taken away. All my orders are to be executed without any evasion; do not act willfully or bother me with nonsense." The same day Colonel V. sent a circular telegram to his subordinates: "Annihilate Chinese appearing on our side, without asking for instructions."

Ataman K. testified that upon receipt of the telegram he ordered that the Chinese be conveyed across the Amur on boats. But as they began to run away, he asserted, Cossack boys who escorted them opened fire and killed most of them. The fifteen or so Chinese who had remained on the barge were bound by the Cossacks and some other people and taken to a wood, behind the village, and there murdered. The sole Chinese survivors in the entire Cossack village were five local merchants, held in protective custody in the school.

Commanders of other Cossack villages sought instructions from Colonel V. on how to deal with the Chinese. On July 16, the *ataman* of Albazinskaia village reported that about 100 Chinese were in the settlement of Rainovskii. When V. telegraphed ambiguously "Remove Chinese side," the *ataman* did not seek clarification, but peacefully conveyed all of the Chinese to the other side (July 18). The commander of Kumarinskaia station, on the other hand, reporting the appearance of 200 Chinese in Sodomon, received more explicit instructions on July

20: "The Chinese are to be done away with. . . . one must be crazy to ask instruction every time." Similar orders went to the commander of Cherniaevaia village the same day.

But when the *ataman* at Pokrovka sought confirmation from General Gribskii for instructions he had received to deport and in the event of resistance to kill the Chinese in his area, the General ordered on July 20, that it be impressed on the local Russian authorities that Russia's struggle was with armed Chinese, who engaged in hostilities against them. "Peaceful, harmless Chinese, particularly unarmed ones, are not to be harmed in any way. To save their lives, they are to be sent to their side on boats or steamers." Colonel V. immediately reversed his position and telegraphed to the Cossack villages that peaceful Chinese not be molested. "Thus all that was needed to end the barbaric slaughter of the mass of completely innocent people," V. wrote, "were literally a few words of General Gribskii, who earlier had not known or seen, what was happening before his eyes."

The findings of the investigation were clear enough. No so the steps taken by the government to punish the guilty. "In vain would the reader seek anywhere in the archives protocols of court trials or accounts of these trials of General Gribskii and his subordinates, for no such trials were held," V. wrote. "It was considered sufficient to limit oneself to the information gleaned from the preliminary investigations and inquiries, solving all these problems by administrative means, quietly and calmly, without any publicity." General Gribskii was relieved of his duties, but in consideration of his otherwise excellent record and his fine military service in the conflict with China, was not dismissed from the service.

The chief of police was dismissed from his position; the police officer Sh. was discharged dishonorably and jailed for two months. Colonel V. also was discharged dishonorably and specifically forbidden to rejoin the service; he was imprisoned for three months. All subordinates who had been accused of killing Chinese, were freed of responsibility.

Yet in the public mind Gribskii and others stood disgraced. As one general noted in his diary, the Amur tragedy was a topic that Russians tried to avoid. The mention of Gribskii's name would end a dinner conversation, and people would lower their heads in embarrassment. "Altogether war is a wild and shocking affair, and such a war as we had all the more so," Kirkhner reflected, "for in the absence of troops and arms, the absence of any kind of definite plan, while the incursion of the enemy with superior forces was possible any minute, the passions were inflamed and everyone did what came to his head."

Not every place were the Manchus ill-treated, however. At Dzhalinda, Ignashina and Markova, where boats were available, they had been put into them after the outbreak of hostilities, had been given oars and told, "Now friends, depart." At Stretenskaia station, through which troops were to pass en route to Blagoveshchensk, Chinese residents were not molested. Russians continued to frequent Chinese shops in preference to Russian establishments because, as N. I. Stepanov recalled, the Chinese were usually satisfied with less profit and though the sons of the Celestial Empire did not shrink occasionally from cheating someone, they did so more politely than other merchants.

The property of the Chinese left behind in Blagoveshchensk was looted. This too aroused much condemnation, but, Kirkhner argued, *"na voine, kak na voine"* (in war one does as in war). What after all is the purpose of war if not to obtain booty?

> War is seizure, the right of power. We shall not go into the fact that war is incompatible with civilization, that it ought not to be, if one looks at the question from the point of view of higher justice. Much has been said about this; the Hague conference had been called specially for this purpose. But what can you do if suddenly, for no reason, you are bombarded?

Chinese aggression and the abandonment of their property by Chinese settlers thus were the roots of the problem, and the blame, if any, fell back on the Chinese, Kirkhner asserted.

> From the Chinese side as well as our own the clash has taken on the character of a national war, a war the more savage, because the combatants are separated by a visible chasm, created by racial, historical and economic antagonisms [the *Amurskii Krai* commented editorially on July 25]. The passions of war have suddenly flared up with hitherto unseen savagery. Not only the common people but even those who are more educated saw in every representative of the yellow race an enemy, whom it was dangerous to leave in the open.

Noting that this hatred of Russia's hard working and normally peaceful neighbors, aroused by panicky fear of a Manchu onslaught, had resulted in the destruction of Manchu villages and property, the editorial reflected that while the destruction of such things was common to all wars, "this war from the very beginning took on the character of a war of annihilation *par excellence*." Now that momentary panic had passed, the editorial wrote, it was time to remember that the task of a civilized Christian nation was to spread culture and civilization and not destruction and racial hatred and that whatever restraint was applied toward enemies among civilized nations must be extended toward the Chinese as well.

Returning to the subject of Russian atrocities, the investigation by the Governor General having confirmed the wanton killing of Chinese who had not left Blagoveshchensk, the *Amurskii Krai* noted on July 27:

But the fact that they had trustingly remained in our midst, only increases our guilt. They confidently believed that the Russian people fought in the battle fields, killing armed foes; they did not know that we can herd together peaceful, unarmed persons, half dead from fear, and slaughter them in cold blood. How shall we atone for our guilt? By what feats of goodness and virtue shall we remove the blemish that we have put on ourselves? What shall we tell civilized people? We shall have to say to them: "Do not consider us as brothers anymore. We are mean and terrible people; we have killed those who hid at our place, who sought our protection."

Defending the City

URING THE NIGHT OF July 16 to 17, a Chinese attack
on Post No. 1 at the mouth of the Zeia was repulsed, and a Chinese junk was sunk by the *Selenga*.
The four field pieces which had returned to the city
were rolled into position and in the morning began to
bombard the enemy, knocking out several guns and
destroying the telegraph station.

In the morning, and on the days to follow, a large
number of Manchu and Chinese corpses came floating
down the Amur. Blocked by the ships and floats and
washed onto sand bars, they polluted the air with a terrible stench. Yet there were those who fished them out
to go through their clothing, occasionally finding gold
coins sewn in the lining. Outraged by the attacks on
peaceful Manchu and Chinese residents and the plundering of the bodies, the Military Governor reminded his
countrymen that "attacking an unarmed and defenseless
enemy is not in the character of a Russian," and
threatened with prosecution and severe punishment all
those molesting, harming or robbing peaceful Chinese.
At the same time he made it a specific duty of the civilian
and military authorities of the Blagoveshchensk region
to recover all corpses and inter them as deep as possible
or to burn them, reporting the exact number to his
office.

The removal of the Chinese and Manchus from Russia did allay public fear somewhat, and as defense preparations were completed and the Chinese guns fell silent, the residents of Blagoveshchensk began returning to their homes. But the lull in fire was deceptive. That night several thousand Chinese crossed the Amur River between Aigun and Post No. 1, and undetected approached to within about 1400 feet of the latter. They took up position in a hollow, their long line stretching perpendicular to the Amur.

The Russian post, as will be recalled, was manned by a handful of professional soldiers, backed by a peasant militia, about 400 strong, some of whom were nearby, others at lookouts elsewhere. At dawn on July 18, the Chinese opened fire at a detachment of militiamen, heading downstream, to Post No. 2, with a string of carts, and forced it to turn back. Awakened by the shots and still undressed, other peasants rushed out from their place near the post to exchange fire with the enemy, but shortly retired toward Blagoveshchensk. The soldiers resisted with greater determination, but upon the wounding of their officer also began falling back, as did the squadron of Cossacks and the two guns. The Chinese followed on their heels with little cannons, which they rolled by hand, and kept up a continuous fire. Except for the casualties exacted by one Russian gun, which halted at a little bridge, the Russians did little to slow down the Chinese advance and when they reached the Zeia some two hours later, panic stricken jumped into the water and swam toward the ferry. The vessel which was approaching shore happened to bring substantial Cossack reinforcements from Blagoveshchensk, and the Russians turned back to face the Chinese. When the troops reached Post No. 1, they found it burned to the ground and the Chinese gone. Part of one Chinese detachment was caught in the process of crossing the Amur and wiped out.

The repulse of the invaders was not known in Blagoveshchensk, where rumors that the Manchus were going around the city to approach it from the rear, from the Zeia side, caused renewed panic, the city having been left once again without its military guardians. As citizens scurried hither and yon, the chief of police tried to calm them with a proclamation, posted all over town.

ANNOUNCEMENT

The head of the internal defense of the city of Blagoveshchensk, Chief of Police Batarevich, calls upon the fainthearted inhabitants of the city of Blagoveshchensk to follow the example of the braver spirits and stop inventing themselves nonexisting danger. There is no danger, if joining together, fearlessly and with concerted effort, arming ourselves with whatever we can and

remembering that God is with us,

we meet the heathen foe should it be necessary, and do not believe every absurd rumor, spread from fear by a stupid person, and do not take to the bushes, where we are helpless.

Stop being afraid; return to the city; and we shall help each other, and will not hurt the cause by scattering individually.

106

Bring to me everyone who frightens [others] with absurd rumors.

Head of internal defense,
Chief of Police Batarevich
6 [19] July 1900. City of Blagoveshchensk.

The citizens returned, but their spirits remained low, for the situation was indeed critical. Moving back and forth between Blagoveshchensk and the area facing Aigun, the military were exhausted, and a large scale Chinese invasion could have inundated the region. Whether it was fear of the Russians, the mercy of God, or just poor strategy, the Chinese did not take advantage of the situation. But the people of Blagoveshchensk could not foresee the future and continued to worry, particularly because the bombardment of the city was resumed. By now the Russian artillery, though vastly outnumbered, replied with some success, and during the night when Chinese fire slackened, about 150 Russian volunteers under three young officers crossed over to explore the Chinese shore. In the fighting which ensued one officer was killed and a soldier left behind, to be found later tortured to death.

On July 19, the Chinese tried to cross over at two places but were repulsed. Their gun fire continued to pound the city and to harrass the Russians, whose defenses had been strengthened and reorganized with the arrival of a number of officers from Khabarovsk. The Russians too crossed over to the enemy side to reconnoiter his position, destroy his outposts and to keep him off balance. "Death in battle is a glorious death," Gribskii declared in encouragement, voicing confidence that all his subordinates, if the occasion demanded, would "without hesitation lay down their lives for Tsar and Fatherland."

Gribskii called on the "valient men of the Amur" to take up arms and deal with the disturbers of peace "in Cossack fashion, resolutely and quickly," removing Chinese border posts "without losing time with needless permission." "Remember, Cossacks, that your forefathers, the heroic defenders of Albazin and the valient atamans Poiarkov, Khabarov and others did not fear the enemy and bravely routed him," Gribskii exhorted. "I am firmly convinced that the Amur Cossacks, imbued with the sacred realization of their duty to preserve order on the frontier will bravely and quickly deal with the Chinese detachments hostile to us and that the name of the Amur Cossack will thunder through all of Manchuria and strike terror among the Chinese population."

Between July 16 and 21, the many little Chinese settlements on the Russian side of the Amur beyond the Zeia were plundered and burned down by the Russians. Though most Chinese, particularly women and children, had gotten across with their cattle before the outbreak of hostilities, some had not been evacuated and perished in the flames.

During the night of July 21 to 22, a Russian reconnaissance party again crossed the Amur and clashed with the Chinese. In the darkness, the *Sungari* made its way to Blagoveshchensk and docked early in the morning with a large quantity of desperately needed ammunition and military supplies from Khabarovsk. Three hundred and eighty additional rifles were brought on horseback from Poiarkova. During the day 700 new recruits were landed by the steamer *Chikoi* at Ignat'evskaia and proceeded to the rescue of Blagoveshchensk, the first troops to do so from downstream. On July 23, a party of migrants arrived from upstream, having traveled by float up to Korsakovskaia Station and from there on foot. They brought word that Russian troops were on their way, the arrival of reinforcements having been delayed by a fall in the levels of the Amur and its tributaries. Now, on the 23rd and on the 25th, rising water on the Amur, Zeia and Shilka reopened navigation and hastened the relief of the city. At the same time it flooded many entrenchments on the Chinese side.

Chinese fire harassed the reinforcements. The 10th East Siberian Line Battalion under the command of Colonel Servianov, for example, was proceeding from Khabarovsk to Blagoveshchensk on several steamers. One of them, the *Aleksei*, carrying the 1st and 2nd companies of the battalion under the joint command of Lieutenant Colonel Vrublevskii, had steamed ahead of the other vessels. On the afternoon of July 24, as it approached the Cossack village Radde, where it planned to take on fire wood and provisions, it was met with rifle fire from the Chinese side of the Amur River. The *Aleksei* docked unharmed, but *Podesaul* Kuz'minskii who was in charge of the Cossack village asked its assistance in removing the Chinese picket.

The Cossack village was guarded by only 72 Cossacks below the ages of 16 or above 50, while over 700 Chinese were at the picket and in the settlement. Unless the Chinese were cleared out of their position, they could cross the Amur and wipe out the Russian village. Furthermore, they could molest the ships that followed. Vrublevskii agreed to attack the Chinese shore and at 3:15 A.M. took aboard the local Cossacks.

The *Aleksei* proceeded 2½ miles downstream and

109

disgorged the 72 Cossacks, the entire 1st Company and 3 platoons of the 2nd Company—a total of 400 men—on the Chinese side. After a quiet prayer, said by the company drummer, the Russians began their advance, led by the Cossack villagers who were familiar with the region. The heavy fog and shrubbery, so thick that the Russians had to cut their way through, made it difficult for the Russians to find their way, but they succeeded and gained the element of surprise. Captain Speranskii headed with the 1st Platoon along the river bank toward the settlement, while *Shtabs-kapitan* Klimenko with the 2nd Platoon skirted the settlement, and moved against the picket on its southern edge. Using bayonets to silence guards whom they encountered, the Russians managed to get quite close to the Chinese before their presence was discovered. The Chinese picket was surrounded by a high earth wall and a moat, however, and the engagement that ensued was costly. Klimenko was seriously wounded by two bullets, one in his chest and one in his right arm. Ten other Russians were wounded, and seven were killed before the picket and the settlement, where ferocious house-to-house fighting occurred, were razed to the ground. But Chinese casualties were much higher: 338 dead, including the commander of the picket and 12 officers. Only seven prisoners were taken and those because Vrublevskii needed information. Among the prisoners there was a Manegr who spoke some Russian. From him Vrublevskii learned that the Chinese had planned to cross over to the Russian side and wipe out Radde as soon as cannons, which were being sent to them, arrived.

Meanwhile the Chinese bombardment of Blagoveshchensk continued sporadically. A girl was killed, her brother wounded, and here and there other casualties were added to the list. No major damage was done to Blagoveshchensk, however, and the Chinese, disappointed in their efforts to annihilate the city, yet secure in the knowledge that the small Russian sorties that continued could not overwhelm Sakhalian either, gradually began moving some of their troops and artillery toward Aigun.

At the same time Manchu ranks dwindled by desertion, the promise of Boxer victory and division of conquered land among the local inhabitants having paled into the destruction of their own villages. Yet though weakened and haphazard, the Chinese rifle and gunfire continued for nineteen days, draining the citizens of Blagoveshchensk of all strength, as they waited and waited for a major onslaught that never came.

On July 27, the steamer *Selenga* reconnoitered the entire line of fortifications of Sakhalian. Steaming through the heavy but aimless fire of the Chinese marksmen without serious damage, the *Selenga* bombarded the enemy entrenchment with devastating accuracy. On the night of July 29-30 a detachment of Cossacks explored the Chinese shore again.

On the evening of July 27 the first echelon of troops, sent to defend the city to restore navigation on the Amur and to clear the right bank of Manchus, arrived in Blagoveshchensk. General Aleksandrov who commanded the units—the 1st Reserve Battalion of a special four company complement, only partly armed, 3 companies of the Stretensk Reserve Regiment and 1 squadron of the Nerchinsk Cossack Regiment—was festively met by the beleaguered authorities and citizens with the traditional bread-and-salt welcome and an ikon. The following noon the arrival of the troops was celebrated with holy mass and vodka aboard the *Selenga* on the Zeia River.

In a special, widely circulated announcement, Military Governor Gribskii assured the Chinese workers of the protection of the Russian authorities as long as they abided by the laws of the country, and called upon the Russian leaders in the gold industry, in their own self-interest to do their utmost to preserve good relations between Russian and Chinese workers.

During the night Major General Subotich arrived. He was assistant to the commander of the Kwantung region, and returning from leave had been assigned temporarily to Gribskii. He was followed by troops from his detachment, which had proceeded up to Ignat'-evskaia by steamers and from there on foot. On July 28, Colonel Servianov's detachment, transported on 10 steamers, stopped at Poiarkova, while the steamer *Batrak* with 900 reservists, 11 officers and two doctors reached Ignat'evskaia. The detachment of Colonel Shverin, proceeding from Stretenskaia Station on 3 steamers, had taken Mo-ho opposite Ignashina Station (July 26), and was heading for Blagoveshchensk. It was followed by the detachment of General Rennenkampf, who was to destroy (and on the 29th did destroy) a concentration of Chinese forces at Zheltuga.[27] Thus by July 28 the relief of Blagoveshchensk was imminent.

Throughout July 31 and the night that followed, the Chinese bombarded Blagoveshchensk, the camp, and Verkhne-Blagoveshchensk Station. They made no last

[27]According to Kuropatkin's report to the Emperor, dated November 9, 1900, Servianov's detachment consisted of 3 battalions, 1 sotnia, 8 guns and 2 mortars; the detachments of Shverin and Rennenkampf had a total strength of 5 battalions, 2 sotnias, and 30 guns.

minute attempt to capture the city, however. That they could have destroyed Blagoveshchensk even at this late date, seemed possible. General Gribskii estimated that Chinese forces in the Aigun-Blagoveshchensk region numbered 18,000 men with 45 guns. Whether the Chinese wanted to lure the Russians into a landing and annihilate them in the process, whether their schemes went wrong, or whether they had no concerted plan of action remained a mystery to the defenders. By the end of the month the opportunity of the Manchus was past, as the above and other reinforcements poured into the region between Blagoveshchensk and Aigun and the Russians prepared to carry the war to the Chinese side.[28]

[28]Three detachments followed to Blagoveshchensk. The first, under the command of Colonel Servianov, commander of the 14th East Siberian Rifle Regiment, consisted of the 14th East Siberian Regiment (2 battalions), the 10th East Siberian Line Battalion (which later became the 20th East Siberian Rifle Regiment), one sotnia of the Amur Cossack Division, the 4th Battery of the 1st East Siberian Artillery Brigade (8 guns) and 2 mortars. It left Khabarovsk on July 18. Transported on Amur steamers till below Aigun, it continued overland, reaching Blagoveshchensk on the evening of August 1. The second detachment, led by Colonel Shverin, commander of the Transbaikal Artillery Division, embraced 1½ batteries of the artillery division (½ battery of the division was already in Blagoveshchensk) and three companies of the 1st Battalions of the Stretensk and Chita Regiments. It too was transported on steamers and following the clash at Mo-ho, mentioned above, continued to Blagoveshchensk, where it arrived on July 29. Upon reinforcement by these two detachments, Gribskii attacked Sakhalian. The third detachment arrived on August 3rd. Commanded by Major General Rennenkampf, chief of staff of the forces of the Transbaikal Region, it was composed of the 2nd and 4th Battalions of the Stretensk Regiment, the 3rd and 4th Battalions of the Chita Regiment, two sotnias of the 1st Argun Cossack Regiment, and the 2nd Transbaikal Cossack Battery. It too was attacked at Mo-ho (July 28) and here and at the Zheltuga gold fields seems to have left behind 1½ sotnias of the Argun Cossack Regiment to secure the places.

The Annihilation
of Sakhalian and Aigun

THE ATTACK ON SAKHALIAN and Aigun was set for the night of August 1 to 2. Major General Subotich and Captain Zapol'skii were in overall command. In an order, dated July 31, Gribskii outlined the plan of action: At 1 A.M. Colonel Pechenkin and Lieutenant Colonel Ladyzhenskii were to cross the Amur above Verkhne-Blagoveshchensk with the 4th and 5th Sotnias of the Amur Cossack Regiment and the 1st Sotnia of the Nerchinsk Cossack Regiment. They were to reconnoiter the enemy positions and then remain assembled on the right flank of the striking force. At 3 A.M. Colonel Friman was to start across at Verkhne-Blagoveshchensk with 4 companies of the 2nd East Siberian Line Battery, 8 guns of the 2nd East Siberian Artillery Brigade, and a half-sotnia of the Amur Cossack Regiment. He was to be followed by Colonel Shverin with 3 companies of the Chita Reserve Regiment, 3 companies of the Stretensk Reserve Regiment, 8 guns of the 1st Battalion of the Transbaikal Artillery Division, and a half-sotnia of the Amur Cossack Regiment. Next, Lieutenant Colonel Poliakov was to cross with the composite Reserve battalion of 5 companies. The steamer *Aigun* and the barge *Kalifornia* as well as 52 boats, 5 scows, and 12 rafts, manned by 207 oarsmen from the Engineer Reserves, were to convey the troops to the right bank of the Amur. During the landing operations from Verkhne-Blagoveshchensk Colonel Servianov was to silence the enemy guns with fire from his own detachment—the 14th East Siberian Rifle Regiment, the 4th Battery of the 1st East Siberian Artillery Brigade (8 guns), and the 1st Sotnia of the Amur Cossack Division. Then he was to follow across, ferried by 132 oarsmen volunteers on 33 boats, the steamer *Sever* with the barge *Iunona*, and the steamer *Grazhdanin* with the barge *Il'da*.

Meanwhile Colonel Fotengauer's Trans-Zeia detachment, composed of the 10th Siberian Line Battalion, half a company of the 1st Blagoveshchensk Reserve Battalion, 2 field mortars, 1 field gun of the 2nd Battery, the 2nd Sotnia of the Nerchinsk Cossack Regiment and 250 militiamen, was to shell Aigun and its powder depot and so cross the river as to step athwart the enemy's route of retreat from Aigun to Tsitsihar. Steamers, carrying additional troops and guns, were to draw fire and to run interference at the mouth of the Zeia and other points, as well as to assist in the troop crossing.

The volunteers who had defended Blagoveshchensk in the absence of regular troops had been disarmed and sent to their homes. Only a few, after some pleading, were allowed to join in the operation. The residents of Blagoveshchensk were not familiar with the details of Gribskii's orders, but it was common knowledge that the invasion had been set for August 2. The terror of the bombardment had driven several townspeople out of their minds. These stayed at the police station, as did a number of persons who were afraid to remain in their homes. Some citizens climbed onto the rooftops to watch the proceedings, while more venturesome souls actually went to Verkhne-Blagoveshchensk. But most people remained peacefully in bed, even when the Chinese opened heavy fire during the night, for they assumed that they were hearing the sound of their own batteries.

The Chinese cannonade was directed at the steamers *Selenga, Grazhdanin, Mikhail* and *Sungari,* which cruised up and down the Amur to deflect attention from the invasion. The Chinese expected a landing opposite the region between Blagoveshchensk and Post No. 1. When the Russians struck vis-à-vis Verkhne-Blagoveshchensk, therefore, the bulk of the Chinese forces in that area occupied a grove about a mile and a half inland. Only a small number of riflemen manned the trenches along the river bank, where the Russians set foot. Thus the Russians encountered hardly any resistance and suffered few casualties, even though their operation was thrown off schedule here and there by high winds.[29] By the time the Chinese realized what had happened and advanced from Sakhalian to meet the Russians, the latter had landed in force and occupied strategic positions. Bombarding the coastal entrenchments from the flank, the Russians drove the Chinese to abandon them. At about 7:30 A.M. the Russians moved against the advancing defenders and bolstered by reinforcements—the landing of the assault forces continued until 11 A.M.

---

[29]During the crossing of the Amur River *Poruchik* Veniamin Ravich-Piglevskii drowned. One of the soldiers, seeing him struggle to keep above water, had swum up and offered his help, but Ravich-Piglevskii, realizing that the soldier, weighted down with bullets, himself barely kept afloat, had pushed him aside with the words "Save yourself, lest we both drown!" Thus, the *Priamurskiia Vedomosti* reported, the young officer laid down his life for "Tsar, Faith, and Fatherland."

—pushed the Chinese back. At first the Chinese withdrew orderly, continuing to return fire, but by noon they began running, across the mountain toward the road to Aigun.

At one o'clock the Russians stopped to rest. For hours after the landing at Verkhne-Blagoveshchensk the Chinese had continued to bombard the steamers before Blagoveshchensk instead of the advancing troops, thinking that the ships carried an invasion force. When they gleaned the truth, they evacuated Sakhalian without a fight, Cossack raiders putting the torch to the few buildings that were still standing. By the time the troops which had crossed at Verkhne-Blagoveshchensk reached Sakhalian at 6 P.M., the Manchu town had ceased to exist.

As a grisly welcome the Chinese had left the head of Filipp Kalinin hanging from a birch tree by his pierced right ear. Captured during the Russian raid on the night of July 18 to 19, Kalinin had been tortured and decapitated. The dangling head was without the left ear, and the right eye was gone. The nose was squashed and the cheeks pierced. Only the hair, mustache and lips and the uniform on the mutilated body found nearby permitted identification.

While Sakhalian was being taken, the military transports and reserves of Major General Aleksandrov were ferried across the Amur. Now the Russian forces were regrouped. Subotich's men, who had borne the brunt of battle, became the General Reserve; Aleksandrov and Lieutenant Colonel Baron Budberg headed the striking force—the 14th East Siberian Rifle Regiment, the 1st Battalion of the Stretensk Infantry Regiment, the 4th Battery of the 1st Siberian Artillery Brigade and one sotnia of the Amur Cossack Division. The same three Cossack sotnias which had given cavalry support to Subotich continued to operate with Aleksandrov.

Falling back toward Aigun, the Chinese forces entrenched themselves in the mountains. The Chinese position was formidable and in the hands of better marksmen would have been impregnable. So heavy was the fire when the Russians attacked on the morning of August 3, that they had to pull back at one point. When the Chinese tried to follow them, however, Russian flanking fire forced them back into the trenches. There they were safe from rifle and artillery bombardment and, as noted, could have held indefinitely had they been better shots. But wild cavalry charges and bayonet attacks disheartened them, and by afternoon the Russians overran the positions. Most Chinese fled directly southward to the shelter of the mountain spurs, in the direction of Tsitsihar. Only a minority withdrew on the postroad toward Aigun, as originally planned. Scattered units offered determined resistance, thereby delaying pursuit and saving their comrades from annihilation. Over 200 Chinese were killed in the mountains, Russian losses remaining remarkably low: one officer[30] and 5 men dead, 10 Cossacks and 14 soldiers wounded.

At 2 P.M. on August 4, after a much needed rest, and reinforced by Rennenkampf's detachment which had arrived during the night, the Russians resumed their offensive against Aigun. Fortifications dotted the approaches to this important commercial town and the

---

[30]*Sotnik* Leonid Volkov, a talented poet and painter from St. Petersburg. He and five of his Cossacks were killed when a wounded Chinese artillery man set fire to the powder of his battery as they approached, and exploding all the shells blew them and himself to smithereens.

Russians expected fierce resistance. Subotich once again headed the striking force, Aleksandrov the reserves.

The many entrenchments between the mountains and Aigun had to be taken one by one. For five hours the Russians advanced against enemy fire. Yet their losses were light. The Chinese would fire aimlessly, their bullets usually flying high over the Russians' heads, and retire to another position, to fire again with no more success. This unintentional shadow boxing delayed the Russians, for they had to change formation again and again, but it did little to stop them. One serious attempt to rush large reinforcements to a mountain position and make a real stand was foiled by Russian shrapnel, and by 7 P.M. the Russian line stood before Aigun.

The town was burning, set afire by the shells of Fotengauer's guns and the bombardment by the striking force. In peasant houses on the outskirts of town some 300 to 400 Chinese infantrymen valiantly fought to the death, here and there committing suicide rather than surrendering. Soon darkness enveloped the countryside and the general assault on the town was left till morning. Fotengauer had encountered heavier opposition than expected and his crossing had been delayed. Consequently he had not moved athwart the road from Aigun to Tsitsihar. Nor had Pechenkin's cavalry done so. With the escape hatch left open, the Chinese abandoned Aigun during the night.

Not all Chinese had left the once proud town, the oldest Chinese outpost on the Amur River. When the Russians moved in the following day, on August 5, they had to fight from house to house, the Chinese dying at their guns or, setting fire to the buildings, perishing in the flames as a final gesture of defiance.

One had to wonder what had happened to the "peaceful" Chinese [Kirkhner wrote]. Many of them conducted themselves like real heroes and had they not had such a corrupt and worthless command, which misappropriated military funds and left it to the soldiers to feed and clothe themselves, the taking of Aigun would probably have cost the Russians far more; indeed Blagoveshchensk rather than Aigun might have been destroyed.

Sakhalian had been razed to the ground. All that was left standing in Aigun were the barrack building and the powder cellar that the Russians needed for the garrison which was to remain here. In Aigun the Russians captured cannons and machine guns and banners and flags of all sorts.[31] They also found and released from jail a Russian couple with two children, who had been taken prisoner by a Chinese patrol following the outbreak of hostilities, when they had been walking from Harbin. Fettered and put in stocks at the neck, arms and legs, they had not been tortured but treated like Chinese inmates.

Meanwhile Rennenkampf's Cossacks rode in pursuit of the troops that had evacuated Aigun during the night. From time to time the Chinese halted in villages

---

[31]In three days of fighting the Russians captured about 50 banners and flags, 4 breach-loading steel cannons, 18 muzzle-loading bronze cannons of different caliber, 13 breach-loading falconets, 2 Nordenfeld guns, 900 rifles of different systems, and a large quantity of ammunition and gun powder. They blew up no less than 26 munition depots. They also found spears, helberts, and battle axes. Chinese casualties must have been high. Up to August 11, the Russians had buried or cremated some 700 Chinese corpses. Russian losses at Sakhalian and in the mountains together amounted to only 2 officers and 10 men killed and 2 officers and 39 men wounded.

and groves and fought back. On August 7, 8 and 9, Rennenkampf briefly engaged the Chinese rear guard, estimated at 800 men infantry, 300 men cavalry, and 10 guns. On August 10, at the eastern slope of the Hsing-an Mountains, he ran into determined opposition. Bolstered by large reinforcements the Chinese decided to make a stand here, putting an estimated 3-4,000 men infantry and 4-5,000 men cavalry and 12 guns in the field. Rennenkampf had only 4½ sotnias and 2 cavalry guns, and the marshy terrain was difficult for mounted operations. Yet Rennenkampf did not wait for reinforcements, lest the Chinese consolidate their position.

Sabers drawn, the Cossacks galloped forward—right into a morass, beyond which the Chinese had installed themselves. In a moment the dashing onslaught had become a pathetic struggle for survival, as the horses floundered helplessly in the quagmire and the Chinese emptied their guns at the Cossacks as if they were fixed targets in a shooting gallery. Two of the Russian officers and ten men were killed, a third officer and other Cossacks wounded. The rest were saved from annihilation when the Chinese were forced back by a flank attack of the other Cossack sotnia and the devastating bombardment of the guns.

Lying on his deathbed in a field hospital, one of the Cossack officers who had been caught in the murderous trap uttered later:

War, how terrible and stupid it really is! Now I am wounded and from the faces of the doctors see that things are bad, and the St. George [ikon] sent to me no longer consoles me much. . . . All that has recently taken place passes before my eyes true to life. My

God, what we had to experience!. . . . I feel how little by little . . . world questions and insignificant earthly considerations and even the tears of my poor wife draw somewhere far, far away from me. I am not sorry for my young, passing life, but regret that its end is not such as I had planned. . . .

The Chinese meanwhile had withdrawn to the Hsing-an pass, from where Rennenkampf could dislodge them only with the help of reinforcements.[32] Upon the arrival of an additional sotnia, six battalions and 20 guns from Aigun, Rennenkampf stormed the position on August 16 and after bloody fighting dislodged the Chinese. On August 17, some of his cavalry took Mergen after a brief struggle. Rennenkampf himself arrived in the city the following day. Russian booty in Mergen included 12 guns, 700 rifles, many pieces of cold steel and huge stores of ammunition. To these Rennenkampf added the 8 guns captured at Hsing-an pass and other guns taken elsewhere, and left them with a garrison which he assigned to this place. From telegrams found in Mergen, Rennenkampf learned that the commander of the Chinese troops which had fallen back toward Tsitsihar and his chief of staff had been killed at Hsing-an pass. Rennenkampf had not annihilated the Chinese forces facing him, but he had made them incapable of further effective resistance.

Governor General Grodekov praised Rennenkampf's feats in a telegram to Gribskii:

[32]The reinforcements consisted of the 1st, 2nd and 4th Battalions of the Stretensk Regiment, the 1st, 3rd and 4th Battalions of the Chita Regiment, the 1st Sotnia of the Amur Cossack Regiment, the Transbaikal Artillery Division and the remainder of the Transbaikal Cossack Battery.

I find no words to thank the brave troops of the Mergen Detachment and its heroic chief. Without rest, without considering the strength of the enemy, and without caring about the number of trophies already taken from the enemy, he had only one main objective in view—the complete annihilation of the opponent. The operations of General Rennenkampf on the way from Aigun to Mergen and the taking of this city are a model of how to fight and pursue restlessly and effectively. Without the least doubt for future success, I permit the Detachment of General Rennenkampf, with God's help to advance further. For every sotnia of General Rennenkampf's Detachment there have been assigned 5 decorations of the military order, for every battery 4 and for every company two of these decorations.

With Grodekov's permission, Rennenkampf continued his advance on Tsitsihar, the capital of Hei-lung-chiang Province. Sending some of his cavalry ahead on August 20, he followed with the main body the following day. About 35 miles from Mergen, he was approached by a bearer of a flag of truce, sent by Shou Shan, the Tartar General of Hei-lung-chiang Province with the proposal to halt military operations. Rennenkampf rejected the offer, and pushed on.

On August 28 he took the city with 460 Cossacks and the 2nd Cossack Battery, while one of his units secured the ford across the Nonni[33] River. The Chinese offered only light resistance, General Shou poisoning himself. The main body of Rennenkampf's detachment entered the city on August 29. Another 31 guns were captured

[33]Also known as the Nun River.

in Tsitsihar, bringing the total of guns captured since Aigun to 65. That day Rennenkampf sent a unit to seek to establish contact with Major General Orlov, who was advancing on Tsitsihar from the Transbaikal Region.

As the Russians pushed into Manchuria, they tried to discourage resistance. Lieutenant General Gribskii proclaimed:

> Inhabitants of Manchuria!
>
> Until recently Russians and Manchus lived next to each other in peace, and this was profitable and useful, especially for you. But a month ago you had the impudence and madness to begin the attack on the city of Blagoveshchensk and the inhabitants of Russia, having forgotten how terribly strong the Great Russian Sovereign is in lands, men and weapons. For this you have been punished terribly. The city of Aigun and the villages along the shore of the Amur, which had dared to attack the Russians, have been burned; your armies have been beaten; and the Amur is dirty from the many Manchu corpses.
>
> No inhabitant of Manchuria will dare to return to the villages on the bank of the Amur!
>
> But inhabitants of those cities and villages, which do not take up arms against us Russians, do not be afraid and listen!
>
> The Russians will soon come into all your cities and villages. But here is a promise: If you will not shoot at us and do not harm our troops and peaceful workers, who are building the railroad, we in turn will not touch you with a finger, and you will live in complete peace on your fields, as you have always

lived before. But if in any village anyone will have the impudence to shoot or stab a Russian, woe be unto you. Such a village or city will be destroyed by fire and not one of the people will remain alive!

I therefore tell you again: Remain where you are, live peacefully, as before, work and trade.

The Russian Tsar loves those who obey.

Do not be confused by bad counsels. Those who force you to fight with us are your enemies. From them you will get destruction and death.

Woe be unto you, if you will not do as we tell you!

This I make known to everyone.

Signed: Military Governor and Commander of the forces of the Amur Province Lieutenant General

Gribskii.

From T'ieh-ling to Harbin

THE MANCHURAIN RAILWAY was being constructed in three divisions, subdivided into 22 sections. T'ieh-ling Station constituted the southernmost point of the 4th Section. Situated some 46 miles north of Mukden, near the junction of the Liao and Wai Rivers, it was connected by rail with Ying-k'ou and Port Arthur. When hostilities broke out in the summer of 1900, track had been laid also for about 15 miles north of T'ieh-ling, to within 6 miles of K'ai-yüan. The Russians who worked near T'ieh-ling—the employees of the 4th Section, a number of officers and the railway guard—did not live at the station or in the city. They resided about a mile and a half north of T'ieh-ling, in a little colony which they called Wai-khe, after the river by that name (usually romanized Wai-ho). T'ieh-ling Station had been built a third of a mile to the south of the city. The northbound line did not go through the city, but skirted the western side of T'ieh-ling at a distance of about half a mile. It passed within 350 feet of the Russian colony.

The Russians who lived here followed news of Boxer activity in Tientsin and elsewhere with concern, but until June there was no sign of trouble at T'ieh-ling or at the neighboring cities of K'ai-yüan and Ch'ang-t'u Fu, and they were confident that the disorders would not spread to their region. They had been on good terms with the Chinese inhabitants, who seemed as polite and friendly as ever, and continued to exchange visits with the Chinese officialdom.

When 15 and 16-year old boys appeared simultaneously in T'ieh-ling, K'ai-yüan and Ch'ang-t'u Fu and exhorted the masses, after entertaining them with knife-wielding magic exercises, to expell the Europeans, the Russians failed to be alarmed at first. Only when their railroad line was damaged in the south and when hostilities began to move up to Liao-yang and beyond, did they realize that the situation was grave. But the Chinese local commanders had posted signs forbidding Boxer propaganda and when A. Silnitskii wrote to them protesting Boxer activities, they responded almost verbatim that there was no Boxer agitation in their cities and that no disorders would occur there. The official replies readily allayed Russian fears, because the Russians could not imagine that the inhabitants of T'ieh-ling, all of whom they knew by sight, should take up arms against them. Yet every day brought new telegrams from the southern part of the line, reporting the burning of temporary railroad bridges, the taking apart of the track, the cutting of telegraph lines, and attacks on railroad stations. The disturbances were increasing in size and were rapidly spreading northward.

When Colonel Mishchenko, the commander of the railway guard of the Port Arthur line, was suddenly called from Wai-khe to Liao-yang on about June 19, the Russian residents became alarmed and no longer felt "at home." Their misgivings were increased by a torrent of ciphered telegrams from places where disorders were most violent. Though they did not understand the numbers and letters of which the wires were composed, they could imagine that they spelled distressing tidings. At the same time they noticed a gradual change in the attitude of the population. No longer did the Chinese greet them with a friendly word; instead, they stared at them silently, as if to say, "What are you doing here?"

On about June 22, a letter was received from Mishchenko, who was still at Liao-yang, recommending that the women be evacuated at once from Wai-khe and other parts of the railway sector to Harbin or to Port Arthur. This was done, some husbands asking leave to escort their wives to a safe place. Only three women remained in the Russian colony: the wife of one of the employees, a doctor's assistant, and an office worker.

With the departure of the women the colony went on a military footing. The night watches were strengthened, and the daytime patrols of the mounted Cossacks through the neighboring region were increased. News arrived that Chinese bands had burned railroad bridges and had damaged the line as close as Hsin-t'ai-tzu, a station only 20 miles south of T'ieh-ling and within jurisdiction of its commander. The latter continued to visit the Russians and to reassure them that they would be safe. He showed them a copy of the proclamation that he had issued, forbidding Boxer agitation. Only later, when an official Chinese document fell into their hands, did the Russians comprehend the official's duplicity. He had tried to put them off guard, while fully informed of plans for their extermination. In fact, he had assisted in the arming of the insurgents and had the anti-Boxer proclamation posted only on the gates of the Russian colony rather than in the Chinese city. He had conferred with Boxer leaders and had made no effort to arrest them.

The Russian defense force was weak. The railroad

Chinese began to shoot at the colony. Throughout the day and through part of the night the Chinese sustained their rifle fire, and although their bullets injured no one, the Russians could neither leave nor rest. The sudden disappearance of the Chinese interpreters in the employ of the Russians was a disquieting sign that they thought the Russian cause lost.

Between the Russian colony and the Wai River there lay a Chinese village and scattered buildings which offered good cover for the advancing Chinese. The Russians succeeded in burning them down, and cleared a field of fire. Shortly before midnight the Russians bayonetted a number of Chinese who had crawled through the high kaoliang to within 35 feet of the Russian firing line. Their pockets were full of matches and they had planned apparently to set fire to the Russian buildings. As the shooting died down, the Russians made preparations to withdraw. Many had not slept for two days and were utterly exhausted. If they stayed another twenty-four hours, they would not be alert enough to prevent another group from burning down their colony. Furthermore, once the Chinese brought artillery into play, their doom would be sealed.

The Russians decided to withdraw northward, to Harbin.[34] That morning they had captured a mule-drawn wagon train of 22 carts with silver and arms. Now they began loading the wounded, women and children,

[34]Iugovich telegraphed that day (July 8) about the retreat of the T'ieh-ling detachment toward Harbin under pressure from the Boxers, behind whom followed regular Chinese troops with artillery, and requested that troops be sent at once to safeguard the railway line between Harbin and Pogranichnaia Station. He communicated the interception of the Chinese Emperor's decree, ordering the armed forces to aid the Boxers in killing Russians. Iugovich's telegram was conveyed to the Emperor by the Minister of War on July 14.

131

ammunition boxes, food, clothing and bedding onto the vehicles. The preparations took two and a half hours and were marked by absolute chaos, for the Russians had been joined by over 200 Chinese Christian refugees—mostly widows and orphans of Chinese Christians massacred in Mukden—and by two French missionaries and two French nuns from the T'ieh-ling mission.

It was pitch-black when the first Russians began to evacuate Wai-khe. By the time the rear guard left the colony, dawn was breaking. Just then the sound of horns and drums drifted from T'ieh-ling. When the Chinese reached Wai-khe, the Russians were gone. The latter had traveled less than two miles when it was completely light. Looking back, they saw billows of smoke rising from the place they had left, as fire consumed the houses and furnishings which they had abandoned.

The northbound caravan was a pathetic sight. It reminded the Russians of Napoleon's retreat from Moscow. Actually it looked worse, because of the women and children. Some of them rode in the carts, but most had to walk on foot, carrying infants in their arms. Exhausted, they desperately kept up with the column, knowing that they would perish if they fell behind. Russians who had horses rode them. Some were mounted on donkeys. One young Russian railroad employee sat astride a bullock on a red blanket. There were some 30 carts which stretched out a long way, because of the Chinese manner of harnessing the horses one behind the other. Reinforced by a half-sotnia of Cossacks, who came to their aid about ten miles north of T'ieh-ling, the caravan consisted of some 600 persons, including the over 200 Chinese Christians, 250 Cossacks and soldiers, and about 150 railroad employees.

At about 3 P.M. the Russians reached K'ai-yüan Station. Two days before everything had been in good order here. Now the station lay in ruins and the once beautiful residence of the chief of the 3rd Railway Section had been reduced to the charred framework of its stoves and black pipes. Only the large, deep well had remained intact, and men and animals drank from it greedily. The place was unsuitable for a night-stop, however, and the Russians continued to the Ch'ing River, stopping at the point where the railroad crossed the river, less than three miles downstream from the city of K'ai-yüan. They found that the telegraph line between T'ieh-ling and K'ai-yüan had been cut in many places, but the line between T'ieh-ling and Hsi-sha-ho-tzu was still intact. They connected a field telephone and asked the chief of the 2nd Section, who lived in Hsi-sha-ho-tzu, to prepare food for them. In the early hours of July 9, they continued their exodus, planning to reach Hsi-sha-ho-tzu at about 3 P.M.

Hsi-sha-ho-tzu was about 20 miles from K'ai-yüan Station. The road led through mountains and the weary travellers and the exhausted animals, pulling the heavy loads, began dragging their feet. Suddenly, as the caravan was emerging from a depression, the Chinese attacked their rear. As quickly as they could, the Russians pulled the carts onto a plateau, while the Cossacks and soldiers formed three lines along the edges of the heights and began to fire back. The Chinese took up position around them—in ditches, in bushes, and behind mounds —and for over an hour fired at the Russians from all sides. Several native Christians were killed as Chinese bullets riddled the carts, and two Russian soldiers were wounded. But after several sorties, in which the Cossacks killed some 60 attackers, the Chinese were repulsed and the Russians could move on again. The Chinese followed and repeatedly shot at the Russians. Had the Chinese been better marksmen, the caravan would have been decimated. It was 5 P.M. by the time the Russians reached Hsi-sha-ho-tzu. They had not eaten anything warm for two days and, tired as they were, pounced with wolfish greed on the food that had been prepared for them.

At Hsi-sha-ho-tzu several carts, a number of employees of the 2nd Section and 23 guards joined the caravan. At 5:30 A.M. on July 10, the motley procession continued to Shuang-miao-tzu, some 8 miles away, and arrived there without incident at about 9 A.M. Around that time a number of Chinese contractors called on the chief of the 1st Section to get paid for work they had done. At about 11 A.M. they hastened away with the money. No sooner had they departed, than bullets began whistling into Shuang-miao-tzu from all directions. The courtyard in which the Russians found themselves besieged was really two yards, divided by an earthen wall. They made a hole in the wall, so that they could rush from one yard to the other, as needed. An earthen wall, ringed by a trench, surrounded the compound.

When the Russians determined that most of the fire came from Chinese buildings about a hundred paces from the gates, they stormed out and counterattacked. The Chinese fell back slowly, halting here and there to shoot from behind bushes, ditches and other cover. As they retreated, other Chinese advanced from the sides and the rear of the compound. Hiding behind the railroad embankment, which passed about 150 paces behind the courtyard, and in the kaoliang and bushes, they unleashed a noisy but aimless fusilade. The defenders fired back from the ditches and the wall and kept the Chinese at bay.

Half an hour after the Russians had stormed out of the gates, one ran back into the courtyard with an injured hand. Soon other wounded followed, carried by their comrades. About a dozen had been hit, none of them critically yet seriously enough, particularly in view of the fact that they had to continue the journey. Although the Russians were superior to the Chinese in hand-to-hand combat and so far had worsted them in every encounter, their situation was deteriorating rapidly. Their supply of ammunition and food was dwindling, while the number of wounded and exhausted was increasing. They could not stay much longer. On the other hand, the carts that were needed to transport the wounded and the supplies dragged like an anchor and hampered their progress.

The telegraph line north of Shuang-miao-tzu was still intact, and one of the senior railroad officials was able to inform Harbin of the situation. When the chief engineer at Harbin asked for an estimate of the enemy strength, the official went to consult the officers. They told him that the Chinese forces off Shuang-miao-tzu numbered about 1,500. When the official returned, he learned that the operator, in the hope of speeding up help, had replied on his own that they were surrounded by 15,000 Chinese. The official tried to correct the figure, but by this time the line had been cut, and he could not get through.

Before connection had been lost, the Russians had been informed that 20 Cossacks were riding to their aid. They waited till they appeared on the horizon, then made another sortie to distract Chinese attention. Three more

Russians were wounded, as were several of the horses, but the Cossacks got through to the compound. By nightfall the shooting stopped.

It was obvious that the Russians could not leave through the gates without heavy casualties. Under cover of darkness, therefore, they made a large hole in the side of the wall and filled in the trench beyond it. At 2 A.M., on July 11, they stole out with their carts and were about a mile away, when the Chinese resumed their attack against the front of the compound.

They traveled for a number of hours, tired and half-asleep, when suddenly, at about 10 A.M., they ran into a Chinese ambush. The fierce encounter lasted for ninety minutes and cost the Russians one dead and one seriously wounded. Finally they overcame the Chinese and continued past bleeding corpses pierced by Cossack lances or hacked to pieces by Cossack sabers. All the attackers had worn the uniforms of Fêng-t'ien Province. One of the captured banners read, "Commander of Infantry and Cavalry of Mukden [Fêng-t'ien] Province, Colonel Shen"; another banner read, "Boxer Soldiers," linking the military with the insurgents.

At 6 P.M. the Russians reached the post where the engineers who repaired bridges had been stationed. They rested, buried their slain comrade, ate, and fed their horses. Fifty Cossacks, sent to their aid from the north with 10,000 cartridges, found them here. At 11 P.M. they continued their trek. Informed by the newcomers that 500 Chinese lay in wait for them at the station which the chief of the 5th Section of the 3rd Division had abandoned the day before, the Russians swung around in a semi-circle, passing some six miles east of the place. When they reached the former residence of the chief of the 4th Section the following day, they found it abandoned and destroyed also. Though once again they had missed their evacuating countrymen by only one day, they could not maintain their pace, much less increase it. Men and beasts were weak from hunger and lack of sleep; a number of mules had fallen by the wayside.

Halting at a huge inn about a mile from the ruins, the caravan stayed put on July 13 and rested, while Cossack scouts reconnoitered the neighborhood. For the five ladies—the three Russian women and the two French nuns—the officers made a hut out of kaoliang, so that they could sleep undisturbed. Not that anyone stared at them anymore. War was no time for ceremony, and ladies and gentlemen took off their footwear to rest their weary feet and reduced their clothing to convenience. As Silnitskii remarked, "*à la guerre, comme à la guerre.*"

At dawn on July 14, the Russians resumed their march north and without incident traveled all day. They spent the night in a grove adjacent to a large inn, about a mile from the burned-down residence of the chief of the 3rd Section of the 3rd Division of the railroad. Early in the morning on the 15th, they continued on their way. At 8 A.M. they were traversing a wide open space near a village, when they blundered into another ambush. The Chinese attackers were dressed in civilian garb, but at their side they carried a linen bag containing a neatly folded uniform with the inscription "Kirin Province, Right Flank, New Infantry, Regiment of Border Defense." Only the aimlessness of the heavy Chinese fire preserved the Russians from annihilation. As the carts rolled on to shelter, the Cossacks counterattacked. This time the Chinese did not melt back, but stubbornly continued their fusilade from the houses in which they had hidden. The Cossacks set fire to the buildings and smoked the Chinese out. As they rushed into the open, the Cossacks dispatched them. Within an hour hundreds of Chinese had been killed, Russian losses numbering 3 dead and 37 wounded. While the ratio was "favorable," the Russians could not afford further casualties. Already two or three wounded were crowded in a cart. Yet Kuan-ch'êng-tzu,[35] where larger Chinese forces were massed, still lay before them.

After debating whether to turn toward Mongolia and head directly for the Russian frontier or to continue toward Harbin, the Russians decided on the latter course, but they swung around Kuan-ch'êng-tzu in a wide semi-circle. Traveling at night by compass, they continued during daylight on the 16th, stopping now and then for a rest. Heavy rain, which began falling in the evening, soon made the roads impassable and at 9 P.M. the Russians stopped at a Chinese village, and forcing their way into several outlying houses slept on the warm Chinese stove-beds in "regal splendor." After paying their reluctant hosts, the Russians moved on at 4 A.M. on July 17. Proceeding without incident, they reached a half-destroyed work place on the railway line, and there spent the night.

On the morning of July 18, they headed for Sungari Station No. 2, which for some time had been connected by rail with Harbin. Suddenly they were attacked again. A Cossack was killed by a bullet that pierced his eye. But the Chinese were dispersed, leaving some 25 dead behind. This was the last battle on the road to Harbin.

[35]Same as Ch'ang-ch'un Fu.

The caravan safely reached Sungari Station No. 2, and from there proceeded to Harbin by train, arriving without further mishap at noon on July 20. Its odyssey had lasted 13 days and had cost 8 dead and 33 wounded.

As the civilian railroad employees stepped into the security of Harbin, they remembered the heroism of the Cossack officers who had escorted them to safety. "One could not but marvel at them," one Russian recalled, "as at the first volleys of the enemy, whose strength we did not yet know, they charged forward at the head of forty or fifty Cossacks into the thickest hail of bullets without a moment's hesitation, encouraging the Cossacks with gay jokes and the example of the most complete personal calm and disdain for danger."

Harbin

THE WESTERN, EASTERN and southern divisions of the Manchurian railway each were under the direction of a construction engineer, with a chief engineer in overall command. Chief Engineer Iugovich was located at Harbin, the headquarters of railroad construction in Manchuria. Founded in 1897 as a construction settlement on the Chinese Eastern Railway, Harbin was at the junction of the main (Nikol'sk-Kaidalov) line and the southern (Port Arthur) branch, and served as distribution point for materials and supplies for the entire project. Here there was a Russian settlement of several thousand railway employees and workers and their families, swelled since the outbreak of the Boxer uprising by refugees from the Liaotung peninsula, including French and English missionaries and large numbers of Chinese converts.

The month of June passed peacefully in Harbin. The Chinese continued working in the city and on the railway and neither the workers nor the population at large showed any hostility. There were individual Russians who darkly predicted the spread of disorders to Harbin, but few people listened to their forebodings. Railway administrators did not think that the troubles of South China would plague Manchuria and anticipated no delay in construction, particularly since 60,000 laborers had just arrived from China for work on the railroad. Reassuring telegrams from the Tartar Generals of Hei-lung-chiang, Kirin and Fêng-t'ien guaranteeing the complete safety of the railway, provided the Russians did not begin hostilities, firmed their peace of mind.

Toward the beginning of July rumors about the spread of anti-foreignism, a flood of coded telegrams, and worried expressions on the faces of some officials aroused anxiety among the Russian residents. A few departed. Others became more cautious in their dealings with Chinese servants. They stopped talking in their presence, and in a number of cases even dismissed them. To calm his countrymen, Iugovich on July 3 made public a telegram from Finance Minister Sergei Witte to the Chinese authorities. In the telegram Witte asserted that Russia was not at war with China; she had resorted to active measures only for the suppression of popular unrest, with which the Chinese Government was unable to cope. "When the disorder will have been quelled, Russia will direct all of her efforts toward preserving the integrity and inviolability of China and her dynasty," the Russian Government promised.

Two days later, on July 5, however, news was received that the Roman Catholic mission in Mukden had been destroyed and the bishop killed. Word spread that the insurgents were heading north, toward T'ieh-ling, and that a message had been intercepted in which the Emperor of China ordered the regular armed forces to join the Boxers in expelling all foreigners. The realization that the insurgents enjoyed government support was heightened by reports of mobilization in Hei-lung-chiang Province and by the receipt of telegrams from the Tartar Generals of the three Manchurian Provinces. The governors warned that they could not vouch for the conduct of their soldiers in the event of an attack on the Russian settlement and advised the Russian agents to surrender the railway and all property to Chinese officials and to leave Manchuria. The Chief Engineer categorically rejected the proposal and together with the senior commander of the railway guard appealed to the Governor General of the Priamur region and the Minister of Finance for troops to protect the Russian railway and its scattered personnel. Private persons and the families of the employees were counseled to leave Manchuria, but the employees themselves were ordered to remain on their jobs.

On July 6 or 7, families arrived in Harbin from Kirin. They told of Chinese posters, calling upon the populace to drive out the foreigners. On July 10, the families of the officers of the railway guard and of the senior agents of the railway were evacuated from Harbin to Khabarovsk on two steamers with barges in tow. Orders were issued also to employees all along the line to discontinue work and withdraw with the railway guards to Harbin, Port Arthur, Nikol'sk or Tsurukhaitui, whichever was nearer, taking along government documents and funds.

An attack on Harbin was believed to be scheduled for the night of July 10 to 11, and a volunteer militia of railway employees was hastily formed to assist the railway guards, of whom not more than a hundred were present at this time. No raid occurred, but this was believed due to the heavy thunderstorm that had raged during the night, and in the morning all offices and the branch of the Russo-Chinese Bank began evacuating the city, moving to the Sungari dock, about five miles away. At the dock there were private and temporary railway buildings. A new city of several hundred brick houses had been under construction nearby, when fear of an attack had prompted evacuation to Russia.

Panic gripped Harbin. Turned down by the militia, into which he had tried to enlist to obtain a rifle, one telegraph official got drunk and put a revolver bullet through his head. Other Russian residents, paying exhorbitant charges for carts from Harbin to the dock hastily left their homes, abandoning many of their possessions. Chinese inhabitants, several thousand of whom lived in Harbin and vicinity, fled also. Long caravans of bullock carts, laden with household goods and women and children on top of the belongings, headed for the interior.

Elsewhere too, the alarm of Russian civilians was shared by their Chinese counterparts. Frequently Chinese servants found themselves dismissed, and Chinese laborers and contractors worried that the Russians might pull out without paying them. At I-mien-p'o Station, in the 10th Subsection of the Chinese Eastern Railway, for example, crowds of Chinese surrounded the residence of Engineer Tikhomirov and demanded their money.

When the Russians packed to leave, the Manchus or "Manzy," as the Russians working on the railway called the native laborers, broke into the houses, sometimes while the Russians were still inside, and plundered what had been left behind. As the last Russian train pulled out of I-mien-p'o Station on the evening of July 11, the populace fought with its own officials and guards over the carpets, wines and other treasures in the Russian warehouses. But the Russians themselves had not been molested.

The voyage to Harbin was marked by anxiety and

hardship. Ever fearful of a Chinese attack, the Russians moved slowly on the sabotage-ridden road, stopping repeatedly to remove obstacles and to repair bridges. On July 15, they reached the Sungari River dock near Harbin. The women and children were at once put on the steamer *Odessa* and two barges and shipped to Khabarovsk, to the safety of Russian territory. The men stayed in the houses that had been vacated by the local employees who had already left for Russia.

Sergei Grudzinskii had remained on his job in Harbin. When the situation became serious, he offered his services as a volunteer, and was assigned to the 7th Sotnia of the Railway Guard. He protested that he could not command a cavalry unit, since he was an infantry officer by training, but he was told that all he had to know was *"sadis!* (mount!), *"za mnoi!"* (follow me!) and *"slezai!"* (dismount!), and the Cossacks would do the rest automatically. The morale of the men was high, and the desire of the younger ones for action was bridled only with difficulty. They received strict orders not to initiate hostilities.

When word was received that superior Chinese forces had surrounded Captain Rzhevutskii, who was coming from T'ieh-ling with 6 officers, 250 Cossacks, several railway agents with their families and a large flock of Chinese converts,[36] volunteers were sent to the rescue. But Rzhevutskii had already succeeded in getting away from the Chinese and on July 18 reached Harbin. His arrival substantially strengthened the garrison, which until then had numbered only between 500 and 600 defenders,

---

[36]Grudzinskii gives the strength of Rzhevutskii's force as 6 officers, 250 Cossacks and several railway agents, as stated above; Doroguntsev gives it as 400 railway guards.

counting 300 persons who had arrived from the Tsi-tsihar line on July 14. The T'ieh-ling detachment was festively received, and on July 22 a special thanksgiving service was celebrated on the square in Harbin.

Volunteers were sent out also to help *Esaul*[37] Savitskii. It was reported that he and 67 Cossacks were battling against overwhelming odds near Kirin. Savitskii's detachment was found at Lao-shao-kou, where it had arrived on July 19, reduced to 1 officer and 38 Cossacks, 5 of them wounded. Savitskii's left eye had been contused by bullet splinters, and his arm was in a sling. Savitskii related that in spite of assurances of friendship and a safe conduct pass from the Tartar General of Kirin, his detachment had been attacked by a Chinese force of about 500 men with artillery. So eager had the Chinese been to wipe out the Cossacks, that they had fired shrapnel over the heads of their own soldiers and inhabitants, killing many. Fighting back desperately, the Cossacks felled some 200 Chinese, themselves losing almost half their comrades and all their horses. Breaking through the Chinese lines, the Russians had successfully evaded pursuit for five days, slushing through the sea of mud into which heavy rains had transformed the tilled soil and discarding their sticking boots and whatever else weighted them down, except their weapons and cartridges. "Tears welled up in our eyes and anger began to boil in our hearts, when we saw the valiant heroes who had arrived," Grudzinskii recalled. "The men walked barefoot, with feet that were skinned almost to the bones, many [clad] only in their underwear, exhausted and emaciated. Truly one could not believe

[37]Cossack Captain.

145

somehow that the Chinese had not succeeded in wiping this handful of men from the face of the earth."

On July 21, a steamer arrived at the dock of Harbin from Khabarovsk with 1,000 rifles and ammunition. Four companies were formed from reservists who had been working on the railroad, the number of fighting men approaching 2,000.[38] The infantry was positioned at the dock, the cavalry sotnias in Harbin, in the new brick houses, and in Shuang-ch'êng-pao to the south of Harbin.

On July 22, the Tartar General of Hei-lung-chiang telegraphed that while he had heretofore cooperated with Russian railway builders in every way, he regarded the Russian drowning of Chinese as tantamount to a declaration of war, and that now both sides were free to attack each other. This part of the message made no sense to the Russians at the time, for news of the Blagoveshchensk massacre had not yet reached Harbin. But the rest of the telegram was crystal clear. The Tartar General declared that military operations against Harbin would begin shortly and exhorted the Russians to fight bravely, for they too would be exterminated without mercy. But he asked them not to kill innocent women, children and old men, and offered safe passage out of Manchuria to all Russian women and children, provided they would not be accompanied by armed men.

Iugovich replied that they were not at war, since neither government had made a declaration of war. He expressed his determination to remain in Harbin with the railway personnel. He did accept the offer of safe passage for women, children and unarmed private in-

[38]According to Kuropatkin, Major General Gerngros had 5 companies and 13 sotnias of guards in Harbin.

146

dividuals, however, and proclaimed that day that all but reservists of lower rank, medical and some telegraph and communication personnel were free to leave for Khabarovsk, Nikol'sk-Ussuriiskii or Vladivostok. The announcement confronted the residents with a dilemma: on one hand it was dangerous for them to stay; on the other hand, the unescorted ships could become death traps, if the Tartar General did not keep his promise. Unable to make up their mind some people went aboard the steamers only to get off again.

During the night from July 23 to 24, some 3,000 women, children, wounded and private individuals left Harbin on two steamers with barges. Their departure ended the torment of indecision, but the husbands and fathers who were left behind ached with worry for their loved ones. They were particularly concerned lest the ships be halted at the city of San-hsing. But the vessels reached Khabarovsk unmolested, whether because the Tartar General remained true to his word or because Russian forces took San-hsing on July 28, before the vessel got there.[39]

Meanwhile military preparations were hastened at the Sungari dock. Chinese laborers dug trenches and erected defense works. Three cannons for firing case shot were made in the railway shop, and the defenders, 2,000 strong, awaited the Chinese onslaught with confidence. The Tartar General of Hei-lung-chiang gallantly telegraphed to the chief engineer that he had refrained from attacking Harbin while it was guarded by only a few soldiers. Now that the Russian force was substantial, he would strike, sparing no one, high or low.

[39]Here and there the vessels were fired upon and sustained minor casualties.

On July 25, the Chinese advanced against railway buildings about a mile and a half from the dock, at a place where the Sungari River had cut deeply into its left bank. The Russians who had gone there were forced to withdraw to the other side of the river. As they departed on a little steamer, an old and sick Cossack could not be found, and had to be left behind.

At 4 A.M. on July 26, the Chinese began firing at the Russian dock from across the river, and pressed toward the brick buildings of the "New City" and against Harbin from the south and east. They succeeded in occupying the railway depot of the First Sungari Station and the permanent way of the railroad between the "New City" and Harbin. But in the afternoon a counterattack by 3 Cossack sotnias drove the Chinese back in the direction of A-shih-ho. A Russian attempt to encircle the Chinese and capture their field guns was anticipated by the latter, and they withdrew in great haste. Soldiers who did not have time to rejoin the main body were cut down by the Cossacks. One group of Chinese at the railway depot and four soldiers in a well concealed ditch offered stubborn resistance. Some of them were killed on the spot; the others were driven to a village and, after it was set afire, into an open field, where Cossack sabers and bullets further decimated the group. Only a few managed to find shelter in a distillery.

Plants in which *hanhsin* was distilled were scattered all over Manchuria. Like the residences of officials, they were surrounded by walls of unfired brick mixed with chopped straw, about seven feet high and five or six feet wide, and constituted veritable fortresses. The walls were provided with loopholes and towers; the gates were of heavy lumber, reinforced with iron.

From this fortification the Chinese showered the Russians with a hail of bullets, wounding *Shtabs-kapitan* Rzhevutskii and a Cossack who stood next to him. But when the Russians scaled the wall, the Chinese opened the gates and fled from the plant. A Russian platoon on the left flank fired several volleys after them. An attempt to cut off the Chinese retreat failed, however. As Cossacks galloped around the distillery to block the way, they ran into a stream with boggy banks into which their horses sank belly-deep.

Meanwhile the *hanhsin* plant presented a strange and wild sight. As Sergei Grudzinskii recalled:

The corpses of men and cadavers of horses lay strewn about everywhere. Sabers and bayonets sparkled. People jostled each other in disorder. All had agitated faces, as if drunk. The noise of voices and swear words filled the air, which was saturated with the heavy smell of blood, sweat and gunpowder. Frightened children, ducks, oxen and horses ran around. Now and then the short, whiplash-like shots of our 20 caliber rifles were heard. The men had gotten all excited. There was no mercy for anyone. Aroused, someone had set fire to a house, and thick, black smoke rose to the sky, as the bright sun beamed indifferently on the picture of death and destruction below.

In the distillery the Russians captured two late model Krupp guns, capable of firing grenades and shrapnel, with all their equipment and ammunition, as well as long-range German rifles and Chinese banners. The guns were of great value, since, as noted, the bronze weapons which had been cast in the Harbin workshops were good for shrapnel only. General Gerngros rode up on his white prancer and personally thanked the Cossacks for their accomplishment. When they returned to the New City and Harbin with their booty, tired but proud, they were received with regimental music and loud, joyful hurrahs.

On July 27 and 28, the Chinese continued to bombard the dock from across the river. They fired at every train that ran between Sungari Station and Harbin. To deprive the Chinese of cover in the event of another attack on the station, the Russians razed some of their own, laboriously constructed, railway buildings and put the torch to nearby villages. As Chinese poured from the blazing houses and tried to drag away cows, pigs and various belongings, mounted Cossacks surrounded them, and drove them to work on entrenchments for the defenders. On the evening of July 28, the buildings on the other side of the river suddenly went up in flames. The Chinese had decided to abandon their position.

On July 29, a Russian patrol reported that a Chinese detachment of 200 foot soldiers and 400 cavalrymen was moving toward Harbin. Cossack sotnias which were dispatched at once, failed to make contact. Then it was learned that the Chinese had moved into a walled distillery about 6½ miles from Harbin. Russian infantrymen and one gun were loaded on a train and departed in the evening, seen off by several tearful wives who had not been evacuated. In the morning on July 30, the cavalry took to the field and by 10 A.M. approached the walls of the distillery.

The Chinese were in a strong position. Their fire was heavy and effective. The 1st Company alone lost 12 men; about 50 were wounded. The Russian gun was knocked out of commission when one of its own grenades exploded in the barrel. Then it was discovered that someone had failed to supply part of the line with ammunition, and panic was barely averted among the Russian troops as the officers assembled them for an orderly withdrawal to Harbin. They did not know, of course, that the Chinese assumed, when they saw them draw together, that they were about to charge, and breaking through the wall at the opposite side themselves were fleeing toward A-shih-ho. Thus the two forces retreated from each other, and the Russians did not learn till the next day that the distillery had been abandoned.

Prisoner of war interrogation revealed that a second offensive against Harbin was scheduled for August 3, and that the Chinese planned to put 25,000 men into the field. As the fatal day drew nearer, the Russians nervously made final preparations. Houses near the New City that might have provided cover for Chinese attackers or hampered Russian fire were leveled, and mines were laid at strategic places. The soldiers were admonished to make effective use of their limited ammunition. They were ordered to remove the clips from their rifles and to fire single shots at enemy soldiers within 400 paces. They were to shoot only three or four volleys, and then charge with bayonets. But the Chinese attack did not materialize.

On the afternoon of August 3, word was received that two Cossack sotnias under Colonel Denisov had cut their way through Chinese lines and were approaching the city.[40] At 6 P.M. steam ships were sighted from the watch

---

[40]Denisov came from Nikol'sk-Ussuriiskii, where he had escorted employees of the 11th Railway Construction Section to safety. Though official reports speak only of his arrival, his sotnias were part of a larger relief

tower of the Harbin police department. The news caused great excitement, and people with field glasses and telescopes clambered onto the watch towers to observe the vessels that were arriving on the Sungari. With baited breath they counted—one, two, three, four, five, six, seven steamers—then rushed to the river bank to join their fellow townspeople in welcoming the Harbin detachment under Generals Sakharov and Alekseev. More and more vessels came during the night and on the following day, till some 22 steamers and 48 barges lined the Sungari dock. It was a magnificent sight, particularly to the residents of Harbin, whose siege was over.[41] Excitedly they milled about the dock at night, feasting their eyes on the illuminated steamers, listening to gay and patriotic band music, and shouting and cheering till they were hoarse. The following day, on August 4, a festive religious service was held on the city square to celebrate the name day of Empress Maria Fedorovna and to give thanks for their liberation.

From the new arrivals, who had come from Khabarovsk and Vladivostok, the residents learned that the steamers with their wives and children and railway employees had reached Khabarovsk. Only now did they hear also of the murder of Baron von Ketteler by

force sent from Nikol'sk-Ussuriiskii under Major General Chichagov. Chichagov's detachment consisted of the 4th East Siberian Rifle Regiment, two squadrons of the Maritime Dragoon Regiment and the 5th (Mountain) Battery of the 1st East Siberian Artillery Brigade. He left part of it at Mu-tan-chiang Station on the Mu-tan River, to allow the resumption of railway construction under its protection. But the 4th East Siberian Rifle Regiment must have arrived in Harbin soon after Denisov's sotnias. Denisov had come via A-shih-ho, where two sotnias had ridden from Harbin to meet him.

[41]The steamers, owned by the Amur Steamship Company, were of invaluable service. They served not only as troop transports but actively participated in some of the battles and, armored, acted as cruisers.

Boxers in Peking and of the dispatch of large German forces to China.

Sources differ regarding the number of troops brought by the steamers. Doroguntsev speaks of some 3,000; Kuznetsov of 6,000. They included cavalry, artillery and infantry from the Ussuri region, and were to be followed by more troops from Russia proper.[42] To the Chinese who watched the flotilla pass, the number of men may have appeared many times greater, since far more troops could have been transported on the barge-pulling ships. On August 13, another regiment arrived from Russia.

As the relief force had approached on the Sungari, General Sakharov had cleared the river banks. He had occupied Lahasusu[43] (July 22), Pa-yen-t'ung (July 25) and San-hsing (July 26).[44] Russians who had worked at the San-hsing dock were rescued by him before he reached the city. On July 19, they had been warned by the commander of San-hsing with whom they had been on friendly terms that a large Chinese detachment which was headed from the lower reaches of the Sungari to Harbin, planned to attack them. Unable to defend the dock with the 49 men under his command, Colonel

[42]Sakharov's detachment was composed of the 17th East Siberian Rifle Regiment (2 battalions), the 3rd and 4th East Siberian Line Battalions (which later became the 18th and 22nd East Siberian Rifle Regiments), the 1st Battery of the 1st and the 1st Battery of the 2nd East Siberian Artillery Brigade (16 guns), the 1st, 2nd and 3rd Sotnias of the Amur Cossack Regiment and the 1st Sotnia of the Ussuri Cossack Division, as well as 10 pieces of position artillery.

[43]Lin-chiang or T'ung-chiang; given in the German summary as Lauschi.

[44]At Pa-yen-t'ung Sakharov had worsted an estimated 2,000 Chinese regular troops and had captured the fortress and with it 19 guns. At San-hsing, which had been defended by an estimated 4,000 Chinese, he had captured 22 guns, including 4 Hotchkiss cannons.

Grigorii Vinnikov had evacuated his little force onto the barge *Chibis* in the morning.

The Chinese detachment was reported advancing on the left bank of the river. Vinnikov, therefore, cast anchor near the right bank. As he did so, some of the soldiers of the Chinese commander opened fire at the *Chibis* while their comrades plundered the abandoned dock. Three of Vinnikov's men, who had been approaching on a boat unaware of the happenings, were seriously wounded, but under the cover of volleys fired from the *Chibis* managed to rejoin their countrymen. With the appearance of the steamer *Voevoda Tolbuzin* the Russians thought their ordeal ended, but so heavy was Chinese fire directed at the vessel that it did not dare to stop and take the barge into tow. When the Chinese saw that they could not hit the barge from the left bank, they crossed over to the right bank and a fierce exchange of fire ensued. At about 3 A.M. on July 21, the Chinese ignited two barges that had been left at the dock and directed them at the *Chibis*. As the current carried the flaming barges toward them, the Russians cut cable and drifted downstream. They passed the fortress Pa-yen-t'ung without drawing fire, but ran aground some 2½ miles below. When the Chinese saw this they hastened from the fortress and began to bombard the stranded Russians from both banks of the river. The situation seemed hopeless. Vinnikov was killed and the two Russian women who were on the barge were advised to change to men's clothing to hide their sex in case of disaster. But at dawn, as the Chinese were bringing up artillery, the rising tide freed the barge, and carried the Russians away. On the morning of July 23, the Russians came upon the steamers of General Sakharov's detachment and greeted them with tears of joy and a throated hurrah! The steamer *Molly* took the *Chibis* in tow and safely delivered its weary passengers to Harbin.

Upon the arrival of large Russian forces, Chief Engineer Iugovich contacted the Chinese Commander of A-shih-ho, where some 10,000 troops were reportedly gathered. He informed him that Russian forces had arrived to restore order and in the name of the friendly relations that had always existed between him and the railway builders, called on him to disband the Chinese troops. He demanded, furthermore, that the commander make the inhabitants return to peaceful pursuits and that he assist in the recruitment of laborers for the rebuilding of the railway. While the Tartar General of Hei-lung-chiang, to whom Iugovich wrote also, responded that he would visit the Russians soon, the commander of A-shih-ho rebuffed Iugovich and fired two cannon shots at the Russian outpost.

At 4 A.M. on August 17, after a religious service, the Russians set out against A-shih-ho. Major General Gerngros with his Cossacks formed the vanguard; Major General Alekseev followed with the main body, about a mile and a half behind. The operation was under the over-all command of Major General Sakharov, and included 16 companies, 12½ sotnias, and 16 guns. It was frightfully hot as the rays of the sun beat down mercilessly from a clear blue sky, and by 10 A.M. the infantry dragged its feet with difficulty. But the Cossacks, who clashed with Chinese forces half way to A-shih-ho, needed no help and the exhausted foot soldiers regained some of their strength overnight.

On the morning of August 18, the detachment approached A-shih-ho. In reply to a demand for his surrender the Chinese commander had bravely retorted that he would disband his troops when General Sakharov compensated China for the destruction of Pa-yen-t'ung, San-hsing, and other places, and withdrew his forces from Manchuria. But his words proved braver than his actions. Like most inhabitants, he had fled from the city by the time the Russian troops arrived at the gates. The soldiers he deserted returned fire only briefly. When the Russian infantry launched an artillery-supported frontal attack and the Cossacks swooped around A-shih-ho to cut off retreat, the Chinese defenders hastened out of the city in the direction of Kirin. A number of them were taken prisoner by Denisov who had hastened after them. Seven guns, many pieces of light ordnance, and a large quantity of ammunition also fell into Russian hands.

The previous night a railway worker who had escaped from Chinese captivity had joined the Russian forces to avenge himself on the Chinese. At the southern gate the Russians found the body of another prisoner who had been less fortunate. It was the corpse of Ostapenko, a Cossack of the railway guard, who had been captured during Savitskii's withdrawal from Kirin. Ostapenko had been tortured to death. His legs bore marks of hastily removed stocks and his entire body was covered with knife wounds.

Upon the capture of A-shih-ho, Alekseev withdrew the troops from the city, and stationed them at the gates and walls. The palace of the Chinese commander and all public buildings as well as the city walls and towers were demolished in punishment for resistance and the torturing to death of Ostapenko. The personal property of the Chinese commander was sold at auction.

The commander of the 4th East Siberian Rifle Regiment was appointed commandant of A-shih-ho. He remained here with his regiment and the 4th Sotnia of the railway guard and 6 guns. All others left on August 22. Gerngros and the cavalry went to meet Denisov, who was on his way from Pogranichnaia to Harbin. Alekseev with the infantry and artillery and Sakharov with his staff departed for Harbin.

On August 28, the 20th East Siberian Rifle Regiment returned to Harbin from Aigun. On the 31st, Alekseev's detachment, consisting of 3 regiments, 2 battalions, a half-sotnia of Cossacks and a lazaret, crossed to the other side of the Sungari and headed for Tsitsihar in support of the Hailar and Tsitsihar detachments, which were attacking it. The 20th East Siberian Rifle Regiment and one battery were ordered to cover Hu-lan-chen. The rest of the detachment followed to Tsitsihar the next day. But Tsitsihar was taken before Alekseev could reach it, and the detachment was recalled to Harbin. From here it was sent to Hu-lan-chen, where Colonel Fotengauer's detachment had encountered resistance. Two battalions, 1 sotnia and 6 guns advanced directly over land; 4½ battalions, 2 sotnias and 12 guns were transported on the Sungari River to the mouth of the Hu-lan River, proceeding from there along the river against the city. On September 12, the commander of Hu-lan-chen submitted without a shot, agreeing to disarm his men and to raze all fortifications. On September 14 the detachment was back in Harbin.

As will be recalled, the residents of the city had been evacuated during the "siege," only the mounted guards remaining to defend it. Passing through Harbin in mid-September, Kuznetsov was shocked by the state in which he found it. "The Cossacks [had] had the place to themselves," he commented. "And they gave free rein to their insatiable greed and dissipation. There was not left, it is said, a single store, not a single house, where the guard did not play the master. The guard did a fine job of guarding!"

On September 21, Gerngros moved against Shuang-ch'êng-pao with the 20th East Siberian Rifle Regiment, the 1st Battery of the 2nd East Siberian Artillery Brigade, a party of sappers, a lazaret and the guard sotnias. A deputation of merchants came out to greet them. The Russians declared that they would keep their soldiers out of the city, if provisions were promptly brought to their bivouac at the southern gates. As the Russians offered to pay for everything, the Chinese complied gladly, and lugged chickens, ducks, geese, eggs, flour, salt, hay, barley, firewood, cattle and even a couple of bottles of champagne to the camp. Would-be-interpreters—*"malo-malo-pelevodchika"* as they called themselves—joined the Russians to cater to their needs. But the friendly atmosphere was shattered when the Russians flushed over 200 Chinese soldiers out of hiding in spite of the fact that a Chinese colonel had assured Gerngros that no troops had remained in the city.

On August 26, Gerngros started back for Harbin, whither Major General Orlov was also headed. On the morning of August 28, Fotengauer departed for Sungari Station with the 20th East Siberian Rifle Regiment, the battery, sappers, lazaret and 2nd Sotnia of the guard, and on October 3, crossed over to the left bank of the river. On the morning of October 9, with music and unfurled banner, the detachment marched into Kuan-ch'êng-tzu, which had been selected as the "permanent" station of the 20th Regiment, as well as of the Priamur

Dragoon Regiment and the Transbaikal Cossack Battery.

Major General Alekseev congratulated the men on their victory and reminded them not to mistreat the peaceful populace. As there were no barracks in the city, the Russians took over inns, connecting them with each other through breaches in the walls. Soldiers were not allowed to wander about freely, and only groups of armed men were sent to the city on official business. Even officers were not permitted to go through Kuan-ch'êng-tzu unescorted. Everyone was instructed where to go and what to do should an alarm be sounded. The Russians remained on the alert for any eventuality.

The Battle of Ongun
and the Taking of Hailar

THE MAJOR OBJECTIVES of the Russians in Manchuria were to defeat the Chinese armed forces and Boxers, to take possession of the entire Chinese Eastern Railway, and to secure navigation of the Amur River. For tactical purposes they divided Manchuria into two parts—North Manchuria (up to the line that went through T'ieh-ling Station), where the forces of the Priamur military district and their reinforcements were to operate under the overall command of Lieutenant General Grodekov, and South Manchuria, where the forces of the Kwantung region and their reinforcements were to serve under Vice Admiral Alekseev. Russian plans called for the recovery first of the main line of the Chinese Eastern Railway, running from the Transbaikal region, from Manchuria Station, to Tsitsihar, Harbin, Pogranichnaia Station and Nikol'sk-Ussuriiskii. For this, Tsitsihar and Ninguta had to be taken. Then, Russian forces were to advance simultaneously from two directions to occupy the southern branch of the railway, from Harbin to Port Arthur. To effect this, Kirin and Mukden had to be captured.

The difficulties involved were staggering. The Chinese Eastern Railway (including the main line and the southern branch) was over 1,300 miles long. Yet this was only part of the distance that the Russian forces had to cover. It was a long way from the Transbaikal region to Manchuria. Men and supplies had to be moved for thousands of miles. The situation was complicated by the fact that there was a shortage of river steamers, so that rafts and barges had to be built, and that a bad harvest of grains and hay had reduced local resources, so that large quantities of provisions and military supplies had to be shipped very far.

The enormous expanse of territory along the Russo-Chinese frontier necessitated the mobilization of large Russian forces for the invasion of Manchuria and the guarding of the Russian border. The troops stationed in Kwantung sufficed only for the maintenance of peace in that region. To have enough men at hand to cope with unrest in Kwantung, the rest of Manchuria and China proper, the Russians needed reinforcements. In June and July aid was rushed from the Priamur military district to Kwantung and Pechihli (16 battalions, 38 guns, 6 sotnias, 2 sapper companies and 2 railway companies). As this left the Priamur region inadequately defended, the mobilization of the Priamur military district and eventually of the Siberian military district became necessary. The Amur River formed the only route of communication between these regions. Had the Chinese succeeded in taking Blagoveshchensk and halting navigation on the Amur, they would have utterly disrupted the mobilization of the Priamur military district.

This was not the first time that mobilization had been decreed in the Russian Far East. In 1895, in the wake of the Sino-Japanese War and the Tripartite Intervention, troops had been called to the colors in the Transbaikal Region, though they were demobilized again when Japan bowed to Russian, German and French demands and gave up the Liaotung foothold on the Asian continent which she had negotiated with China.

The mobilization of 1900 was carried out with remarkable speed and inefficiency. It was decreed by the Emperor on June 23; it was publicly announced and begun on June 25. Like the mobilization of 1895, it did not go off like clockwork. In the Transbaikal Region it was executed, as Major General Nikolai Orlov observed, not with German precision but with "typically Russian peculiarities." Instead of calling up the number of men needed, the Russian authorities assembled many times more. After selecting the required number, they sent back the rest.[45]

There were in the Transbaikal Region at the turn of the century some 25,000 persons of working age. From these it was planned to outfit 5 cavalry regiments, 4 cavalry batteries and 4 infantry battalions, and to draw reinforcements for organizations and depots already in existence. Several of the newly formed units were grouped together in the Hailar Detachment, so called because the detachment was to advance on Hailar. Fairly small at first, the Hailar Detachment grew eventually to a force of over 5,000 men.[46] It consisted primarily of

[45]The same happened in the Priamur region. As the Minister of War reported, the percentage of people who failed to muster in response to mobilization orders was less than expected and thus there were for a number of days more men per unit than needed. On the other hand, the readiness of a number of military organizations ran behind schedule.

[46]The Hailar Detachment consisted only of Cossacks of the second and third levy. It was composed of the 3rd, 4th, 5th, and 6th Battalions of the Transbaikal Foot Brigade (910 bayonets per battalion), the 3rd Verkhneudinsk Cossack Mounted Regiment of 6 sotnias (899 sabers), and the 2nd Transbaikal Cossack Battery (6 cannons), as well as of railway guards—the Ural Sotnia (128 sabers), the 6th Tersk Sotnia (116 sabers), the

Transbaikal Cossacks who were uncomely in appearance but had endurance, high spirits and pride. Though they all had previous military training, their discipline was very peculiar. They would smoke in front of a superior and when saluting would nod their head with familiarity. Nor would a common Transbaikal Cossack let an officer strike him, as was the custom in the army, and an ataman of a Cossack village had to be addressed as "you" (rather than as "thou"). But they were satisfied to live on meager rations, were crack shots and bold warriors. Furthermore, they knew the land and the people along the Chinese border and were on good terms with the Mongols who for a fee would graze the cattle of the Transbaikal inhabitants in the rich steppes of Mongolia between spring and autumn.

There were not enough Transbaikal officers to staff the Hailar Detachment; not more than two for every battalion. The other officers were drawn largely from the Kazan military district. The detachment was under the command of Major General Orlov, commander of the Foot Cossack Brigade, who learned of his appointment to that position on July 12, when he arrived in Chita. Lieutenant Colonel Volozhaninov served as his chief of staff.[47]

The Hailar Detachment's transport consisted exclu-

18th Tersk Sotnia (72 sabers) and the 8th Foot Company (174 bayonets). It numbered a total of 3,814 bayonets, 1,205 sabers, and 6 cannons.

[47]Volozhaninov had been Senior Adjutant of the district [oblast] headquarters and had been detached to Orlov by General Matsievskii, head of the Cossack forces. Matsievskii also assigned to Orlov his personal adjutant. Matsievskii's own son Georgii, a shy and tactful but brave and intelligent young cadet served as messenger with the staff. He had just completed the course of the 3rd Moscow Cadet Corps and had gone to Chita on leave to visit his father, when the hostilities had overtaken him and as a Cossack he found himself on active duty.

sively of two-wheeled carts, drawn by horses and oxen. The latter not only pulled supplies, but themselves ultimately became supplies, as they were eaten. From the Chinese eventually the Russians obtained also camels, hinnies and mules, so that they could load their packs onto the animals and advance at a surprisingly rapid pace.[48]

The railway guards, like the Transbaikal Cossacks were excellent fighters. They did not belong to the imperial army and were not under the jurisdiction of the Ministry of War, for neither China nor the Western Powers would have tolerated the stationing of regular troops in Manchuria. But they were former members of the regular Cossack and infantry forces, recruited from among the best volunteers at very high pay.[49] Thus the railroad guards were professional in training, if not in name and status. Although the Ural Cossacks were grey-haired men with dignified beards, they were seasoned veterans. The Tersk Cossacks were superb shots; they were brave, intelligent, and carried out orders faithfully. The officers of the mounted sotnias were excellent. Though they were former infantry officers, they had learned the cavalry business well. The 8th Foot Company was also an effective fighting force. Its commander, an intelligent and calm officer, was of

[48]Generally speaking, the Hailar Detachment was inadequately "serviced." The 9th Mobile Hospital caught up with the detachment two weeks after it had crossed the border and proved very useful, but the large field hospital with the detachment doctor did not arrive until the detachment was already in Harbin and was no longer needed. The "flying" ordnance depot did not reach the detachment until August, when two major victories had already been attained. The field bakery joined the detachment at Hailar when it was already returning from the campaign.

[49]Common railway guards earned about 40 rubles a month, officers as much as 3,000 to 4,000 a year.

particular value to the Hailar Detachment, because his service on the railroad line had familiarized him with the terrain and the inhabitants of the region.[50] All in all, the Hailar Detachment embarked on the campaign with seriousness of purpose. In the words of Orlov: "Here one did not look at the war as a pastime or a means for achieving personal ends, but as a sacred cause."

Mobilization orders called for the assembly of the Hailar Detachment at Staro-Tsurukhaitui by August 14. But when word was received that the Chinese, on July 11, had driven the Russians away from the Chinese Eastern railroad and might even violate the Russian frontier, Orlov obtained a speed-up in the mobilization and changed the point of assembly to Abagaitui. On July 25, Orlov presented the banner to the 3rd Verkhneudinsk Cossack Mounted Regiment, and with the 4th and 6th Battalions of the Transbaikal Foot Brigade crossed the border. He left the regiment and the 2nd Transbaikal Cossack Battery behind for two days of rest, since they had assembled at Abagaitui only the previous day after exhausting forced marches.

Proceeding from Abagaitui across the Chinese border and following along the left bank of the Hailar River, which formed the upper reaches of the Argun, Orlov took a longer route than had he proceeded from Staro-Tsurukhaitui to Hailar, as originally planned. But in so doing he was sure of water, which the other route lacked, and avoided two major crossings on floats over the Argun and Hailar Rivers. Furthermore, he might succeed in

---

[50]By the time of Orlov's departure, only the 18th Tersk Sotnia had reached Abagaitui. But the officers of the other units had hastened ahead and provided Orlov with valuable information about the region, so that a sketch could be drawn of the route to Hailar.

surprising the Chinese, who had become accustomed to the other route, along which the railroad guards assigned to his detachment had withdrawn.

The first day Orlov penetrated with the two battalions to the Dalai Nor railroad station, a distance of almost thirty miles. He stopped for a day's rest, and on July 27, advanced to Hoerhungte, the next station, about twenty miles away. With the two battalions and the 6th Tersk Sotnia which had joined him, he captured without resistance 51 well-armed Mongols and 2 officers, with 58 horses, and sent them to Russia to work on the construction of the Transbaikal railroad.

At the stations telephone communication was restored and small garrisons, chosen from the weakest soldiers, were left behind for protection. Oats and flour had been found and bread was baked. A herd of 170 oxen was purchased at Abagaitui and sent after the detachment. The oats, the rich grass of the steppe, and the freshly baked bread restored the strength of horses and men, and the dysentery that had broken out among the troops was halted.

Orlov remained at Hoerhungte Station for a day, because the foot battalions needed a rest. But he dispatched the mounted Tersk Cossacks to the next station, Ongun,[51] about 20 miles away, and brought up one mounted sotnia of the 3rd Verkhneudinsk Cossack Regiment. When a message was received during the night of July 28 to 29, that Ongun was held by four Chinese cavalry squadrons, Orlov sent the Verkhneudinsk Cossacks in support of the Tersk Cossacks. The two Cossack sotnias attacked the Chinese, galloping up to a position, dis-

---

[51]Also called Wankung.

mounting, firing three volleys, leaping back onto their horses, galloping to the next position, dismounting, firing again, and advancing anew. By 5 A.M. the Chinese withdrew, leaving behind a number of dead.

On July 29, the foot battalions followed to Ongun and bivouacked near a little lake, under cover of the heights on the left bank of the Hailar River. Although the Chinese had withdrawn before the Cossacks that morning, they must have noticed the small number of the Russians, and decided to counterattack the following day. At 4 A.M. on July 30, Russian guard posts reported the approach of a considerable enemy force. The foot battalions at once took up position behind the ridges and sandy hillocks, which provided excellent cover. The 1st Sotnia of the 6th Battalion was sent to protect the Russian bakery, which was at the railroad station, Orlov's adjutant, *Poruchik* Kublitskii-Piottukh, being put in charge of the defense of the bakery.

In the distance the Chinese cavalry, including Mongols, spread out in two orderly lines of single rank, their right flank extending to the plain of the Hailar River. Infantrymen followed. Fluttering banners and galloping messengers could be discerned clearly, as could be the smoke of camp fires in the valley beyond, where the Chinese main bivouac was situated. According to a prisoner whom the Russians had taken, the Chinese were under the commander of the forces in the Hailar region, whom the officers of the railroad guard knew as a bright and very energetic person. The total Chinese host was estimated to number over 10,000 men.

As the Mongols advanced, they opened fire from a great distance, so that the bullets fell harmlessly in the sand before the Russian positions. When the Russians did not respond, the Mongols drew closer, rending the air with terrifying whoops. They remained in good formation, and their bullets began hitting the bivouac, punching holes in the tents of the Cossacks. The Russians returned fire, but the Mongols continued their attack, deftly taking up positions in the sand and digging individual fox holes. The exchange of fire lasted for hours.

The Russians took turns eating and prepared food for the 3rd Verkhneudinsk Cossack Regiment and the 2nd Transbaikal Cossack Battery, which were on their way from Hoerhungte and had been ordered by telephone to hasten their arrival. Orderlies served tea and sundries to the officers, who ate and drank with gusto as the bullets whistled past overhead. While the Russians waited for their reinforcements to arrive, the Chinese brought up their artillery. Two guns appeared on a height, and grenades with percussion fuses began to explode over the Russian bivouac.

At 11:45 A.M. at last the Verkhneudinsk Cossack Regiment and the Transbaikal Cossack Battery appeared on the scene, boosting Orlov's forces to 2,000 bayonets, 1,000 sabers and 6 cannons. With the aid of the infantry, the battery was moved up the difficult, sandy incline onto the heights, while the regiment took up position in the dead space, where it could eat and rest, and feed and water the horses. Meanwhile Orlov met with the newly arrived commanders and with the commanders of the 6th Foot Battalion and informed them of his plans for attack.

The Chinese artillery had moved up to about 5,000 feet and the riflemen to between 800 and 1,200 paces, when the Verkneudinsk Cossack Regiment rode out on the right flank at 1:50 P.M., its appearance on the plateau serving as the signal for a general attack. On the left flank, whither Orlov had proceeded, the 4th Battalion opened rapid fire, while a sotnia advanced in a small envelopment movement. In his orders, Orlov had called for a bold and bloody strike, the Russian troops to fight without their packs and to pursue the enemy as far as possible, returning not before dark.

At 2:10 P.M. the Russian artillery went into action. Its fire was effective, and the Chinese guns soon evacuated their position, though the bombardment of the infantry had to be continued longer. At 2:25 P.M. Orlov took off his cap, crossed himself, and ordered the 6th Battalion to advance. The entire detachment moved out, leaving two and a half sotnias of the 6th Battalion in general reserve and half a sotnia to guard the bivouac.

Kublitskii-Piottukh and his men charged across an open space and drove the Chinese from a hill position, five Cossacks being wounded in the attack. The mounted Cossack regiment turned back and chased the Chinese cavalry, while the foot Cossacks pursued the retreating infantry. Since the Chinese had ventured rather close to the Russians, they found it difficult to get away. As they fled, they threw away heavy sacks with cartridges, clothing and boots. Some hid in bushes, others in foxholes, and fired at the Russians as they passed nearby. The Chinese were terrible marksmen and their fusilade from afar had been harmless, but now, at close range, they felled a number of Russians.

Orlov himself was almost killed this way. "Sir! You're being shot at!" he heard his adjutant shout, and saw a Chinese taking aim at him from a distance of only ten paces. The bullet barely missed him. Before the Chinese could fire again, a Cossack cut him down with two saber blows—one across the skull and one on the neck.

The Chinese who had holed in fought with exasperation. A Cossack sabered a Chinese who had hidden in the bushes; another Chinese shot the Cossack; another Cossack killed the Chinese, and yet another Chinese gunned down the Cossack. A tall Chinese in a blue robe and a uniform jacket, wearing a headband and a very long queue, stood in front of a crowd of Chinese, holding high a huge black banner with a red border. As he stood there against the background of the green steppe he looked most picturesque and seemed to inspire the men behind him with courage. Aleksei Starodubov, a sturdy, fifty-four year old Cossack volunteer with a grey, closely cropped beard, went up to him, shot him point-blank and grabbed the banner from his hands as he fell mortally wounded.[52] At the same time the other Cossacks charged the panic-struck Chinese. *Shtabs-kapitan* Bodisko, the commander of the 18th Tersk Sotnia also captured a banner. A breech-loading Krupp steel gun was taken that day, and another one the following day. For over ten miles Orlov followed close on the heel of the retiring Chinese, then turned his detachment back, as he did not wish to go farther without packs or bread. Only the hussar Bulatovich with 20 Cossacks continued to Urdingi and there spent the night, returning the following day. Russian casualties were 8 dead and 17

[52]For this act of heroism Starodubov was awarded the Cross of St. George, thereby becoming the first cavalier of the Hailar Detachment. He distinguished himself again and again in battle, leading and inspiring the younger Cossacks by his example, and was decorated repeatedly. His own son served in the 6th Battalion. Mikhail Aleksenov also received the St. George's Cross, but posthumously. He had cut down four Chinese at Ongun, laying down his own life.

wounded.[53] Chinese corpses numbered between 800 and
900.[54] The Chinese commander had saved himself with
60 chosen cavalrymen.

Orlov now sent Bulatovich with his "flying horse-
patrol" to reconnoiter Hailar's defenses. When he received word that the city had been abandond by soldiers
and inhabitants alike, he ordered the mounted Cossack
regiment and the Cossack battery to Hailar during the
night of August 1 to 2. He himself started with the
foot battalion for Urdingi in the morning. The road
was littered with discarded Chinese clothing, cartridges
and wagons. The following night a messenger arrived
with the disquieting news that Hailar had not been
abandoned and that the forces which he had dispatched
there requested immediate aid.

Bulatovich's original report had not been incorrect.
The city had been deserted when he had gotten there.
But a Chinese detachment returned and attacked him,
cutting off four of his Cossacks, who disappeared without
news. What happened was that two detachments had
been sent from Hailar—one to Abagaitui and one to
Tsurukhai. The former was defeated at Ongun. The
latter, hearing of this, hastened back to Hailar and
coming upon Bulatovich's horse patrol clashed with it.
Bulatovich could not hope to hold the city with his
handful of men and withdrew onto a hill, from where his
tiny unit could fire effectively. The horse-holders with

---

[53]The dead included the interpreter Maksimov, who died from his
injuries. Among the wounded were Lt. Col. Razhev of the 6th Transbaikal
Battalion and *Podesaul* Gorokhov of the 3rd Verkhneudinsk Cossack regiment.

[54]According to a report of Kuropatkin, dated August 3, only 200
Chinese bodies were counted. Two Chinese were taken prisoner. The
report erroneously states that the Chinese commander was killed.

the animals took cover in a nearby depression with a lake, where the horses could be watered. The Chinese showered Bulatovich's men with a hail of bullets, every Chinese soldier firing hundreds of rounds. Yet they did not take proper aim and the Cossacks laughed at the ineffectiveness of the fusilade. Nevertheless some bullets were bound to find a target, and two of the Cossacks were killed. The Russians had little choice but to stay put and wait for reinforcements; they were short of ammunition and their horses were tired.

Having received the call for help, Orlov sent out two foot sotnias of the 4th and 6th Battalions on two-wheeled carts during the night and himself with the others followed at about 3:30 A.M. on August 3, arriving before Hailar around 11 A.M. When the reinforcements appeared, the Chinese fled, and Orlov occupied Hailar before dinner.

Hailar was only a small district city, but it was of importance to the Russians because it had been the administrative seat of the western section of the Chinese Eastern Railway. Under the protection of a garrison which Orlov left behind,[55] construction of the railroad could be resumed. Furthermore, Hailar was a rich prize. From the enormous quantity of provisions which fell into Russian hands, Orlov formed a supply depot, which included more than 360 tons of flour, oats, millet, vermicelli, soap and candles, over 3,000 chests of tea, as well as skins and tobacco. It was able to supply not only the Hailar Detachment during subsequent operations but all forces that passed through Hailar in either direction.

---

[55]Orlov assigned the territory between Hailar and the Russian border to the 2nd Military Section of the Transbaikal Region, and put it under the command of the *hetman* of this section.

One byproduct of the Russian victory at Ongun and the taking of Hailar was the realization by the Mongols that the Russians were stronger than the Chinese. They, therefore, left the side of the Chinese, and for the duration of the hostilities Mongolia remained quiet.

When the Russians entered Hailar they did not find the four missing Cossacks. Then one of them, Butorin, appeared unexpectedly. A tall and slender man with a long and somewhat foolish-looking face, he was an experienced and typically roguish Transbaikal Cossack. Many a time he had ventured into the steppe to have business dealings with the Mongols, had learned about their life and habits, and spoke Mongolian well. He related that when he and his comrades had been cut off from their unit, they had separated to find their own ways back. Seeing that Chinese roamed throughout the valley, he lay down in a ditch, covered himself with straw and dung, and did not move until dark. Though a Chinese bivouac was nearby and though the Chinese guard posts which were situated between him and the Russian lines were close to each other, he managed to get through. At one point, a dozing Chinese guard sat in his path. Stealing up behind him, Butorin took careful aim and struck him with his saber on the head, slightly from the side so as to miss the thick queue, and the man expired without a sound. But Butorin did not know what had happened to his three comrades who were still missing.

One day Orlov and some of the officers surveyed the environs of the city. They rode up to a large temple and while their horses rested in the shade stepped inside. They were fascinated by the collosal statues that stared down at them mysteriously. When they went out, they noticed that their horses were very restless, neighed and dug the dirt with their hoofs. As they rode on, the uneasiness of the horses increased. Not far to the left a large flock of grey eagles rose. The Russians trotted through the temple grove and enjoyed the shade of its trees. Suddenly they stopped short. Before them lay the corpses of the three missing Cossacks without their heads.

Meanwhile General P'ao, one of China's most able commanders, realizing the significance of the loss of Hailar, was approaching from the Greater Hsing-an Mountains with a force of 7,000 men. When the mounted Cossacks, whom Orlov had sent some 80 miles ahead, reported P'ao's advance, Orlov went out to meet him. On August 13, he proceeded to Dzhaimete and on the 14th, after a grueling hike during which the thirsty troops found only one well and one watering pond, reached the position that his cavalry had taken up at Ya-k'o-shih,[56] some 23 miles east of Hailar. In the ensuing battle, which began at about 2 P.M. and which raged for several hours, the brunt of the fighting was borne by the Transbaikal Cossack battalions, which advanced against the left flank of the Chinese. In front moved the 4th Battalion and side by side with it the 5th, with the 6th following behind them in support. A severe thunderstorm with sheets of rain and hail brought sudden darkness, so that nothing could be seen at 100 paces. Orlov took advantage of the unexpected cover to throw the battalion which had been held back in reserve against the right flank of the Chinese and then mount a general assault.

[56]Also known as Yakeshi.

General P'ao, who had been Commander of the Chinese railway guard before the upheaval and was recognized during the battle by the Russian guard sotnias by his overcoat, was killed and his detachment turned to flight. Though the Russians were terribly fatigued from the 23 mile march, the intense heat, and the fierce fighting, they pursued the Chinese for almost ten miles and shortly after 10 P.M., in complete darkness, fell upon the Chinese rear guard and routed it. Only then did they stop and bivouac. The Cossacks had been outraged by the decapitation of their comrades. Now that they had inflicted heavy casualties on the Chinese, they felt avenged.[57]

During the night the Cossacks were aroused by shouts that the Chinese were attacking. In the dark they groped for clothing that they had been drying, for their weapons, and for their horses. But there was no attack. Some Chinese stragglers, who had not realized that the Cossacks were sleeping in the bivouac from which they had driven the Chinese rear guard, had blundered into the Russian outposts and been shot.

That very night Orlov sent two sotnias of Verkhneudinsk Cossacks and the Ural Sotnia of the guard to Mien-tu-ho, the next station. The following day, near the place of battle, the Russians found a Chinese soldier who had a terrible neck wound, just below the back of the head, so large that his brains were exposed. The wound had been inflicted by his Chinese captain, when he had failed to advance against the Russians, as ordered. Though they were certain that the Chinese was on the brink of death, the Russians decided to give him a last

[57]Russian casualties numbered 3 dead and 9 wounded. Three Chinese flags and 1 gun were captured.

good meal. But he lived through the day and the next, was bandaged up and sent back with the wounded to the field hospital, where he recovered and even asked to be baptized.

The Battle of Hsing-an Mountains

THE VICTORY AT YA-K'O-SHIH gained the Russians all of western Manchuria up to the Greater Hsing-an Mountains. There a newly formed Chinese detachment with reinforcements sent by General Chou Mien held a heavily fortified position. Bulatovich with his flying detachment proceeded to I-lieh-k'o-te[58] Station, near Hsing-an, and before dawn on August 19, approached the Chinese position on the Greater Hsing-an Mountains. A patrol of 12 Cossacks under the personal command of Bulatovich rode ahead and drove away a Chinese post from a bridge across the river at the foot of the mountains. As they galloped about on the other side of the river, they were subjected to heavy artillery and rifle fire. Though the main body of the flying detachment had come up to the river, the swampy terrain and the evident numerical superiority of the enemy forced the recall of the scouts, and the flying detachment withdrew to I-lieh-k'o-te. But outposts were left in full view of the enemy. The reconnaissance of the Hsing-an position had begun.

As Bulatovich's flying detachment had advanced some 40 miles ahead of the Hailar Detachment, Orlov decided to follow suit on August 20, without further waiting for the two companies of the battalion of the Chita Infantry

[58]Also known as Irekte.

177

Regiment, which were on their way to Ya-k'o-shih from Hailar. He ordered the main body of the detachment to move up to Mien-tu-ho Station, about 12 miles away, and the mounted Cossacks another 15 miles or so, to Ha-la-kuo[59] Station. It was only about 10 miles from here to I-lieh-k'o-te and the cavalry would be able to rush to Bulatovich's aid anytime. A garrison was left behind at I-lieh-k'o-te and the 18th Tersk Sotnia was broken up into several parts with different assignments— to protect some of the railway workers, to remain at the Hailar River ford and assist peaceful Mongols in returning to their grazing grounds, and to serve as headquarters cavalry of the Hailar Detachment.

On the morning of August 20, the Hailar Detachment passed in review before Orlov as it moved out. The main body was headed by the 5th and 6th Battalions. Then came the 8th Company of the guard, and the 3rd and 4th Battalions together with the wagon train and a herd of cattle, guarded by a platoon of the mounted Cossack regiment. *"Zodorovo, Verkhneudintsy!* [Well done, Verkhneudinsk (Cossacks)!]" Orlov shouted as the detachment marched past. Then he took off his cap, and saying, "With God!" crossed himself, and with a platoon of the 18th Sotnia that escorted him rode to the head of the detachment. "Let's see what the mysterious Greater Hsing-an is like," he remarked.

At Mien-tu-ho there was a little stream which flowed into the Hailar River. Its water was excellent and the kitchen was set up on its bank. The Transbaikal foot brigade stopped to the right of the railroad station, on the slope of the mountains, as the place was drier, protected from the wind and free from the fog that settled

59Also known as Khorgo.

in the lower area. The mounted regiment with the battery halted in back of the foot brigade and somewhat below it, in order to be closer to the excellent pastures which covered the picturesque, mountain-ringed valley. Headquarters was established in a three room barracks building, guarded by the escort and the 8th Company. Mounted patrols protected the camp, and outposts were set up on the road ahead and at strategic places, including the mountains, whence the entire plain could be seen for a great distance.

After a rest, the mounted Cossacks with the Cossack battery moved on to Ha-la-kuo. But two sotnias of the 3rd Cossack Battalion soon joined Orlov. They came from Hailar where they had stayed as garrison until relieved by two companies of the 2nd Battalion of the Chita (Transbaikal Cossack) Foot Regiment. Two other companies under the personal command of Lieutenant Colonel Nadkhin, the battalion commander, were on their way to Mien-tu-ho. The wagon train with provisions and the cattle, escorted by three sotnias of Transbaikal Cossacks, also came up, as did another herd of cattle driven from Abagaitui by a sotnia of the 4th Battalion and a large wagon train of provisions from Hailar with goods obtained in Nerchinsk. It brought enough soap for everyone to wash their clothes, as well as writing materials, preserves and wines and vodka for the officers, which the latter divided with great care and almost religious ceremony. In wartime the meat ration was usually doubled and the soldiers given one pound of meat a day. So many heads of cattle did the Hailar Detachment now have, however, that the Cossacks often got two pounds of meat a day.

On August 22, the Hailar Detachment continued to

Ha-la-kuo Station, preceded by the 6th Tersk Sotnia of
the guards. They left behind a small garrison of weak
Cossacks of the 3rd Battalion, with *Zauriad-prapor-
shchik*[60] Novikov as commandant. He was to take care
of the supply depot, bake bread, and dry and gather
the hay cut by the detachment, and cut, dry, and gather
more. There remained at Mien-tu-ho also the doctor of
the 5th Battalion and a Cossack who had contracted anthrax. The anthrax had developed on the neck, the Cossack probably having slept on the collar of the stricken
horse. The infected spot had been cut out and the Cossack seemed to be recovering satisfactorily, but Orlov
could not take any chances lest the disease spread among
the battalions. It would demoralize the men and could
arouse panic. In spite of everything the Cossack died,
though apparently not of anthrax but of catarrh of the
stomach.

The distance to Ha-la-kuo was not great and the detachment arrived at its resting place for the night in
the afternoon. Orlov proceeded in these easy stages to
give the two companies of the 2nd Battalion of the Chita
Regiment time to catch up with him. The mounted regiment and the Cossack battery stood before the station.
The foot Cossacks settled behind it, on the slope of the
heights. One of the buildings at the station itself was
used for headquarters.

Before leaving Mien-tu-ho Orlov had read a report
from Bulatovich. Bulatovich had gone all the way up
to the Chinese positions and had sent two mounted patrols of 8 Cossacks each around the enemy flanks to reconnoiter the positions and the approaches leading up to

60Acting *Praporshchik*, the lowest officer rank in the Tsarist army.

them. Now Orlov did not even dismount at Ha-la-kuo, but rode straight on to the bivouac of the mounted regiment to question Bulatovich personally and to work out the general plan of attack on the Hsing-an stronghold.

It was pouring when Orlov and his staff reached the bivouac of the 3rd Verkhneudinsk Regiment. There, in a spacious, water-proof tent that the Cossacks had captured from the Chinese, he conferred with the commander of the regiment, the chief of staff and Bulatovich. As they drank aromatic tea, Bulatovich related how his Cossacks had ridden close to the Chinese positions and dismounting had made their way on foot to within 75 paces of the enemy bivouac, and had observed everything that the Chinese were doing and saying.[61]

Orlov had already been acquainted with the terrain before them by the railroad engineers and guard officers who were familiar with the region. Engineer Bocharov had provided him with an excellent map. On the basis of this knowledge and the information that Bulatovich now added, Orlov worked out a plan of action. He told Bulatovich that he would be given four sotnias of Verkhneudinsk Cossacks and that he was to lead them and some Ural Cossacks around the left flank of the Chinese the following day (August 23). About 20 miles south of their position he was to cross over a mountain pass and appear in the rear of the Chinese, athwart the road to Tsitsihar. Orlov planned to attack the Hsing-an mountain ridge at dawn on August 24. Bulatovich was to be in position by noon to cut off the Chinese retreat. If the Chinese were not falling back by then, Bula-

---

[61]It is not clear whether any of the Cossacks understood what they heard, but it is quite possible that some of the Cossacks knew a little Chinese or Manchu.

tovich could attack them from the rear or take whatever action he deemed desirable.

That night Orlov broke the good news that, according to unofficial reports, Peking had been taken by the allied forces on August 14, and that, according to news from the telegraph agency, Harbin had been occupied by the Russians.

At 5 A.M. on August 23, Bulatovich began the envelopment maneuver. At the same time the main body of the detachment set out for I-lieh-k'o-te, with orders to camp beyond I-lieh-k'o-te without lighting any fires. At the head rode some of the mounted units that were with the detachment, then followed a company of the railroad guards, the 3rd Battalion, the battery with its nine cassons, the field forge and a spare gun carriage, and the 4th, 5th and 6th Battalions, with the transport wagons following their respective units.

The wagons were laden with all kinds of belongings. The officers, for example, did not limit themselves to the authorized weight, but included in their baggage sofas and easy chairs and colorfully painted Chinese tables on low legs. Orlov did not object, for he could always junk the stuff when the space was needed for provisions. The appearance of the wagon trains was no less striking than their content. Not only was there a variety of harnesses—the standard government ones, those used by the Transbaikal Cossacks, and even Chinese yokes—but the wagons were pulled by horses, mules, hinnies and camels. The Transbaikal Cossacks themselves were a motley lot. Small of stature, with sunburned faces and sweat-soaked tunics, their feet in roomy, soft and heelless *ichigi* instead of regular boots, they looked the opposite of parade-ground heroes. Yet, as mentioned, they were excellent shots, thought nothing of traveling over 25 miles a day, and attacked the enemy with calm self-confidence.

Orlov rode ahead of the main body of the Hailar Detachment to reconnoiter the enemy position in person. The Tersk Cossacks who escorted him were mounted on small but sturdy Transbaikal and Mongol horses, laden with strapped-down felt cloaks and all kinds of belongings. Orlov was accompanied by his staff and by the battery commander, *Voiskovoi starshina*[62] Folimonov. The latter had a thin, sun-burned face with lively eyes that were hidden in deep, sunken hollows, yet sparkled from behind bushy eyebrows in such a way as to give the gentle-hearted man a ferocious appearance. His pride and joy was the huge, dark-bay stallion on which he rode.

It was a hot morning and the sun beat down mercilessly. Even the white service caps and tunics seemed burdensome. The fog lifted and only scattered clouds crawled along the gullies of the spurs of the Greater Hsing-an Mountains. The road was climbing imperceptibly, and it was difficult to realize that the strategic pass which the Chinese held was only a few miles away. After lunch Orlov found to the left of the road a gully for which he had been looking. Here the detachment could be concealed for the night. From their position the Chinese would not be able to see the Russians enter the gully, particularly since the Russians were moving eastward and the western side would be in the shade by afternoon. The east side of the gully was hidden by a mountain on which the artillery could be positioned as a safety measure. Nor would the Chinese see the detach-

[62]Army sargeant major or master sargeant.

ment spread out in the morning, for the Russians would do so while it was still dark; furthermore, fog shrouded this area in the early morning hours. Orlov had appropriate orders sent back to the detachment, and continued his reconnaissance.

Soon he came to the shabby buildings of I-lieh-k'o-te Station, near which the horses of the 1st Sotnia of the 3rd Verkhneudinsk Regiment, the reserve of the forward posts, were grazing. The preceding night the Cossacks of this sotnia had sat motionlessly within 70 paces of the Chinese bivouac; nothing eventful had happened. They provided Orlov's reconnaissance party with several old, experienced Ural Cossacks of the guard as guides. The Ural sotnia, under the command of *Shtabs-kapitan* Iakimovskii, had operated in the sector near the Greater Hsing-an before the war and its Cossacks knew the region well. But when Orlov asked for more guides to direct the detachment during the attack, he was told that Bulatovich had taken most of the sotnia with him to go around the Chinese.

Looking at different approaches and weighing where the artillery could pass and where his units could push forward without being noticed, Orlov got all the way up to the Russian advance posts. He dismounted and crept up to a Cossack lying behind a bush. As he peered through the leaves, he could see the Chinese position spread out before him.

The Chinese trenches had been dug absurdly. A line of square holes across the main road, they could only have hindered a frontal attack. But a frontal attack in the mountains was unlikely and the Chinese riflemen were exposed to fire from the heights. Yet over-all the position was strong. Between the heights occupied by the Russian advance posts and the higher ridges held by the Chinese, there lay a swampy valley, cut through by a stream. There was a bridge across the stream, but the Chinese trenches had been dug opposite it. The Ural Cossacks knew of two other points at which the river could be forded, however, and the Tersk Cossacks now reconnoitered them. The Chinese heights were covered with forest; only in the center was there a treeless valley through which the main road led. In the valley there were a number of large log cabins which belonged to the railroad. Used as warehouses and as living quarters for the workers and railroad authorities before the hostilities, the solid buildings now were occupied by Chinese troops. Piles of railroad ties at different points in the valley also provided cover for Chinese riflemen. Beyond the trenches and in the forest Orlov could espy low, blue and white vehicles, around which soldiers milled. Through their binoculars the Russians could clearly make out their long, black queues. They also saw the kettles of food, hanging over the campfires. A Chinese soldier squatted down near one of them and defecated. "What a scoundrel! Right where the kitchen is!" the Russians whispered.

From his place of observation Orlov spotted a temple which lay near the pass. He asked the battery commander whether he could hit the temple from this place. Folimonov remarked that it was rather far away, but that his guns could probably reach it. A few trees stood in the way, but these could be cut down and a field of fire cleared.

Unable to see the left flank of the Chinese from where they were lying, Orlov and his escort moved to the right, to a height occupied by another half-sotnia of Tersk

Cossacks, the Russian advance posts stretching out for some three miles. Orlov was surprised that the Chinese had made no more serious effort to hold these strategic heights and had withdrawn after an attack by Bulatovich, since from here their positions were open to observation and fire. From the new location Orlov could overlook the entire left flank of the Chinese. They occupied the railroad headquarters buildings behind the swamp and stream. In the background there was a wooded mountain on which the Chinese had hidden a number of guns. Cannons could be seen also near the trenches. Yet the trenches offered no protection against fire from the height on which Orlov now was. Although he could not see the temple from this place, its direction was known, and the mountain that blocked the view would not obstruct its bombardment. There was a better field of fire here than on the height from which Orlov had watched before, and he decided to move his artillery to this spot to support the attack.

In the process of looking for a good artillery position the Russians had become quite careless, stepping into the open, their white tunics and caps standing out against the greenery. When *Praporshchik* Koritskii reported that a Chinese had been seen galloping to the rear, Orlov realized that they had probably been spotted, and started back. Before he and his companions could reach their horses, however, the clatter of rifle and cannon fire was heard. The Chinese were advancing on a broad front to the stream. Although Orlov ordered the outposts to withdraw in the event that the Chinese attack threatened to claim heavy Russian casualties, the Cossacks managed to contain it without loss. Orlov and his colleagues meanwhile had the opportunity to verify exactly where the Chinese forded the river and to pinpoint their artillery positions, thus working out the final details for the Russian attack. Then they rode back to the bivouac near I-lieh-k'o-te on a better, more concealed road, very satisfied with their reconnaissance.

When the Chinese had opened fire, Orlov had sent back a messenger, and one sotnia of the 3rd Cossack Battalion and part of the 8th Company of the guards had set out at once to reinforce the advance posts. Now the 1st Sotnia of the Verkhneudinsk Cossacks also hastened in support of the Tersk Cossacks to secure the heights from which the Russian attack was to be mounted in the morning.

It was a cold night. Back in camp, Orlov put on a heavy overcoat and those who had them, donned fur jackets. A new engineer by the name of Serbskii had just arrived as a specialist on the region and Orlov conferred with him briefly, but they had already passed through the sector where Serbskii had worked. Orlov then called the chief of staff and asked him to read the order that had been given to Bulatovich. Bulatovich with a flying detachment from the cavalry regiment and men of the Ural sotnia was to envelop the enemy. He was to hasten through the mountain pass onto the Tsi-tsihar road and block this route of escape. The instructions were clear and did not have to be modified. Orlov thus could dictate the orders for the attack.

Reviewing the disposition of the enemy, Orlov had his forces advance as follows: the 6th Battalion, guided by the Cossack Savin, was to proceed to the left, by way of the gully and the forest, around the right flank of the Chinese, and strike it from the rear, in the direction of the temple. The 4th and 5th Battalions, under the joint command of *Voiskovoi starshina* Ogloblev and guided by the Ural Cossacks Maksin and Solodovnikov, were to move along the same route and attack the Chinese right flank. The battery was to take up position on the height from which Orlov and Folimonov had observed the Chinese. To the left of the battery the 8th Company was to advance against the trenches. One sotnia of the 3rd Battalion was to be near the battery. The other sotnias of the battalion were to act first as general reserve,[63] then to advance on the right of the battery, against the occupied railroad administration buildings, and remaining on the right side of the road to envelop the Chinese left flank. The Cossacks Guzikov and Borodin were to serve as their guides. The 6th Sotnia of the guard was to protect the Russian right flank. Units of the Verkhneudinsk Regiment were to secure the main road, across which the Chinese had dug trenches, but to remain outside firing range. Orlov himself would be to the left of the battery. The forces were to move out at 2 A.M. without packs.

Meanwhile Orlov dispatched the entire 3rd Battalion in support of the forward posts, lest the Chinese capture these heights and thwart his plans. Furthermore, by acquainting the 3rd Battalion with the locality ahead of time, Orlov hoped to facilitate getting the battery into

[63]According to the German summary of Russian General Staff reports, Orlov left two companies of the Chita Regiment as well as the company and the Tersk sotnia of the railway guard as reserve. Two sotnias of the Verkhneudinsk Regiment stayed with the wagon train. The two companies of the Chita Regiment belonged to the 2nd Battalion which had been sent as reinforcements for the Hailar Detachment together with the 3rd Battalion of the Stretensk Regiment. These battalions seem to have joined Orlov at Hailar, where he had stayed from August 3 to 13, perhaps in expectation of their arrival. They did not advance with him, however, remaining at Hailar to rest from their march and perhaps delaying Orlov at Ya-k'o-shih again.

position the following day. It was already dark when the various commanders received copies of their orders and studied them by candlelight.

The two companies of the 2nd Battalion of the Chita Regiment arrived in the evening. Orlov instructed the battalion commander, Chitinskii, to set out half an hour after the general advance and following the artillery, cover it until it got into position. There the 3rd Battalion would take over its defense, and the companies of the 2nd Battalion should join the general reserve.

That night the soldiers slept dressed. The officers lay down too, yet in the brief hours rested uneasily, mulling over the plans for attack. At 2 A.M. on August 24, the black lines of Cossacks filed out quietly, the still of the night broken only by the noise of the artillery wheels. The expected fog had not settled during the night, but the early hour gave them the cover of darkness while passing through some of the open areas. Gradually it became lighter, and the Russians could move more surely and faster. By 5:30 A.M. the battery reached its position.

The commander of the 3rd Battalion, *Voiskovoi starshina* Stankevich, a calm and reliable yet lively man, was already there, as were Captain Smol'iannikov and his subaltern, *Poruchik* Shevich. Fulimonov with his expert gunners and *Vakhmister*[64] Vologdin were running up and down the height and even climbed a tree devouring the Chinese positions with hungry eyes.

As Orlov inspected the disposition of his forces, he found Captain Choglokov's 8th Company a little too far to the left to direct enfilade fire at the Chinese trenches and ordered the unit to move to the right. It did so and barely reached its destination, when the battle broke

[64]Cavalry sargeant major or master sargeant.

out and Choglokov advanced directly against the left flank of the trenches.

Orlov and his staff headed for the small, boggy open spot on the height, where they were to be. As they crossed an open place, the Chinese sighted them and opened heavy fire. Soon shots were heard everywhere. Orlov and his staff dismounted at the position selected the previous day, and as their horses were led to the back, advanced to the ridge and began to watch events through their binoculars. It was only 6:45 A.M. and not yet time for the scheduled attack.

But Chinese riflemen had moved forward on the right flank, and caught the entire Russian position in enfilade fire. A hail of bullets wounded one of the artillerymen near the caissons and killed several horses. The whistle and thud of bullets hitting trees and the crash of falling branches and limbs filled the forest. But the Cossacks had lost respect for the aimless Chinese fire and paid little attention to it. The weather was beautiful. It was cool and fresh in the forest and the deep shade was very pleasant. It became too warm for the fur jackets and overcoats, and the officers handed them to their orderlies to take back and attach to the saddles. Soon even the tunics seemed too warm.

Stankevich sent a sotnia of his battalion against the Chinese infantry, and Smol'iannikov who was on the extreme right flank also went into action against them. Before long Stankevich's entire battalion was engaged. The Cossacks had marched through the bitter-cold night without rest for over four hours, crossing mountains and ravines and swamps. Yet they charged with zest and after a brief exchange of fire resorted to their bayonets. Folimonov, amply supplied with ammunition, opened rapid fire with shrapnel, and by 7:30 a.m. silenced the Chinese artillery, which had managed to fire only several rounds. The sudden appearance of three Cossack sotnias on their right flank at this time, threw the Chinese into confusion, and they withdrew their cannons hastily to the temple at the mountain pass. The Chinese riflemen tried to get out of the trenches, but were pinned down and were ripped apart by the shrapnel. The rapid fire of the Cossack battery, echoing and re-echoing in the mountains, filled the valley with a hellish roar, as Chinese riflemen died by the tens in the trenches, and piled up in heaps of corpses in the woods. The shrapnel splintered and broke trees, tore into the railway buildings and showered the temple grounds. Chinese messengers galloped back and forth as the Russians mounted their offensive.

The battle was brief. Unprepared for assault from different directions, the Chinese wavered and after only fifty minutes of battle turned heel, closely pursued by the 6th Tersk Sotnia of the guard. Had the 6th Battalion adhered to plan and rushed to the temple in the rear of the Chinese instead of going to the aid of the 4th and 5th Battalions in their attack on the right flank, the defeat would have been total. Even so, at 12:20 P.M. the fleeing Chinese ran into Bulatovich's Cossacks, who had ridden almost 60 miles to cut off their escape. The Chinese wanted to turn back, but there were confronted by the Tersk sotnia, commanded by Shevich, Smol'iannikov, one of the finest officers of the Hailar Detachment, having fallen during the pursuit. The Chinese were trapped and most of them were killed, the remainder scattering to the nearby forests and swamps, followed here and there for some 25 miles. Russian casualties numbered 3 dead and 9 wounded. Russian booty included 23 banners, 5 cannons, and 120 carts with various goods, as well as many rifles, cartridges and shells. The Russians also freed one of their countrymen and his wife from captivity.

The Capture of Tsitsihar and Kirin

WHILE THE HAILAR DETACHMENT had crushed the Chinese forces in the Greater Hsing-an Mountains, the Bolsheretsk Detachment was moving against Tsitsihar, the capital of Hei-lung-chiang Province. Tsitsihar was regarded as a major center of opposition to Russian interests, because of its strong garrison and the presence of Tartar General Shou Shan, who had voiced bitter hatred of Russia.

Orlov had orders to be at Fu-la-erh-chi[65] Station on September 2, when the Bolsheretsk Detachment was expected to approach Tsitsihar. His detachment then was to coordinate its action with the Bolsheretsk Detachment to capture the Tsitsihar garrison. On August 25, Orlov buried the dead. On the 26th he advanced to Ya-lu[66] Station; on the 27th to Pa-lin[67] Station. On August 28, he reached Cha-lan-t'un,[68] resting there for one day. On August 31, his cavalry reached Fu-la-erh-chi. On September 2, he himself arrived there with the main body of his detachment. When Orlov entered Tsitsihar on September 4, he found that several mounted sotnias of the Bolsheretsk Detachment had already taken Tsitsihar

[65]Called Fuliardi by the Russians.
[66]Also known as JAL.
[67]Also known as Barim.
[68]Also known as Ya-lu, but not the same place as the Ya-lu mentioned above.

193

on August 28, and that the Chinese garrison had withdrawn southward, toward Pe-tu-na.[69]

The capture of Tsitsihar had been effected by General Rennenkampf with skill and daring. He had with him 5 sotnias or a total of about 460 Cossacks and 8 guns. Sending only patrols and small units on the expected line of approach, where the Chinese had dug in, Rennenkampf succeeded in getting around the Chinese position with the main body of his detachment. Suddenly he appeared in the south, athwart their route of withdrawal, and demanded their unconditional surrender. When a thick column of Chinese infantry—the reserve, numbering about 2,700 men—tried to march away past him, Rennenkampf brought his guns into play and stopped them in their tracks without serious resistance. When Tartar General Shou Shan heard the artillery fire, he decided to commit suicide and swallowed some gold to rupture his intestines. He fainted and was put into a casket to be taken out of the city, but shortly regained consciousness. Thereupon, he made his cavalry escort swear that they would carry his body out of the city, and ordered the officer in command of the escort to kill him with three bullets in the chest.

When the Chinese officials who called on Rennenkampf following the surrender found out that his entire detachment consisted of less than 500 men, they were stunned. The brazen conduct of the Russian patrols and individual Cossacks whom they had spotted everywhere the day before had tricked them into believing that they were surrounded by a host of between 15 and 17,000 men. They at once began to accuse each other of treason and the late Tartar General's military assistant

[69]Spelled by the Russians Bodune; also known as Hsin-ch'êng.

became so distraught that he threw himself into the Nonni River and was barely saved by the Cossacks. His shame was understandable. In addition to the 2,700-men reserve, which had been halted by Rennenkampf's artillery, there were 4,500 Chinese soldiers in the trenches before the city, and another 1,500 were expected the following day. Forty-three guns fell into Russian hands.

When the Hailar Detachment and the Bolsheretsk Detachment joined forces at Tsitsihar, 12 battalions, 14 sotnias and 22 guns were assembled. Orlov sent Rennenkampf with 12 sotnias and 6 cavalry guns ahead to Pe-tu-na, following himself with the main body of troops.[70] Pe-tu-na was almost 200 miles from Tsitsihar and two wide rivers—the Nonni and Sungari—had to be forded. Yet Rennenkampf managed to race to Pe-tu-na in five days, and on September 11, approached with one sotnia the city which sheltered 1,500 Chinese soldiers and 150 cavalry men. A Chinese official by the name of Li rode out to meet Rennenkampf asserting that there were 5,000 troops inside and asked him to delay his occupation of the city for two days. Rennenkampf replied that his detachment would be in Pe-tu-na that evening and that the following morning at 6 A.M. the Chinese—first the cavalry and then the infantry—must come to the Russian bivouac and lay down arms.

At 6 A.M. on September 12, the Chinese cavalry,

---

[70]The main body consisted of the Transbaikal Foot Brigade, parts of the Stretensk and Chita Regiments that had not been left behind as garrisons in Tsitsihar and units of the Transbaikal Artillery Division. It took the infantry so much longer than the cavalry to reach Pe-tu-na because the Sungari River was about a mile wide at this point and the detachment had neither pontoons nor sappers. It was time consuming to ferry the troops across in the few boats that were available.

wearing new uniforms and fully armed, approached the place where the 75 or so Russian Cossacks had camped. Rennenkampf rode out to greet them. At his request they demonstrated Chinese cavalry drill before surrendering their arms. Next came the infantry and handed over its weapons. The captured arms were destroyed and the men assigned to the Chinese commander were herded away for use in railroad construction.

On September 19, the bulk of the detachment arrived in Pe-tu-na. From Pe-tu-na the Russians moved against the city of Kirin, the capital of Kirin Province. As in the case of Tsitsihar the attack was to occur from two directions in an attempt to capture the garrison. The mounted Cossacks were sent south of the Sungari River, through the cities of Lung-wan[71] and Kuan-ch'êng-tzu,[72] to attack Kirin from the south. The main body of troops, reinforced by a detachment sent by General Sakharov and commanded by Lieutenant Colonel Durov, was to advance on the northern side of the Sungari River and attack Kirin from the opposite direction.[73]

Determined to make a personal reconnaissance of the situation, Rennenkampf set out for Kirin on the morning of September 22 with two sotnias, leaving part of his detachment at Kuan-ch'êng-tzu. At 3 P.M., at the village of Ta-shui-ho, the junction of the imperial and commercial roads between Mukden and Kirin, the Russians

[71]So spelled on F. and A. Hosie's map of Manchuria; also given as Nung-an Hsien. Orlov calls the place Luan-van-chen.

[72]So spelled on Hosie's map; also called Ch'ang-ch'un Fu.

[73]Kuropatkin reported that the forces sent against Kirin from Tsitsihar, Ninguta and Harbin numbered 18 battalions, 25 sotnias and 78 guns. In addition to these, the 3rd Rifle Brigade was held in reserve at Harbin; it consisted of 8 battalions and 24 guns. To suppress Chinese opposition in Kirin the Russians thus had a total of 26 battalions, 25 sotnias and 102 guns *plus* 12 mounted and 2 foot sotnias of guards.

were attacked, and Rennenkampf himself was almost killed when a Chinese thrust a spear at him. He was saved by a Cossack who threw himself in front of him and took the blow in his own shoulder. The Chinese were overcome, as was a larger force at dawn on the 23rd.

When Rennenkampf appeared before Kirin at 7 A.M., a bearer of a flag of truce came out of the city and asked him not to enter. But Rennenkampf rejected the request and trotted into Kirin, directly to the Governor's mansion. The 220 Chinese horsemen who guarded the place were quietly surrounded and disarmed, and their Winchester carbines thrown into the Sungari River.

In Kirin the Russians captured 69 late-model guns. They threw into the river some 5,000 rifles and about 1 million cartridges. That Rennenkampf succeeded in taking a fortified city of 120,000 inhabitants with only about 200 Cossacks was no doubt due to the fact that the day before, the governor of Kirin had received orders from Prince Ch'ing to suspend hostilities with the Russians. But Rennenkampf knew nothing of these orders, even though they had been conveyed through the Russian Foreign Ministry, and his action was heroic.[74]

With the fall of Kirin to the cavalry, the main body of Orlov's detachment turned to Harbin, where it soon received orders to return home, so that the Transbaikal

[74]According to Orlov, Kirin had already been occupied by *Shtabs-rotmister* Volkov and 26 Cossacks of General Chichagov's detachment, when Rennenkampf reached the city; according to Elets, Cornet Vasil'ev and three dragoons from the Maritime Dragoon Regiment had arrived in Kirin the day before Rennenkampf's coup as truce bearers from General Aigustov. Trusting in the protection of the Sungari River against a large scale attack from the north and confident that his artillery would keep any enemy at bay, the Tartar General refused to surrender the city. The thought of a cavalry raid from the south never occurred to him.

Cossacks could get back in time for harvesting. Rennen-kampf remained in Kirin until the arrival of Major General Kryshanovskii with 4 squadrons of dragoons, 1 Chita Cossack sotnia, the 3rd Transbaikal Cossack Battery and a mounted train of mountain artillery on September 26. Rennenkampf then proceeded to Ta-ku-shan, whither one of his sotnias had been sent already from Kuan-ch'êng-tzu. On September 28, his entire detachment was assembled at Ta-ku-shan. From here he moved to join the Russian forces that were coming from Mukden. They met in T'ieh-ling on October 6.

Reviewing the great speed with which his forces had covered enormous distances during the Manchurian campaign, Orlov found that the foot battalions had averaged about 20 miles per day of march, maintaining the pace of the mounted Cossacks. The commander of the armed forces of the Priamur military district telegraphed Orlov that he could not keep up on the map with the Hailar Detachment's "eagle flight" (a play of words on Orlov's name), and Lieutenant General Matsievskii, commander of the Transbaikal Cossack Forces, wired that Orlov's men had broken all records in their marches and campaigns. Casualties in the Hailar Detachment's four foot battalions of the Transbaikal Cossack Brigade alone numbered 468 dead and wounded.

The Chinese had been routed, but not because of cowardice. They had fought bravely and had been well armed. They had lost in part because the soldiers had not been trained adequately in marksmanship. But above all, they had failed because their officers had not provided efficient organization and were ignorant of modern military science. Thus the Tartar General of Hei-lung-chiang had sent troops simultaneously in three directions—against the Hailar Detachment, against the Bolsheretsk Detachment, and against the Khabarovsk Detachment—not to mention the considerable forces he had dispatched to Harbin. In Orlov's judgment, the Chinese would have had a far greater chance of winning, had they concentrated their armies and thrown them against one Russian force at a time.

With the capture of the capital, Russian operations in Kirin Province came to an end, except for occasional bandit suppression campaigns. Chinese officials tried to ingratiate themselves with the Russians, and Lieutenant General Kaulbars, who established his headquarters in Kirin, was wined and dined by the local governor.

The Fall of Hai-ch'êng

THE FINAL RUSSIAN OFFENSIVE was mounted in the south. Major General Fleisher, the commander of the 1st East Siberian Rifle Brigade, had been appointed also commander of the newly formed South Manchurian Detachment, which embraced the heretofore independently acting detachments of Colonels Khorunzhenkov, Dombrovskii and Mishchenko. On August 8, after the capture of Ying-k'ou, Mishchenko was ordered to join Dombrovskii near the village of Ta-shih-ch'iao and with him advance on the Chinese forces that occupied the heights to the north and east. The Chinese numbered only 4 battalions and 4 guns, with a like force in reserve at Hai-ch'êng, twenty miles away. But the few mounted Cossacks who were available were used primarily for messenger service, and the reconnaissance patrols which traveled on foot did not discover this. As a result the Russians overestimated the breadth and strength of the line of opposition before them and embarked on a grand maneuver, Fleisher sending out three solid columns: in the center, Colonel Aurenius, with the 3rd East Siberian Rifle Regiment with 8 guns and one section of Cossacks; on the left, Mishchenko with two companies and two Cossack squadrons of the railway guard and the 1st Transbaikal Cossack Battery; and on the right, Dombrovskii with four and a half companies of the 11th East

Siberian Rifle Regiment, 4 guns and 1 platoon of Cossacks.[75]

It was hot—up to 132° Fahrenheit—when the men set out from Ta-shih-ch'iao Station on the morning of August 10. Bathing in sweat, they hastened after the retreating Chinese, who now and then made a brief stand, then withdrew farther. They crossed mountains and ravines and rivulets and vast fields of kaoliang. They tried to keep up with their horse-drawn cavalry; they tried not to lose contact with each other. Not only was it stifling in the high kaoliang, but the stalks were tall enough to hide a man on horseback, and it was easy to get lost. Hot and thirsty, the soldiers continued as long as their legs could hold them. Here and there men collapsed unconscious, five of them dead. But the columns pressed on to isolate the Chinese units and cut them off from each other and from Newchwang.

The center outpost of the Chinese, which was withdrawing within view of Aurenius' center column, changed its direction and veered north toward Hai-

[75]According to Ivanov, Aurenius' center column was composed of 5 companies of the 3rd East Siberian Rifle Regiment, 3 companies of the 11th East Siberian Rifle Regiment, the 1st Battery of the East Siberian Rifle Artillery Division (4 guns), the 1st Mortar Battery of the 1st East Siberian Artillery Brigade (4 guns), 1 section of the Verkhneudinsk Cossack Regiment, and half a company of Kwantung sappers—a total of 8½ companies, 8 guns and 1 section. Mishchenko's left column embraced two foot companies and 2 mounted sotnias of the guards, the 1st battery of the Transbaikal Cossack forces, and 10 men of the Kwantung Cossack Company—a total of 2 companies, 2 sotnias, 6 guns and 10 men. Dombrovskii's right column consisted of a battalion (4 companies) of the 11th East Siberian Rifle Regiment, a raiding and scouting party of the same regiment of half a company, the 1st Battery of the East Siberian Rifle Artillery Division (4 guns), 1 troop of the Verkhneudinsk Cossack Regiment, and 10 men of the Kwantung Sapper Company—a total of 4½ companies, 4 guns, 1 troop and 10 men. The general reserve under Lieutenant Colonel Dubel't numbered 4 companies (the 2nd, 3rd, 4th and 6th) of the 1st East Siberian Rifle Regiment.

ch'êng, when it found Mishchenko athwart its route to Newchwang. Dombrovskii's right column meanwhile hastened over the most difficult mountain roads around the eastern outpost of the Chinese and threw them back against the 3rd Regiment. But Aurenius had fallen behind collecting stragglers, and the Chinese managed to get through in front of him and to join the forces that were retreating before Mishchenko. Strengthened, and with only Mishchenko's outfit on their heel, the Chinese decided to make a stand at the city of Hu-chuang-t'un.[76]

The Chinese artillery was excellent. It knocked down some of the horses pulling Mishchenko's gun and smashed one of the wheels. But the Chinese had not reckoned with the breakneck speed and agility of the 1st Cossack Battery, which tore from hillock to hillock blasting apart any troop concentration. So quickly did the battery move about that the Russian troops could not keep up with it, and galloping ahead of its own lines the battery almost singlehandedly forced the enemy back. Yet attempts to destroy him were unsuccessful again, the Chinese slipping away before Aurenius, who had fallen behind once more, could close in.

The foot soldiers were exhausted from the hot, rapid march through the stifling kaoliang. When they stopped for a breather at a well on the outskirts of the burning city, some fainted away. Water had to be forced into their tightly closed mouths. Drained of expression, with a vacant look on their pale, dusty faces, they failed to recognize their officers and comrades, and mumbled in-

---

[76]The place is not certain. Kushakov calls it Khuduchen, Ivanov Khudutun.

comprehensible words. Two of them, a Tartar and a Jew, reverted to their native tongues.

But the Chinese did not know of the vulnerability of the Russian troops and continued their evacuation of Hu-chuang-t'un. As they blew up the ammunition dumps, the earth shook with mighty explosions and the most spectacular fireworks rended the sky. The Russians put the torch to the remaining buildings, and by morning the city was a heap of ashes.

When the Russian columns, reunited, bivouacked for the night, the supply train had not caught up with them. The soldiers went to sleep hungry, without having eaten all day. On the morning of August 11, they moved out again, still unfed.

The Russians headed for Hai-ch'êng in two columns. The main column, commanded by Fleisher, consisted of his detachment, that of Dombrovskii and the Don Cossack guard sotnia. It proceeded northward along the railway line. The other column was under Mishchenko. It traveled on the left, parallel with the main column.

General Shou planned to withdraw before the Russians without a major engagement, to lure them toward Newchwang and there spring a trap. But his subordinates refused to abandon Hai-ch'êng without a fight. Yün, who assumed command over the militia, constantly molested Mishchenko's weaker, left column, forcing it to advance in combat formation. When Fleisher halted for a rest and the distance between the two columns grew to about three miles, Yün set an ambush for Mishchenko in the high kaoliang. But the Chinese battery which drew the Russians into the trap was overrun, and the soldiers who opened fire at the Russian back from entrenchments concealed in the kaoliang were decimated by Russian case-shot. While Mishchenko was fighting in the kaoliang, a hoard of Boxers from Hai-ch'êng tried to recapture the Chinese artillery, and to the sound of horns rushed onto the mountain chanting and waving banners. Wearing the usual yellow sashes and stripped to the waist and greased with oil for hand-to-hand combat, the Boxers ferociously charged the Russians. Their ranks included old men and boys, even girls. It was pitiful to watch how these children would grab a battle-hardened Cossack by the leg and try (and occasionally succeed) to pull him off the horse and bite him. Sweeping upon the Boxers from the flank, the whooping Cossacks with their sharp sabers made short shrift of them.

At 2 A.M. on August 12, the Russians resumed their advance. The Chinese forces, estimated at 4,000 regular troops with 8 guns and 1,000 Boxers, had retreated to a fortified height half a mile from Hai-ch'êng, and the Russians tried to sneak up under the cover of darkness. Slowly their columns groped down the mountain in the early twilight like the fingers of a large hand. The 2nd and 6th Companies moved against the center of the Chinese position, Kushakov's unit around the right flank. The Kuban Cossacks rode to a village in the west to strike the Chinese from the rear and to deny escape.

It was getting light when the Russians stole up to the enemy position. They could discern the mountain entrenchments and heads, popping up here and there, silhouetted against the sky. Quietly they drew nearer. Coming to an open field, they crouched down and ran across swiftly. Not a shot was fired at them. As they stopped to select the points of attack, they could hear the sound of wheels and the tread of horses behind the mountain. Realizing that the Chinese were pulling out, the Russians left their cover and clambered up the steep cliff. The entrenchments were empty. A signal flare was shot from the main column and a huge mortar shell flew over their heads. The bombardment of the city had begun.

With practically no resistance the Russians broke into Hai-ch'êng. Retreating artillery men abandoned their weapons and galloped away. There was sporadic rifle fire from the outskirts and gunfire from the northern heights, but these were quickly silenced. The city was theirs.

Kushakov sent patrols through the city to assemble the peaceful inhabitants. Only some 40 old men, women and children were found. They had lived and worked near the Russian station, knew some of the railway guards, and trusting in their connections and background had remained behind. The railway guards did indeed treat them well. Kushakov housed them in the buildings at the fortress gate and posted sentinels to protect them from violence. Gratefully the Chinese brought chickens and eggs and potatoes and vegetables and helped to prepare dinner. But with the arrival of the main detachment, which marched into the city, band playing, the railway guards were relieved, and regular troops took over.

When Kushakov returned to the city from the bivouac area to acquaint himself with the general disposition of the various units, he dropped by the house where a Chinese acquaintance had been living. The sentinel at the door had been removed, and inside, on the floor, two old men lay in puddles of blood, bayonetted to death, while a young boy, about eight years old, with his belly ripped open, squirmed in agony. Outraged, Kushakov asked a sargeant major where the other Chinese were, and was told they had been sent out of the city, "farther away from [their] sin." That day the doctor in Kushakov's regiment was called upon to revive an old woman and a girl of great beauty. Expelled from the city, they had run into soldiers who had killed the old woman's husband and raped the girl. In agony the two had thrown themselves into the river to end their miserable lives. The old woman was revived, the girl not. Once again victory claimed the lives of innocent bystanders.[77]

[77]Engineer Girshman complained to Vice Admiral Alekseev on August 27, 1900, about the plundering and burning of which the Russians had been guilty in the offensive against Hai-ch'êng. When Kuropatkin demanded an investigation and the punishment of the guilty, Alekseev replied that Girshman's accusation had been exaggerated. He asserted that the inhabitants themselves had managed to remove the most needed things and that Boxers and Chinese troops had plundered the city even before the arrival of the Russians. Upon further investigation, Alekseev reported that there were only isolated instances, and that the culprits had been court-martialled.

The Battles of
An-shan-chan and Sha-ho-p'u

THE FALL OF HAI-CH'ÊNG brought Mishchenko's detachment a period of rest. Not enough men were available to launch an offensive against Mukden, and the arrival of reinforcements from Europe had to be awaited.[78] For forty-three days the Cossacks remained inactive, at first recuperating, then waxing increasingly bored and restless. They looked forward to the coming of Lieutenant General Subotich, commander of the

[78]Before the Boxer uprising the 3rd East Siberian Rifle Brigade (composed of the 9th, 10th, 11th and 12 East Siberian Rifle Regiments) and the East Siberian Rifle-Artillery Division (consisting of 3 batteries), the 1st Verkhneudinsk Cossack Regiment (composed of 6 sotnias) and 1 sapper company were stationed on the Kwantung tip of the Liaotung Peninsula. When the 9th, 10th and 12th Rifle Regiments, the 2nd and 3rd Batteries and three sotnias were sent to Pechihli, they were replaced by the 1st, 3rd, 8th and part of the 15th East Siberian Rifle Regiments (the latter being then formed out of the 9th Line Battalion), three sotnias of the Chita, one sotnia of the 1st Nerchinsk Cossack Regiments, the 2nd Foot Battery and the 1st Mortar Battery of the 1st East Siberian Artillery Brigade and the 1st Transbaikal Cossack Battery. These forces were sent from the Maritime Region. The 8th Rifle Regiment was designated as garrison for Port Arthur.

The forces on which Mishchenko could draw totalled only 7½ battalions, 9 sotnias and 28 guns—not enough for an attack on Mukden, where heavy Chinese resistance was expected. The reinforcements which came from Odessa by ship and were to be assigned to the Mukden campaign arrived at Port Arthur on September 6. They consisted of the 13th and 14th Rifle Regiments and 1½ batteries of the 4th Rifle-Artillery Division, and were commanded by Lieutenant General Subotich.

armed forces of the Kwantung region, under whose command they would fall, for he respected and treated railway guards like regular troops.

Cossack patrols utilized the lull to reconnoiter enemy positions thoroughly, supplementing their personal observations with information obtained from the populace. Having lived in Manchuria for three years, many of the Cossacks had contacts, even friends, among the inhabitants and could communicate with them. The civilian officials and engineers also gathered data about the Chinese armies. The estimate that emerged by September was that some 50,000 well-armed troops with 60 of the newest Krupp, Maxim and Nordenfeld guns stood between Liao-yang and Mukden.

Subotich, an observant and thoughtful officer, who had personally familiarized himself with Manchurian terrain and conditions, reached Hai-ch'êng on September 21. He had at his disposal in the Ying-k'ou-Hai-ch'êng region 47 companies and 2½ sotnias or about 9,000 men and 28 guns. The numerical strength of the Chinese forces with their modern European weapons and vast stores of ammunition did not impress him. He knew that the Chinese lacked leadership and discipline, and did not command the respect and support of the people. Living off the land, they appeared to the population not as guardians but as plunderers, no better, at times worse, than the foreign intruders. The inhabitants, therefore, hid food from their own troops and tricked them into leaving by firing rifles and then reporting falsely that the Russians were coming. When the Russians did come, the villagers hoisted white flags, even Russian ones, and went out to meet the invaders to assure them of their submission. Naturally Chinese soldiers resented such conduct and when they withdrew, often set fire to the villages. This in turn deepened the hostility of the populace. The militiamen vanished to their own villages and the armies were left with men from other provinces and homeless vagrants who had no respect for other people's property.

Subotich took full advantage of the situation. He curbed the passion of young firebrands and protected the populace. He announced: "Notwithstanding the repeated orders of the military command and the Imperial Sovereign's desire, proclaimed to everyone, under no circumstances to burn down villages, there are scoundrels who do not hold dear the Tsar's will and have no regard for other people's property, acquired by the sweat of peasants, Chinese though they may be. Such scoundrels will be shot." The warning was crystal clear and did not have to be enforced. Dousing fires instead of setting them, and helping rather than hurting the peasants, the forces of Subotich won an important psychological victory, for the population began to clamor for peace and to dismiss its own troops as marauders.

Tactically, too, Subotich understood how to deal with the enemy. The Chinese armies were provocative and aggressive until the Russians advanced, then they fled; as soon as the Russians halted, the Chinese regrouped and attacked; when the Russians pushed forward, they melted away again. To defeat them effectively it was necessary to pursue them without let-up, depriving them of the opportunity to regroup. One could not be as cautious as textbooks required, a fact which many Russian commanders could not accept. But Subotich appreciated the difference in conditions and followed through punch after punch, not giving the Chinese a chance to bethink themselves.

Subotich planned a three-pronged advance. The center column was to make a frontal attack on the An-shan position. The left column was to move against the western detachment at Newchwang; after defeating it, it was to envelop the right flank of the eastern detachment at An-shan. The right column, light and mobile, was to envelop the left flank of the enemy; it was to go east by rail, through the mountains.

On September 23, the left column set out for Newchwang under the command of General Fleisher. It was composed of the 1st, 2nd[79] and 11th East Siberian Rifle Regiments, two sotnias of Verkhneudinsk Cossacks, one infantry battery, a platoon of cavalry battery,[80] and a mobile section of the Red Cross. The Chinese forces in this area were commanded by General Shou. They numbered about 6,000 men.

Newchwang lay in a plain, covered with kaoliang that was high enough to conceal a rider on horseback and dissected by a multitude of narrow, winding roads. The Russians found it difficult, therefore, to keep their bearing and remain in touch with each other, the Chinese doing all they could to add to the confusion. Small Chinese detachments nimbly moved from village to village, forcing the Russians to wheel about almost blindly in the high kaoliang. Unable to see where they were going, the Russians had to stop repeatedly and try to determine by the sound whether they heard Russian or Chinese shots and from where they came. When they fired they did so by instinct, the target remaining hid-

[79]According to the German summary of Russian reports, the 3rd East Siberian Rifle Regiment.

[80]According to the German summary, there were 10 guns of the 1st Battery of the East Siberian Rifle-Artillery Division and 2 guns of the 1st Transbaikal Cossack Battery.

den in the kaoliang. Yet the Chinese occasionally fell victim to their own strategy, as Russians unexpectedly loomed up before them. In such a confrontation the Chinese were no match for the European marksmen. It was in ambushes, where even their aimless fire could be effective, that they killed or wounded 2 Russian officers, 1 doctor and 24 soldiers that day.

The Chinese chose not to defend the city itself, and in the morning, on September 24, General Fleisher entered Newchwang. Expecting the Russians to stop in the city for some time, General Shou had halted for the night only four miles away, and in the morning of September 25 continued his withdrawal at a leisurely pace. But General Fleisher left only a small garrison in Newchwang, and hastened to envelop the right flank of the An-shan position, where 14,000 Chinese were entrenched. Soon Fleisher's left column came upon Shou's detachment and turned an orderly retreat into a rout. Chinese plans to withdraw eastward into the Ch'ien-shan hills to let the Russians go past toward the main force at Sha-ho and then fall in their rear were shattered. Fleeing directly toward Sha-ho, the Chinese brought the Russians into their own camp, though the Verkhneudinsk Cossacks and their battery scattered two thirds of Shou's force and only 2,000 men reached Sha-ho.

Meanwhile Colonel Artamonov, the chief of staff, personally reconnoitered the approaches to An-shan with two guard sotnias. He rode along the fortified heights and made a sketch of the artillery emplacements, forcing the Chinese to reveal their positions by approaching to within 300 paces of their forward detachments and drawing fire. The Chinese were stretched out for over 4½ miles. The right flank of their line leaned on a

211

fortified hill, the left flank on a fortified temple. Their trenches were arranged in tiers, and defended by an estimated 14,000 men and 30 guns.

At 5:30 A.M. on September 26, the Russian main force broke bivouac, and advanced from Hai-ch'êng toward An-shan-chan in two columns. The center column, commanded by Artamonov, consisted of the 13th and 14th rifle regiments and two companies[81] of the 15th East Siberian Regiment, three and a half batteries,[82] a machine gun battery and a platoon of Verkhneudinsk Cossacks. The right column, under Mishchenko, was composed of two companies and two sotnias of guards and four guns of the 1st Transbaikal Cossack Battery. Thrusting northeastward, Mishchenko easily took the village of Ta-t'un, An-shan-chan, the An-shan pass and a terrace on the northern slope. Yet though this put him behind the An-shan heights, he did not hear any battle raging there. Soon he was informed by the center column that the enemy had abandoned the fortifications during the night. His own opposition, too, seemed to have evaporated into thin air. As a result he had advanced so swiftly, that he was over four and a half miles ahead of the main force, and decided to wait. His companies stacked rifles and were about to scatter, the officers sat down to have a snack and discuss the mysterious disappearance of the Chinese, while he himself went to the foot of the hill to choose a route for getting the artillery up, when suddenly the eastern hills exploded with artillery salvoes and rifle volleys, and thick lines of Chinese

[81]The 1st Battalion of the 15th East Siberian Rifle Regiment.

[82]Twenty-six guns; probably the 2nd Foot and the 1st Mortar Battery of the 1st East Siberian Artillery Brigade and 1½ batteries of the 4th Rifle-Artillery Division.

troops covered the hills, which but a moment before had looked unoccupied. Banners fluttered on the heights, cavalry detachments galloped along the slopes and the eerie tone of long, Jericho-like horns wafted across the plain.

The men hastily unstacked their rifles and dropped to position. Before the officers had time to descend to Mishchenko and inform him of the size of the enemy forces, which were stretched out along the mountain ridges for two and a half miles, he ordered Strakhov and Denisov to chase the Chinese from the hill which he could see from where he was. Assuming that the two Cossack sotnias, consisting of not more than 40 men each because many were still out on patrol, had been sent merely to reconnoiter the enemy positions, the officers returned to their men without talking to Mishchenko. They could not believe their eyes when the two tiny sotnias of Kuban and Don Cossacks galloped across the plain in column formation and charged up the slope against the very center of the formidable position. Eighty men against 14,000! The Chinese hastily abandoned the hill, but no sooner had the Cossacks taken it, than they became the target of murderous crossfire. Without hesitation Mishchenko led the rest of the detachment to their aid. This time the Russians ran into determined opposition, and gunfire from the west seemed to indicate that the Chinese were attacking them also from the rear.

Unexpectedly the Chinese began to fall back and cleared all the heights. Only isolated shots rang from the north. It developed that the gunfire in Mishchenko's rear had not been Chinese, but Russian, that of the Transbaikal Cossacks pursuing General Shou. Fleisher thus had rounded the An-shan position as planned. The wild Cossack charge had cost the life of *Shtabs-kapitan* Valerian Strakhov, commander of the Kuban sotnia. Seven others were killed or wounded. Had Fleisher not appeared, however, the entire sotnias might have been wiped out. No longer were the guards annoyed with Fleisher for having been too slow at Hai-ch'êng.

After burying their dead, Mishchenko's men settled down for the night at the very place where some months ago they had waited for reinforcements for five days without ammunition. In the evening Captain Orlov joined them with two companies of the 14th Regiment and a section of the Red Cross, staffed by Akhriutina and the Countess Ignat'eva. The soldiers were particularly pleased to see the ladies, for they brought not only medical help but everything from writing paper to salt and a warm informal atmosphere lacking in military hospital units.

Unable to halt the Russians, the Chinese had withdrawn northward, toward the Sha River. It was their intention to draw the Russians into a huge horseshoe, formed by the village of Sha-ho-p'u at the top and the railroad embankment and the Ch'ien-shan hills on the west and east respectively. Together with the Mukden reserves and the remnants of the Newchwang detachments, they planned to meet the Russians in an embrace of death.

On paper the Chinese position was impregnable. Some 53,000 men were to give body to the 8 mile long horseshoe into which the Russians were to be drawn. About 3,000 of Shou's men failed to appear, and the 14,000 strong An-shan force arrived too late to join battle effectively. Still, the Chinese main reserves numbered 30,000, dwarfing the 18½ companies and 2 sotnias which the Russians put into the field against them. Yet statistics can be deceiving. In peacetime the Chinese battalions had been full strength on paper only, the commanders pocketing half or more of the salary funds. Upon the outbreak of hostilities, the battalions had been hastily refilled with bodies rather than soldiers. There were boys of 15 and men of 50; there were thieves and marauders, eager to strike out on their own. Few were steeled in the discipline of war and dedicated to a cause. Nor were the trained soldiers that were available used effectively. The Chinese command was a many-headed monster at cross purposes with itself.

With the Russians on his heels, General Shou reached the Chinese position only shortly before the battle. The various commanders had positioned their troops at their own discretion, as far away as possible from the expected point of Russian attack. Shou's attempts to tighten the overextended line ran into opposition. Many commanders refused to accept his authority; others said they would not listen to a man who had run away. His prompt decapitation of several officers was no boon to morale, and attempted last minute shifts in position proved futile. Guns and units that were moved from one place to another did not reach their destination before the Russian attack and merely compounded the confusion of command.

So extended was the Chinese position that the Russians lacked the manpower to strike at the front and flanks both. But they had 30 pieces of artillery, not counting 4 machine guns, and Subotich gave the battle the character of an artillery duel. He shifted his artillery now to the left flank, now to the middle, and pounded the Chinese out of one position after another, while the infantry massed for a breakthrough at the center.

At 6 A.M. on September 27, Mishchenko set out with his two companies, two sotnias and 4 guns to locate the enemy position. The plain that extended from the An-shan heights to the Liao and Sha Rivers was a blind of thick, red kaoliang, over which the Russians could peer only from scattered trees and from the roofs of isolated temples and villages. To the east, some two miles away, the plain was framed by a ridge of blue rocky mountains, which descended toward the Russians in a tier of terraces. Here, Mishchenko discovered, the Chinese had en-trenched themselves. To get a better view and to estab-lish an observation post for keeping the main forces in-formed, Mishchenko ascended the nearest hill, on which several flags and a handful of men could be seen. The heavy artillery fire that met him revealed, however, that he had tackled more than a mere outpost. Yet the Trans-baikal Cossack artillery blasted the hill clear and the companies occupied it without casualties. The battery quickly took up position on what became known as Mt. Mishchenko, and engaged in an artillery duel with the Chinese guns along the mountain ridges.

Suddenly the railway guards found themselves sur-rounded by masses of Chinese. On the eastern heights, behind the railroad embankment, in the western village, even in their own rear, everywhere Chinese infantrymen were crawling near, while Chinese cavalry raced toward their flanks. Grenades and bullets swished through the air and momentarily flattened the stunned Russians. But as the grenades burst among them, they scattered to the ridge of the hill and fired volley after volley at the ad-vancing Chinese. Yet they kept on coming in waves, the neighboring height looking like a giant anthill. What the Russians had mistaken for a minor outpost was the very center of the enemy position, and the 400 men had blundered into the midst of a force of 30,000.[83]

From the edge of the village of Sha-ho-p'u, some 4,200 feet away, Chinese guns lopped delayed action charges at the Russian guns. These the Transbaikal Cossacks deftly picked up and threw away. But other grenades exploded. Here a Cossack bent over in mortal agony, there a comrade pressed his wound closed with his hands, while a third Cossack began jumping on one leg, the other dangling helplessly from a piece of clothing. The Chinese artillery had zeroed in and fired with deadly accuracy. When the Russian ammunition began to give out, the end of Mishchenko's detachment seemed at hand.

The expected charge did not materialize. The appearance of a cloud of dust and the sound of gunfire in the south at the critical juncture, stayed the Chinese death blow. Though they intensified their bombardment, the Chinese halted their advance. Soon Artamonov arrived on the mountain with the vanguard and by 11 A.M. the battery of Colonel Golov stood alongside that of the Transbaikal Cossacks. Amply supplied, twelve guns now opened rapid fire at the Chinese. The latter courageously continued the duel until the machine gun battery of Lieutenant Colonel Gaitenov showered them with a deadly stream of lead. When the Chinese realized that the Russian reinforcements were small—only the 1st Battalion of the 14th Regiment under Colonel Lesh had arrived with the batteries— they resumed their flank attack. But by now it was too late. Leaving the flanking

---

[83]The Chinese had destroyed the railway station at Sha-ho-p'u and had occupied the railway embankment and the heights to the east of it. They numbered 30 battalions with 20 Krupp and Maxim guns.

Chinese to the main forces that were approaching, Artamonov, Mishchenko and Lesh mounted an all-out push
against the enemy center.

Supported by steady cannon and machine gun fire,
Artamonov with 2½ companies of the 14th Regiment
beat the Chinese out of Sha-ho-p'u, while Mishchenko
with 1½ guard companies and the 4th Company of the
14th Regiment drove the Chinese from height after
height all the way across the Sha River. As expected,
the forces of General Subotich, who hastened to the
aid of Artamonov and Mishchenko, crushed the flank
attack. By mid-afternoon the Chinese had been dislodged
everywhere and by nightfall, when General Fleisher's
column arrived, they were in full retreat toward Liao-
yang.

At Sha-ho-p'u the usual numerical superiority of the
Chinese had been cemented by courage and bolstered
by skillful artillery marksmanship. If they succumbed
nonetheless, it was due to lack of discipline and, above
all, due to the absence of a unified supreme command.
On the Russian side, there had been many acts of bravery. None were more praiseworthy than the calm,
healing work under fire of Dr. Khmara-Borshevskii and
of the nurses,[84] who to the weary, wounded warriors
were angels of mercy.

[84]Labutina, Eremina and Kuzmina in addition to Ignat'eva and
Akhrutina.

The Fall of Liao-yang

GENERALS HSÜ, YÜN AND FEN were among China's best commanders. Yet at Sha-ho-p'u they had proven unable to control their own men, who wantonly deserted their ranks and plundered the countryside. Mortified, the commanders withdrew to Mukden, and from there sent their resignations to Peking. But outraged as they were with the pillage and desertion of their subordinates, they paid them the compliment of imitation. Instead of defending the Manchurian capital of Mukden or negotiating its surrender to preserve the imperial treasures, the generals hastened from the city with wagon trains, laden with loot from the Imperial Palace, the bank and treasury. Deserting their soldiers, they left them free to scatter across Southern Manchuria and Mongolia. The detachments of the northern provinces headed for Mukden, T'ieh-ling and Fa-k'u-mên like a swarm of locust, denuding the countryside. Only the units formed in Liao-yang Province stood fast to give their people time to remove or hide their belongings in Liao-yang city, against which Subotich was advancing rapidly.

Russian patrols had determined that the Chinese were entrenched on heights half-way between Sha-ho-p'u and Liao-yang. At 6:30 A.M. on September 28, General Fleisher moved out with the left column to round the right flank of the Chinese and storm the western face of the Liao-yang fortress. Colonel Mishchenko, with the right column, departed at 8:20 A.M. to travel through the mountains around the left flank of the Chinese and force the eastern gates of the fortress. The center column, under Colonel Artamonov, set out at 8:30 A.M. to strike the southward-facing heights from the west. Ahead and to the left of Fleisher's column, a flying detachment of men from the 1st, 3rd and 11th companies with two cavalry guns and a sotnia and a half of Verkhneudinsk Cossacks prodded along retreating bands of Chinese marauders. Two attempts by Chinese cavalry to crush the small detachment were cut short by Cossack sabers. As the Russians drove Chinese soldiers before them, pushing them northeastward, into the muzzles of the vanguard, many Chinese scattered, doffed their uniforms, hid their guns and masqueraded as peaceful villagers.

While Artamonov approached the height where the Chinese were entrenched and bombarding them distracted their attention, Fleisher approached the walls of Liao-yang at about 2 P.M. Two companies of the 3rd Regiment secured the river crossing. As the 11th Regiment advanced against the western face of the wall and the 3rd against the northern, the defenders of the fortress fired merely a few shots, felling 7 Russians, then fled eastward, into the mountains.[85] In spite of their

85According to Dugald Christie, Dr. A. Macdonald Westwater, a missionary from Liao-yang, had accompanied the Russians as a Red Cross surgeon. "When the army was encamped south of Liao-yang, he went forward into that city to represent to its authorities the hopelessness and suicidal folly of resistance, and persuaded them to open the gates and let the Russians enter quietly. Thus the city was saved." According to the German summary of Russian reports, an English doctor who had lived in Liao-yang for eighteen years (apparently Dr. Westwater) calmed the Chinese residents when the Russians entered Liao-yang, assuring them that they had nothing to fear.

prompt withdrawal, they were unable to save all their artillery. Rapid fire by Gromov's battery from one side of the river and shooting by the two companies under Lieutenant Colonel Iablochka, who had crossed the river, from the other side, forced them to abandon several modern Krupp and Nordenfeld pieces.

Once Fleisher had rounded the heights, Artamonov stormed the position and drove the defenders to a village, from which their comrades had been shooting at Fleisher's column. Finding themselves hemmed in on two sides, the Chinese fled, abandoning more modern weapons. By this time the Russian flag had been hoisted over the fortress, and Artamonov's men merely pursued the running foe.

Mishchenko, on the other hand, had a talent for smacking into opposition. The mountains through which his light, right column was to make its way unobtrusively harbored about 6,000 Chinese soldiers who had fled there from Sha-ho-p'u and from the heights. Reassembled by a fanatic Boxer, they tried to block Mishchenko's path. But fearful of being enveloped, they overextended their line. Firing rapidly, Mishchenko's 4 guns and two companies drove the Chinese out of their way, ever deeper into the mountains. Ordered not to pursue the enemy farther, Mishchenko turned to Liao-yang, where all detachments received a day's rest.[86]

[86]Russian casualties in the three days of fighting (September 26-28) amounted to only 10 men dead and 3 officers and 64 men wounded. The remarkably low rate was due in part to the poor marksmanship of the Chinese. It was due also to the skillful planning and execution of the Russian attacks and to the soft ground which left many Chinese artillery shells unexploded. "One notices here the lessons of the South African [Boer] War," the German major who summarized the Russian reports observed. "Flank attacks and envelopments are the major means by which one tries to drive the enemy out of his defense positions or to weaken him

Having returned in force—with 6,000 men, powerful artillery, and large military supplies—Kushakov and his comrades recalled with wonder how on July 5 to 7 their small detachment of 224 railway guards had weathered the assault of some 7,000 Chinese. Revisiting the places of battle, the barracks where they had defended themselves, and the graves of their comrades, they were angered to find all the graves dug open and the bones strewn about in the field. Carefully they collected the remains and together with the bodies of their recently fallen comrades and six Russian heads, including that of the unfortunate engineer Verkhovskii, which they had found displayed on the fortress wall, buried them that night with full military honors.

From a guard of the 2nd Company, who had been taken prisoner by the Chinese and only recently released by the Tartar General of Fêng-t'ien, Kushakov learned some gruesome details. Held in the Liao-yang jail, the soldiers and fellow-captives had been served foul water and stinking excreta for food and had been beaten until they consumed it. Their wounds had been neither cleaned nor bandaged, and became infected. Soon they began to smell so bad that Chinese convicts who were locked up in the same jail complained. Irritated, the Chinese commander had those with festering wounds decapitated. The head of one of the victims was brought back to jail and put in the middle of the floor. As punishment for the complaint, the prisoners were ordered onto their feet and forbidden to lie down to sleep unless they

in front. Only after this has succeeded and the artillery has effectively pounded the way does the frontal attack take place. Furthermore, the enemy positions always seem to have been reconnoitered beforehand very exactly."

used the severed head for a pillow. For a long time the prisoners shunned the ghoulish cushion, but eventually fatigue got the better of revulsion and the broken men took turns sleeping on the head. "After two days and nights I had become so weak from this punishment," the soldier recalled, "that I could no longer stand up. Then I alone was put onto the festering head. How long I lay on this head I do not remember, since I rarely regained consciousness, but probably for a long while, because there were worms on the neck and on the back of my own head as of that of the corpse." He showed Kushakov the scars on his neck and the spot where his hair had been eaten. Then he related how from time to time he and the other prisoners were put on public display near the city gates, to be beaten and spat upon by the passers-by. There were joksters who amused the crowd by painting the faces of the prisoners. Some made them hold banners with various inscriptions, others forced them to eat pancakes smeared with filth. But the greatest mirth was aroused by those who made them kiss a squealing piglet in all places.

The Chinese did not stop with the humiliation of the prisoners. One Russian soldier with chained arms and legs was laid near an open window in the jail. Then his forehead, cheeks, chest, stomach and legs were cut open with a knife, so that worms would get in and eat him alive. The tortured soldier did not utter a moan, but tears streamed down his face. When he tried to shorten his agony by not eating, the Chinese forced porridge into his mouth. Mercifully he choked to death. Another Russian, a civilian foreman, bled to death after his arms and legs had been cut off. The heads of the victims were always shown to their comrades to remind them of the fate in store for them. It was only their transfer to Mukden that saved the survivors, the Tartar General releasing them after pressure from Colonel Mishchenko and Engineer Girshman.

The Taking of Mukden

FROM LIAO-YANG LIEUTENANT General Subotich headed for Mukden, the capital of Fêng-t'ien Province and cradle of the Ch'ing Dynasty. Here the first Manchu rulers of China had held court until the transfer of the capital to Peking in 1644. The tombs of the early Manchu emperors were in the northern outskirts of the city. Mukden had a population of about 200,000. Situated at the junction of main roads leading into Manchuria from the interior of China and Korea, it constituted a major commercial and industrial center. The city was surrounded by an outer earth wall about 11 miles in circumference and an inner brick wall with towers and gunports, about 3 miles in circumference. The population was densest in the center, where most of the commercial activity took place.

Prison interrogation revealed that the disunity of enemy command was supplemented by friction between northern and southern Chinese and that resistance was not likely to be stubborn. "We regarded Liao-yang as iron and Mukden as paper," a captured Chinese officer told the Russians. "If our forces were unable to defend Liao-yang, they will abandon Mukden." Subotich himself felt that the Chinese forces were on the run, their stand at the heights before Liao-yang being an exception, local troops there having fought tenaciously for their native region, believing that Russia wanted to annex it.

The final Russian offensive, which began on the morning of September 30, was spearheaded by Colonel Mishchenko's guard detachment, reinforced by the 5th Verkhneudinsk Cossack sotnia, a military raiding and scouting party from the 11th and 14th Rifle Regiments and the 1st Cossack Battery. Next followed Colonel Dombrovskii with the vanguard, composed of 3½ battalions of infantry, 16 guns, 4 machine guns, sappers and a platoon of Cossacks, and finally the main forces in two echelons.

The Russians proceeded along the imperial highway without resistance. Completely demoralized by their many defeats, the Chinese fled before them. Inhabitants of the villages along the way related that the Chinese troops, deserted by their generals, were withdrawing in complete disorder. At first they took from the populace only food and whatever animals they could ride; eventually, like the generals and officials in Mukden, the soldiers extended their reach and turned their flight from the Russians into a foray against their own people. They were not satisfied with taking what they craved. The countryside was littered with discarded and destroyed loot. If the marauders were not only greedy but mean, the Russians had contributed to this indirectly. The proclamation which they had issued at Hai-ch'êng guaranteeing the safety of peaceful inhabitants, had reached this area and had prompted the peasants to deny food and assistance to their own troops, thereby arousing their ire. Robbed and mistreated in consequence, the villagers went out to meet the Russians with little white flags and asked them to track down the culprits, in turn adding to the anger of the military. Some European commanders and soldiers behaved no better than their Chinese counterparts, but they could argue at least that they were depriving the enemy, rather than their own countrymen. Seeing what the common people had to endure at the hands of their own soldiery, Subotich's men sought no retribution from the populace for the attacks and atrocities that had occurred. On the contrary, they helped them douse the fires set by their compatriots. When they appropriated Chinese property, it was mostly food—chicken, geese, and vegetables—which they truly needed.

All of September 30, Mishchenko followed the path of destruction left by the retreating troops. There was no opposition, no need even to reconnoiter the route ahead, the fires ignited by the marauders lighting the way like beacons. A disgruntled Chinese officer who fell into Russian hands that evening stated that Mukden too was already aflame. Like other informants he asserted that no measures were being taken to defend the city and urged the Russians to hasten there without delay to save it from plunder and destruction. Similar sentiments were expressed by inhabitants with little white flags the following day.[87] The Russian officers did indeed plan to take Mukden quickly, lest the enemy recoup his strength. But they did not tell this to the Chinese, nor to their own soldiers. Announcing that they would spend the night at Pai-t'a-p'u, about 12 miles from the fortress of Mukden and close to 30 miles from where they still were, they sent their cavalry ahead.

---

[87]Subotich received a petition in English from the merchants and Christians in Mukden, asking him to occupy the city as soon as possible, since complete anarchy reigned there.

The 8th Don Cossack Sotnia of *Podesaul* Denisov forced the issue. Dispatched by Mishchenko merely to secure the ford across the Hun River and to reconnoiter the approaches to Mukden, it had its heart set on being the first unit to enter the capital, confident that Mishchenko would come to its support as soon as fighting broke out. Mishchenko and Artamonov, who were to catch up with Denisov the following day, realized the likelihood of having to rush to his aid. This consideration, plus the calculation that it would be easier to take Mukden by surprise, while the Chinese troops were in the midst of plundering, induced the Russians to strike without delay. Mishchenko and Artamonov thus trotted toward the city with the 3rd Kuban and the 5th Verkhneudinsk Cossack Sotnias and the Transbaikal Cossack Battery; Captain Kushakov followed with the foot detachment at a quick pace.

Intelligence that the Chinese would not defend the city was correct. They were ready to abandon it. But in the process they planned to blow up the city and the Russians. Feverishly mines with electric lead wires were being laid in government buildings and ammunition dumps, at the gates and in private homes. The populace was chased out of the city and did not know of the preparations. Looting continued and merchants and home owners believed that they had been driven out for this reason. But the generals were informed, and warned the officers not to withdraw into the fortress, which had been mined also. Strict orders were issued to the populace not to set any more fires and arsonists were shot without mercy. When fires broke out here and there nonetheless, the Tartar General and others who knew about the mining fled with their families for fear of being trapped in a premature inferno.

Expecting the Russian attack to take place on October 2, as originally planned, the Chinese were so absorbed in plundering and mining Mukden that they had neglected to post guards on the walls, when Denisov's patrols appeared before the city on the afternoon of the 1st. Embittered with their own authorities, who had driven them out of their homes, some inhabitants informed the Cossacks that they were not expected yet and that the city gates were open. No doubt there were others who would have reported to the fortress the arrival of the Russians, had they deemed an attack imminent. But the scattered groups of horsemen appeared to be only reconnaissance parties.

When Denisov assembled the entire sotnia, Chinese mounted patrols caught sight of it, and began shooting from the outskirts of the city. Ignoring them, the Cossacks galloped toward Mukden. Within several minutes they flew through the southern gates, chopping down the sentries. Quickly they occupied the tower and part of the wall and opened rapid fire at the tents of the Chinese guards, set up on the street below. Frantically the guards scurried away, dropping their weapons, and shouting that the Russians had taken the gates and were galloping through the streets, butchering everyone. Panic-stricken, Chinese soldiers and officers stampeded from the fortress and other buildings. Shooting at random, they hit their own countrymen. Seeing the dead and wounded, those who came from behind assumed that the Russians were here too and turned back, compounding the confusion of those who headed their way. The Cossacks did all they could to give the illusion of great strength. Running about on top of the walls, now to the right, now to the left, they fired everywhere. Then, when a cloud of dust signalled the approach of Artamonov and Mishchenko, Denisov, who knew Mukden well, had his men remount, and galloped into the heart of the imperial city directly into the palace, occupying all the gates of the imperial quarter and shooting at the fleeing Chinese. Before the latter could recover their senses and realize that they had been fooled by the bravado of a handful of daredevils, Artamonov and Mishchenko had arrived with reinforcements. Fighting among themselves for horses and mules, Chinese Boxers and soldiers fled to the northern outskirts of the city. Some were unarmed, others carried new rifles hastily taken from the arsenals, often with the wrong ammunition.

In their hurry the Chinese had not tried to detonate the mines. Only at one of the gates did they bury a box with powder and strewed powder and phosphor matches on the cobble stones. When the Cossacks galloped through, the hoofs of their horses ignited the matches and the scattered powder relayed the fire to the hidden box, which exploded as the last Cossacks rode past. Six of Denisov's men were burned, two of them seriously, and their horses perished. But this was a small price to pay for the victory, particularly in view of the holocaust planned by the Chinese.[88]

At sunset Kushakov's foot detachment arrived and occupied the eight gates of the fortress and the inner walls of the imperial city. The Cossacks manned the guard posts in the Imperial Palace; raiding and scouting

---

[88]In their eight day advance from Hai-ch'êng the Russians had lost a total of 123 men, including 1 officer and 41 men killed or mortally wounded or shell-shocked. The Chinese force which they had routed was estimated at 50,000 men with 60 guns.

parties protected the palace of the Tartar General. Additional reinforcements, including half a company of sappers, were sent by General Subotich from Pai-t'a-p'u, since the pacification of the city remained yet before them. To secure their escape, the fleeing Chinese soldiers had ignited walls of fire between themselves and their pursuers. Entire quarters of Mukden were aflame, and the city was rocked by explosions. The Russians gunned down all arsonists and forced the peaceful inhabitants to fight the fires. Thus they managed to save the Imperial Palace and other buildings of note. When order was restored, Kushakov had reason to needle Chinese officials that Denisov deserved a monument as the savior of the imperial city.

The Pacification of Manchuria

THE FALL OF MUKDEN did not end the war. The Chinese did not surrender or come to terms at once. Some scattered to their homes; others formed into roving bands and attacked Russians and Chinese alike. Seeking to protect the railway and related enterprises, the Russians became involved in the pacification of the entire region. By this time Russian forces in Manchuria and Pechihli had grown to 3,900 officers and 173,000 men. With the capture of Mukden such a large force was no longer necessary and a reduction in size and demobilization were decreed on October 3.

The Russians hunted down armed bands, dismantled mines and destroyed ammunition depots—a dangerous undertaking, 27 men and 9 horses being torn to shreds in one explosion. Though the Chinese had succeeded in removing some of their artillery, the Russians found in the Mukden arsenal 50 modern guns and many thousand rounds of ammunition, including 20 million rifle cartridges, among them expanding bullets, sold by an unscrupulous European manufacturer.

To clear the railway line and insure the safety of repairs, Colonel Mishchenko continued northward, to T'ieh-ling, in October. There he met a Cossack sotnia belonging to General Rennenkampf's detachment and thus restored contact between the south and north Manchurian armies. Pillaged by Chinese marauders, the inhabitants of T'ieh-ling responded favorably to Russian assurances of protection and willingly carted back rails, ties and spikes, which had been removed but not thrown into the river as elsewhere. Leaving Captain Kushakov at T'ieh-ling, Mishchenko forded the Liao River with two sotnias and two guns and doubled back to Mukden and Liao-yang, ferreting out hunghutze or "redbeards," as the bandits were commonly called after the flaxen beards behind which they hid their identity. Colonel Kondratovich cleared the area between Mukden and Newchwang; Colonel Kvetsinskii operated some 50 miles northeast of Mukden; General Shtakel'berg crossed the Liao River and after joining forces with General Volkov moved against Chinese detachments in the northwest, along the Mongolian border. There were many other operations. Kushakov, for example, pushed east of T'ieh-ling to free two French missionaries and some 2,000 Christians, besieged for twenty-three days. Before long the restoration of the railway and new construction were in full swing.

The Tartar General of Fêng-t'ien meanwhile wrote to General Subotich from Hsin-min-t'ing of his willingness to enter into peace negotiations. In so doing he blamed the anti-foreign upheaval exclusively on the Boxers, asserting that he himself had done everything in his power to preserve the centuries-old friendship between Russia and China. Like other officials he asked the Russians to continue their anti-bandit campaign. But peace cannot by imposed by military force. As the Russians realized, the roots of unrest were to a large extent economic. So long as the people went hungry, their bellies would be filled with bitterness. Only the

233

Chinese could solve this problem, and the fact that the officials who by their timidity, if not their connivance, had contributed to the catastrophy now tried to shift the blame onto the shoulders of the masses, forebode ill for the future.

Throughout the winter the Russian troops in Manchuria remained on the alert. Two-wheeled carts laden with supplies were ready to leave at a moment's notice and the men kept on their bodies cartridges, biscuits, tea, sugar and salt. The bands of hunghutze which they tried to eradicate were not a postwar phenomenon. For decades bandits had defied Chinese authority and plundered the countryside. They had been so strong and organized that officials had found it necessary at times to make deals with them, and supply them with foodstuffs and occasionally even bestow a military rank on their leaders. But the war had swelled their ranks. The bands had many hiding places and were experienced in vanishing from the scene. Repeatedly Russian troops would be summoned to a place only to find the bandits gone.

The end of the fighting did not bring rest to the Russian soldiers. They had to build their winter quarters with their own hands. Meanwhile, service in Manchuria began to bore the officers, and they thirsted for entertainment. When the Slavianskii choir visited Mukden, the officers took in every note and longed for "Little Mother Volga" as the singers, arrayed in 16th and 17th century Russian costumes, sang "Ei ukhnem," the song of the Volga boatmen.

Fear of the Russians, of the Boxers, and of the blind fury of war had compelled most Chinese to flee from the cities in the path of the Russian armies. The fields had gone unharvested. By the time the hostilities were over, most crops had been burned by the autumn sun if not by the fires set by the Boxers or else had been trampled by the armed forces of both sides. Thus the end of war did not mean an end of suffering for the peaceful population. Hunger stalked the land.

In Tsitsihar the shortage of food was evident in the fall of 1900, and by winter a large number of women and children were begging in the streets. Captain Nekrasov of the 21st East Siberian Rifle Regiment, accompanied by a Chinese interpreter who spoke English and French fluently, made a tour of inspection. His heart melted at the sight of the frightened, dirty children with pale lips, and he was distressed by the abject poverty, filth and stench in which cripples and blind people lived at a nearby temple. With the aid of the interpreter, Nekrasov raised funds from Chinese officials as well as from his fellow officers, and a welfare committee was set up to distribute food among the needy. Donations were obtained from individuals, the military authorities and various organizations, the Manchuria Railway transporting the large quantities of grain free of charge.[89]

The Russians did not assume the government of Manchuria directly. They had garrisons in a number of cities and dominated key officials as their advisers. For example, General Tserpitskii was the commander of the Russian forces in Mukden; Colonel Grombchevskii was the adviser, attached to the Tartar General. "The duties of the colonel are broad and demand much tact in the continuous cooperation, and frequently opposition, of

[89]Kuropatkin reported to Nicholas II on January 21, 1901, that the Russo-Chinese Bank had distributed to poor Chinese in his name in the presence of the Russian Consul 1,200 pieces of warm clothing; another 1,000 would be distributed soon. There were 5 eating places, where 15,000 portions of boiled rice were distributed every day.

the two authorities—Russian and Chinese," Ivanov noted. "He must play the role of a buffer. . . ." The Russians assisted the Chinese officials in various ways. Thus at the request of the Tartar General of Fêng-t'ien Ivanov's detachment escorted the final payroll to the Chinese troops on the Mongolian border.

The military occupation brought economic stimulus. The Russian officers were good customers of various establishments. Quickly Mukden and other cities were rebuilt. As Ivanov paraded through the streets of Mukden on Coronation Day (May 27), 1901, he marveled at the reconstructed shopping areas, patrolled by Russian and Chinese military policemen. Crowds of small boys walked alongside the soldiers, trying hard to keep in step. Others saluted with their dirty little hands, then stretched them out with the words: *"Kapitana, davai den'gi* [Captain, give money]!"

Ivanov saw no hostility in the eyes of the spectators who watched the parade. But he reflected that the Tartar General past whom he marched, must have been thinking that the Russians deserved the appellation "foreign devils." "They truly are devils," Ivanov remarked. "There are only some 7,000 to 10,000 of them in Manchuria, while he, the Tartar General, has in Mukden alone 200,000 inhabitants, while in all of Mukden [Fêng-t'ien] Province there will be found up to 8 million descendants of the brave Manchus, and yet he, the Tartar General feels that he is unable to do anything with these allies. . . devils. . . ."

In most of Manchuria the Russians did as they pleased. Only in Ying-k'ou, where other foreigners resided, were they subject to allied pressure and criticism. While the Russian consul was appointed governor of the city there was set up a council on which foreigners and Chinese merchants were represented. The Russians still were in control but foreign protests repeatedly modified their policies.

Western views of the Russian occupation usually were unsympathetic. In a report on Russian activities in and around Ying-k'ou, Captain G. F. Napier, British Special Service officer, wrote in May, 1901:

During August and the first days of September the Russians were undoubtedly guilty of a considerable amount of needless brutality, not to call it by a stronger term. The rights of foreigners appear to have been respected, and the Chinese are now treated with comparative fairness. As none of the Russians, however, can speak the Chinese language, they are entirely in the hands of their native interpreters, who use this power to squeeze the Chinese freely, and who are probably largely to blame for the defective police arrangements of the port. Unchecked crime became so rampant here during the past winter that in January last the Consular Body addressed a joint letter to the Civil Administrator and Admiral Alexeieff on the subject. Matters subsequently improved for a time, but during the month of April there were eleven cases of burglary in the houses of British residents.

A drunken Russian soldier shot the Chinese watchman of the British Consulate through the gateway on the 10th February last, and the man is at the time of writing under trial. Armed piracy is at present rampant within 5 miles of the port, junks being boarded and robbed, and murders being committed in broad daylight.

Early in the present month the Russians sent out two expeditions against these pirates, by land and sea, but, as much time was wasted in ostentatious preparation, both expeditions returned empty-handed. There is also grave reason to believe that the Civil Administrator's interpreter is in with the gang and gives them early information. . . .

The Russians have done a certain amount of municipal work in the native town, each Chinese householder being now kept responsible that the street in front of his house is kept clean and watered. They have also appointed a Dr. Daly, a British subject, Sanitary Inspector, with an assistant, and have sanctioned the construction of a paved road through the European Settlement to the east gate of the town, at a cost of 900 taels, this and all other expenses being met by levies on the Chinese guilds. . . .

At the instance of the Russians . . . the Chinese Military Governor of Mukden deputed Magistrates to return to many of the more important towns occupied by the Russians (e.g. Tieh-Ling, Liao-Yang, Hai-cheng, and Kai-chow), and in some cases these Magistrates have been allowed to organize police; in others Russian police are still at work, while in many towns remote from the railway the Chinese officials have been in power throughout the trouble. In the case of the port of Newchwang no Chinese officials have returned, and it now appears to be the sole town in Manchuria entirely administered by the Russians. . . . The policing of Newchwang is performed partly by Chinese police, organized by the Russians, and partly by Russian military police.

The policing of the country round the town is performed by Chinese mounted militia, armed with rifles, who are maintained by the town guilds with the sanction of Russia. The ease with which the Russians have succeeded in administering the place, in spite of the faulty methods, is a striking answer to the theory which I have frequently heard expressed, that the Chinese would be a difficult people to rule by foreigners on account of their obstructive methods. Broadly speaking all defects of the Russian administration of this part (i.e., disorder due to defective police) are traceable to the fact that they are in the hands of corrupt Chinese interpreters, who are in league with the thieves.[90]

An American report by Captain James H. Reeves, Military Attaché of the United States Legation in Peking, who visited Ying-k'ou toward the end of 1901, was similar in tone:

The Russians are in full control of the town, with a Civil Administrator as chief officer. This Administrator is supposed to be exercising the function of a Chinese Taotai, till such a time as the Russians are able to turn the government over to the Chinese. They are also still holding the Imperial Custom House. The Russian custom flag is hoisted at the custom wharf and also flies on all custom launches. The Chinese Imperial Custom Staff is still doing the work. The revenues are turned over to the Russo-Chinese Bank. The Russian Administration claims that an accounting

[90]During the Russian occupation many Chinese learned to speak a form of pidgin-Russian and some of the Russians acquired a smattering of Chinese, but usually this sufficed only for the most elementary communication.

for all the funds will be made to the proper authorities when the country is turned over to the Chinese. It is safe to say that no accounting will be made unless forced by the various powers to whom the custom revenues are pledged as payment for the recent indemnity. Some improvements have been made in the condition of Newchwang, the principal being the building up of the bund and the cleaning of the Chinese city. To stop the street nuisances of the Chinese, the novel method was adopted of allowing the soldier detecting the perpetrator to assess a fine of twenty-five or fifty cents according to the gravity of the offense. In default of payment the Chinaman was put in the street gang for a certain number of days.

There is not a single Russian connected with the city administration who can speak the Chinese language. Consequently they are at the mercy of the Chinese interpreters, and these perpetrate the usual frauds. As an example, it is said that it was desired to issue a proclamation stating that all Chinamen obeying the laws would be protected and all offenders punished—but when the proclamation came from the interpreter it stated that the native Christians had been the cause of all the trouble and that they would be severely dealt with.

Considerable friction existed at Newchwang between the Consuls and settlement people on one side and the Russian Administrator on the other side. Apparently the Russian authorities desire to make themselves felt and are trying to compel the settlement people to recognize this fact, irrespective of rights granted by treaties.

The sort of friction that developed between Tim-chenko-Ostroverkhov and the settlement people is best illustrated by a letter that the Russian civil administrator wrote to the British consul:

June 28, 1901

Sir,

A few days ago I received a letter from Mr. Omel-vina of the Irish Presbyterian Mission in which he states, that a Christian Chinese named Chia Wen Hsi was unfairly charged with the . . . town revenue fees.

I requested Chia Wen Hsi to come to my office and asked him why he had not applied directly to me but complained to the Missionary. The Chinaman said that he did not think of complaining but simply went to the Missionary to borrow money to pay the tax as he had none at the time. Mr. Omelvina advised him not to pay the tax and promised to write to me re this matter. From the above it is plain, that Mr. Omelvina allowed himself to interfere in the relationship of the natives toward the Administration in a matter which has absolutely nothing to do with Christianity, and even dared to recommend disobedience to legal orders of the Authorities.

Similar conduct of Missionaries residing in China has always caused just indignation of the Chinese Government and is one of the reasons of the dissatisfaction of the population and Authorities with the native Christians, and the hatred toward Missionaries particularly and all foreigners in general for their interference with the Civil relationship of the Chinese Authorities toward their subordinate population.

Esteeming rights of the population, now under control of the Imperial Russian Civil Administration, our Government wishes first of all to establish close and sincere connexion with the natives, so as to be enabled to come to their assistance in all cases of need.

This can only be attained by direct negotiations between the population and Authorities, and the interference of mediators may only lead to misunderstandings and cause mutual distrust between the natives and Authorities. The Imperial Russian Government therefore will not bear any interference of Missionaries and foreigners in general in its dealings with the natives, especially when such interference goes against legal demands.

Informing you of this fact, I have the honour to ask you to call Mr. Omelvina's attention to his action, which is entirely against the treaty rights of the Missionaries in China, and to warn him that in case of a repetition of a similar case of his interference with the native population's business, not concerning him in the least, the Imperial Russian Government will be obliged to take most energetic steps to protect the right of the natives to apply direct to the Authorities.

Hoping that you will use your influence with your nationals to prevent similar misunderstandings in future.

> I have etc.
> sign: Ostroverkhow
> Civil Administrator

An English traveler who visited Manchuria in 1903 described the Russification of Manchuria as a myth. "The Chinaman is as untouched and as unregenerate, according to the Western standards, as he ever was before,"

B. L. Putnam Weale wrote. "The Chinaman has not cut off his pig-tail; has not changed his dress or his habit; has not been influenced either externally or internally, mentally or morally." He asserted that "the Chinese officials have as little to do with the Slav as possible—the gentry despise him—the traders bleed him—the common people learn his language along the railway, only to insult him in their own. . . ."

In appraising the Russian position in Manchuria, Captain Reeves found the Chinese Eastern or Manchurian Railway to be "the great central feature." He commented:

In her commercial expansion there seems to be an utter lack of that wisdom and foresight with which Russia is accredited in all diplomatic transactions. With that magnificent disregard for the opinion of the tax payer as to the expenditure of money, which absolute monarchies are supposed to be possessed of, she blunders on, now selecting this port as her grand outlet, now that one, developing one and after partially abandoning it selecting another and now spending enormous sums of money in dredging harbors and building docks. Finally the railway interests, probably fearing the overwhelming influence of militarism, decide to have their own city, harbor and all accessories complete. The huge empire goes cheerfully on, spending all she can collect, spending all she can borrow, apparently expecting to reap grand returns from the development of the country without exactly knowing how she is going to do so. The present policy in that country might be described as a combination of the traditional "bull in a China shop" and "the dog in the manger" policies. The industrial force for the development of the country must be the Chinese, yet every plan and every action could not more fully antagonize the Chinese if they were conceived for that very purpose.

A very different view was expressed by Senator Albert J. Beveridge, who toured Manchuria in 1901 "with as full liberty as is accorded a foreigner on a tour of observation throughout the United States." To Senator Beveridge the Russian town-building in Manchuria was "a comfort and a delight to behold."

It is more than a hundred miles into Manchuria that you encounter this striking material evidence of the Russianization of the country—a Russian town being built side by side with the decaying, germ-infected collection of hovels which compose the Chinese town. The residences of this Russian town are of wood perhaps, or stone, as taste determines. They are pleasant to look upon, too. Indeed, the homes of merchant or miner or officer, or even of moujik in Siberia are often much handsomer than those ordinarily occupied by the same class in Russia; and it would seem that this comparative superiority is to be repeated in Manchuria. Generous verandas circle the home of a railway official; cool awnings of blue, shifting with the sun, protect these porches from its rays. Young trees are planted along the new-made streets. Occasionally a block is reserved for a miniature park; and, again, there are trees fresh planted, and the color and fragrance of flowers. This, in contrast, is the order, the loveliness, the system, the cleanliness which Russia in Manchuria is building over against Chinese aggregations of corruption, disease, disorder, and all unsightliness. If the Russian is uncivilized, as it has been the fashion to declare, at least in Manchuria he is erecting precisely those very things which, in America, we look upon as the results and proofs of civilization.

Senator Beveridge was impressed by the way in which the Russians had pacified the population of Manchuria. Men who but a year ago had been "frenzied fanatics" and "demons," now were "peaceful and happy laborers, apparently not only pleased with their lot, but . . . rejoicing in it." The secret of the Russian success, Beveridge wrote, lay in their method of pacification.

What, then, is that method? It is the simple and traditional method of Russia to strike when you strike, and to spare not when you are striking. It is to wage war while war exists, and to employ the methods of peace only when war is over. . . .

And so in Manchuria, when the great Boxer uprising began . . . the smiling Russian, with his mild blue eye and his kindly bearing, became, in truth, what rumor pictures him to the Anglo-Saxon world—a man of the sword and of blood. . . . It was fire and sword and death. It was war. There were no attempts to pacify or cajole while villages were burning. While the conditions of war lasted, Russia waged war. And she waged no "milk-and-water" war; she waged a war of blood. And when she had finished, she had finished indeed, just as everywhere Russia's task has been finished when once she has concluded a border conflict.

For it is worth the attention of all men that when Russia has once inflicted her punishment there has seldom been any recurrence of insurrection. Where Russian law and order and system have been established they have remained, upheld not by the bayonets of the soldiers who established them, but by the hands of the very people among whom and against whose resistance they were planted.

The flight of Chinese officials left the bandit-threatened populace no choice but to turn to the Russians for protection. They did not resent the quartering of Russian officers in Chinese homes as much as might have been expected, for it kept Chinese marauders at bay. Russians refrained from administering the occupied places themselves. They even used Chinese troops, under the supervision of Russian officers, to restore peace in the countryside. The Russian high command sought to insure the good conduct of the Russian forces in China. As Kuropatkin ordered General Grodekov and Admiral Alekseev in September 1900: "See to it that the troops do not coerce the population in any way. With the last shot of battle the life of the natives, their honor, property and customs must become inviolate for our troops."

In a top secret letter to Foreign Minister Lamsdorff, in October 1900, Kuropatkin agreed to the restoration of the Tartar General of Mukden to his old position, as requested by Engineer Girshman, even though he had been Russia's chief opponent. Only a "native" administration could put an effective end to the anarchy that prevailed.

The Russians knew that the other powers resented their influence, but attributed this to jealousy. They

246

were proud of their civilizing mission. Their self-satisfaction was bolstered by the Chinese, who honored them for the pacification of Manchuria. On May 6, 1901, the Tartar General of Fêng-t'ien, in the name of the Manchu Emperor, bestowed 42 decorations on the Russians. Among those decorated with the highest orders were Vice Admiral Alekseev, Lieutenant General Subotich, Lieutenant General Tserpitskii, and Major General Fleisher. "No doubt the Chinese government was forced by circumstances to bestow decorations on Russian generals, officers and officials who in one way or another had participated in the crushing of the rebellious Boxer movement," Ivanov commented, "But *'faisant bonne mine au mauvais jeu,'* it evidently wished to single out those Russian figures in Manchuria who had distinguished themselves by fairness and lack of prejudice against the Chinese."

When the Russians first arrived in Manchuria, they noticed only the stench of the Chinese cities and the primitiveness of Chinese industries. Gradually they comprehended also the high productivity of Chinese agriculture and the artistry of Chinese architecture. The feelings of many Russians changed from disdain to respect. What Europeans held most against the Chinese was their cowardice, but as P. Vetlitsin wrote toward the end of his experience in Manchuria:

The modern military European slights the Chinese as cowards who cannot even defend their native land. They are, of course, guilty of this. But how else could he be? For thousands of years the Chinese was taught respect for productive labor, for quiet country life and all its best manifestations; they have re-educated

247

also the Manchus converting them from a militant tribe to an agricultural one; for thousands of years too there was being created a unique cult, in which there is no place for war. Can one then regard the Chinese with contempt?

Everywhere Chinese and Russian officials exchanged visits. Thus the governor of Hsin-min-t'ing entertained Colonel Aurenius, the commander of the 3rd East Siberian Rifle Regiment and chief of one of the occupation districts, and Captain Fedorov, the chief of police of the city. The Russians enjoyed the quaintness of the affair—the Chinese bowls and chopsticks—but not the food. "Many Chinese dishes could have been sufficiently palatable even for our European taste," observed Ivanov who attended the repast, "if the cook had not flavored them with sugar instead of with salt." Nor did the Russians care for the aromatic Chinese tea, served with bad American granulated sugar.

Inevitably the question of war guilt cropped up during conversations. One day General Hsü, who had fought against the Russians at Newchwang, Sha-ho and Liaoyang, passed through Hsin-min-t'ing. He had been arrested by a Chinese officer and was being taken to Peking for punishment.[91] Eager to talk to him, Aurenius invited him to the dinner which he was giving for the governor of the city. Hsü spoke freely through his interpreter "Misha," who had a good command of the Russian language. Alluding to the fact that the Manchu government, while publicly instructing the civilian officials to live peacefully with the foreigners, secretly

---

[91]Hsü was exiled to Irkutsk, where he became an alcoholic and eventually shot himself.

ordered the military commanders to support the Boxers, Hsü stated: "The Russians too have colonels and generals . . . . If they fight, it is not their fault. They are sent. . . ."

When one of the officers complimented Hsü that his troops had fought well, the general covered his face and uttered: "I am ashamed for my officers and men." He added: "What could I do? When the first grenades fly past, the generals run away. When the Russians begin to fire their rifles, the officers run away. And when finally the Russians begin to draw near, the soldiers run away."

Dressed in a blue silk robe with a fur lining, the tall, stately young general, with his energetic, open countenance aroused the sympathy of the Russians. Ivanov in particular felt drawn to him. Suddenly he was filled with goodwill toward the Chinese whom he had always regarded as inferior. "Some instinctive prejudice had repelled me from these people, clad in feminine jackets and skirts, with their queues and shaven faces, which made men look like women, he recalled. "And it had been not only the outward appearance that had repelled: the Chinese people are most strange to us in spirit and blood. . . ." Now that he sat and fraternized with his recent enemies, a poem came to his mind:

Koli sporit',	If you quarrel,
tak uzh smelo,	do so bravely;
Kol' kaznit',	If you execute,
tak uzh za delo,	get down to business;
Kol' prostit',	If you forgive,
tak vsei dushoi,	do so with the whole soul;

Koli pir,	If you have a feast,
tak pir goroi!	have a mountain of a feast!

There were many other instances during the occupation of Manchuria when the gulf between conqueror and conquered was bridged as the passion of war gave way to the compassion of peace. More slowly cooled the ardor of those who had stayed behind in Russia and had not experienced the emotional release of battle. Their lingering chauvinism was given voice by the Senior Scribe of the General Staff in St. Petersburg. Flushed with victory, he addressed a general letter to the Russian soldiers in the Far East:

> Greetings dear comrades! Russian knights—soldiers of our dear fatherland! . . .
>
> As I congratulate you on the new year and the new glory, I must convey to you also the deep gratitude of all those who here, in the native land, followed your victories and treasured your bravery.
>
> Honor and glory be unto you for those audacious feats which you accomplished in China.
>
> Like eagles you flew from one place to another, everywhere defeating the Chinese horde. . . .
>
> You sure gave it to the Chinese. . . .[92]
>
> What will the foreigners . . . say now?
>
> Fate brought all nations together in China for a bloody feast and here it was found that the Russian soldier was stronger and fiercer than any other, and Russia now constitutes for all nations a dreadful giant. . . .

[92]"*Nu, i zadali-zhe vy pertsu etoi kitaishchine,*" as it is phrased colorfully in Russian.

May God let you complete your service satisfactorily, to carry out faithfully and honorably your oath and duty before God, Tsar and fatherland, to return home healthy and unharmed to your dear parents, wives, brothers, and sisters, and to labor again in peace for the good of your native home and fatherland.

Hurrah! Hurrah! Hurrah!

Epilogue

EVERY MILITARY OCCUPATION lasts too long. The Russian occupation of Manchuria was no exception. Peace between the allied powers and China was officially concluded in September of 1901, with the signature of the Peking Protocol. But though she withdrew her forces from China proper, Russia failed to evacuate Manchuria completely. Civilian statesmen were willing to abide by the pledge, given repeatedly to the world, that Russia had no territorial designs on Manchuria and would withdraw as soon as order was restored. But the military demurred. They reported on September of 1901 the revival of various political sects and secret societies, which like the Boxers the year before, spread anti-foreign and anti-Christian propaganda. Although Russia had not invaded Manchuria with plans for its retention,[93] once she was in Manchuria, she found it increasingly difficult to pull out. Inexorably pressures and events pushed her in deeper and deeper until she became involved in another war that was to undermine the very

[93]In response to a query from General Grodekov, Kuropatkin had received imperial permission on August 24, 1900 to reiterate that Nicholas II had decided "with a view to re-establishing friendly, neighborly relations with China as soon as possible . . . not to annex any part of China to the Russian possessions." Nicholas wanted the disturbances quelled and communication by rail and river secured, but once this was done the occupation forces were to be withdrawn.

foundations of the Russian state and topple the Romanov Dynasty.

While Russian interest and involvement in Manchuria antedated the Boxer uprising, the Russo-Chinese War turned Russia's investment into one of blood as well as of money.[94] Her efforts to protect this investment—"so that these men will not have died in vain"—brought her into conflict with the other powers. As Russia sought to insure her dominance in Manchuria by presenting China with a series of "conditions" for her withdrawal,[95] the other powers protested. But foreign objections merely hardened the Russian outlook, the Russians insisting as a matter of "principle," that their negotiations with China were of no concern to anyone else. Western and Japanese suspicion of Russia increased Russian suspicion of the West and Japan, and played into the hands of the Russian military who opposed withdrawal from Manchuria.

The view of Vice Admiral Alekseev was typical. In a top secret letter to the Minister of War, dated March 16, 1901, he urged that the occupation of Manchuria be continued indefinitely, without a fixed time limit, until the region was truly pacified. He brushed aside foreign protests:

As regards the international significance of the

[94]Russian casualties for the entire campaign in Manchuria and Pechihli consisted of 22 officers and 220 men killed and 60 officers and 1,223 men wounded. This does not include losses incurred after October 14, 1900, in the pacification of the occupied regions.

[95]The text of the various conditions and agreements may be found in G. A. Lensen (ed.), *Korea and Manchuria between Russia and Japan 1895-1904. The Observations of Sir Ernest Satow, British Minister Plenipotentiary to Japan (1895-1900) and China (1900-1906)*, Tallahassee: The Diplomatic Press, 1966.

occupation, the protest of the powers against our intention to retain Manchuria can be regarded as [a protest against] a fact, long ago foreseen by them. In recognizing our agreement with China concerning the construction of the Manchurian Railway, they recognized our right to defend this [rail]way with the means most suitable for it. The actual manner of defense, i.e. the replacement of the guard by troops, is an internal matter, a military-technical [matter] so to speak, which cannot arouse serious objections. Considering the position taken by us in Manchuria on the strength of extraordinary circumstances, one must keep in mind, that the occupation of Egypt and Bosnia, instituted allegedly in the interests of order and peace, had in its time called forth strong protests from all sides, including our own; but these protests had gradually lost all significance in the face of the firm determination of England and Austro-Hungary not to recall their troops.

The only serious objections against our military occupation can be presented by Japan, who has large commercial interests in Manchuria and, perhaps, will take advantage of this convenient pretext to attain her objectives in regards to Korea. In view of this, we ought to forestall the possibility of active measures on the part of Japan, enter into an agreement with her on the basis of the Korean question, and obtain for ourselves full freedom of action in Manchuria, even [if this has to be done] by means of concessions and temporary compromises.

Western views of Russian intentions and accomplishments in Manchuria differed widely. Many had mistrusted Russia from the very beginning. As early as May 30, 1900 *The New York Times* had written: "It would perhaps be ascribing too much Machiavelism even to Russian diplomacy to suggest that the uprising of the 'Boxers' are stimulated from St. Petersburg. But yet it is certain that nothing could suit Russia better in the present juncture than just such risings, which make all foreigners in China apprehensive for their safety." *The Japan Weekly Mail,* a British-owned, Japanese subsidized newspaper, voiced the same feeling more moderately (July 28, 1900): "Disorder and violent unrest in Manchuria at present can only inure to Russia's ultimate advantage." Western merchants regarded the Russian attack on Ying-k'ou "an outrage . . . from start to finish," and an American businessman, labeling Russian methods as "varied, devious and uncertain," declared that there was "a total absence of faith in anything Russian." "The Siberian army is composed—as admitted by the Russians themselves—of the dregs of her population," Mr. H. J. Bush wrote from Newchwang in a letter to the London *Times.* "Discipline is an unknown quantity, the very passes issued by the civil and military authorities are unintelligible to the bulk of the rank and file. . . . Is there any hope of order being restored to a country through the means of such rabble?"

The American Minister to China, Edwin H. Conger, never believed that Russia would evacuate Manchuria. As he wrote to Secretary of State John Hay from Peking on September 13, 1900:

I do not believe that all the Russian troops will be withdrawn. If they are, I apprehend it means that she will plant herself at Shan-hai-kwan, Newchwang and places in Manchuria and easily finding that the actions of the other powers are "obstacles" in the way of her withdrawing, say to China: When you pay, we will withdraw, otherwise we hold everything north of the great wall. If China does agree, Russia's settlement is made. If China does not agree, it is made all the same, and it will neither be necessary for her to join in the military occupation of Peking or to take part in a general conference.

Less hostile views were expressed by other observers.

Never was a great nation taken more by surprise than were the Russians last summer by the outbreak of hostilities in Manchuria [wrote Professor George Frederick Wright from personal observation]. It is difficult to realize the suddenness with which this storm burst upon the Russians. To meet it there was no preparation. The engineers with their families were not adequately guarded, and the vast property of the railroad was everywhere exposed. To the extent of their ability, the Chinese destroyed this property, and it was only by the most hasty flight that any of the foreigners escaped. These facts ought definitely to dispel the impression that has prevailed in many quarters that the war in China was fomented by the Russians in anticipation of the great advantages which they were going to reap from it.

An English consul testified that the construction of the Manchurian railway had benefited Manchuria. "In the space of eighteen months a Chinese hamlet has been transformed into a fair-sized Siberian town," he wrote about Harbin. "Thousands of Chinese coolies have flocked to the spot, workshops and wharves have been erected along the shore, shops and streets, lighted by electric light, have been built, while a church, a park, a bank, and numerous other spacious red brick offices and houses attest the presence of civilization." Another observer noted in the fall of 1903: "Russia has spent, in Manchuria, at least sixty millions sterling, and this enormous expense, we must avow, has profited that country much more than Russia—at least, so far."

That the acquisition of Manchuria would be tempting for Russia was well understood by the English, who had amassed a world empire:

> For when one considers the position of a rich and fertile country like Manchuria, with its mines and forests almost untouched, and a climate eminently suited for Europeans, dividing Russia from two of her most valued possessions, and these from each other, and containing the railway system that connects them together, and when in addition one reflects that the acquisition of this country, while firmly consolidating the eastern Empire of Russia, and rendering her the dominant influence over China, is in itself an easy task and in itself justifiable by the gains of civilization that would accrue to 20,000,000 people, one cannot but feel that even a nation without the "terrae saera fames" would be impelled to profit by such a golden opportunity.

That the annexation of Manchuria might prove necessary from a Russian point of view regardless of original plans, also was understood by the English.

It is not impossible [Charles Hardinge wrote in 1900] . . . that Manchuria may eventually prove as difficult to the Russians to abandon as Egypt has proven to us, and that it may be found impracticable to withdraw the Russian Military Administration now established in that province and to again expose the important and valuable Russian interests concentrated in their railway to the risk of further destruction at the hands of savage hordes which the Chinese authorities may be unable or unwilling to control.

To Professor Wright the prospects of the annexation of Manchuria by Russia were not alarming. "Even if she should be compelled to retain Manchuria," he commented, "it need not seriously affect the other interests in China. Manchuria is a country by itself, with vast undeveloped resources, forming a natural connection between Siberia and the open waters of the Pacific." Senator Beveridge wrote in 1903 that "it may be accepted as a settled fact that Russia has already acquired Manchuria, if she concludes to remain there, although it is still nominally Chinese, and not Russian, and its governors are still appointed by the Chinese Emperor." But he was favorably impressed by the application of Russian law, order and system in Manchuria. "An achievement so vast, so quietly accomplished, so cheaply secured, so easily consummated, so important in itself, and so beyond calculation in its influence upon the rest of the world, compels the admiration of every thinking mind, no matter whether you regret or whether you applaud while you admire."

There were those who thought less highly of the Russian occupation, yet dismissed it with a "serves-the-Chinese-right" gesture. Equating the Manchus with the Mongols, an article in *Current Literature* stated: "There is a certain political justice in the occupation of this borderland of China by Russia. For the ancestors of these Manchurians for centuries devastated all Russia, burning Moscow and carrying away captive numberless Russian women. So now the Slavic hour of vengeance seems to have come."

Western newspapers were full of accounts of Russian atrocities in China. Some were false, others were true. But Russian behavior did not differ markedly from that of the allied forces in general. "A horrible lust of cruelty developed amongst the private soldiery of all nationalities, and pervaded them like some subtle miasma emanating from this evil-smelling land," wrote eyewitness George Lynch. E. J. Dillon elaborated:

> During the war that was waged, but not formally declared [between the foreign powers and China], no quarter was given to Chinese regular soldiers; in battles and skirmishes no prisoners were taken, and after easily-gained victories wounded enemies, instead of being cared for, were put to death like venomous reptiles; nay, thousands of defenseless and well-meaning Chinamen were slaughtered in cold blood, and not always, it is said, with the swiftness or the minimum of physical pain with which the man of average humanity would snuff out the life of a wild beast. In Tungtschao and Pekin Chinese girls and women of all ages were raped first and bayonetted afterwards by men whose governments were wrapping themselves up in the soft wool of Mary's little lamb. . . .[96]

[96]Prophetically Dillon warned: "The policy of the Powers is a sowing of the wind, and the harvest reaped will surely be the whirlwind. . . ."

Missionary reports from Manchuria showed that the Russians protected native converts and allowed that "mission work should be carried on to the extent of instructing the Christians" even though they "discountenanced proselytising, at least in the meantime." "The Christians found the cross a useful badge of Christianity, had placed them in their houses and found them effective in preventing the Russians from looting," a missionary observed, adding: "It soon became apparent that while it saved them from Russian extortion it brought down upon them afterwards the enmity of their neighbours."

Whatever may be said of the five hundred Cossacks who drove three or four thousand Chinese into the river at Blagovestchensk [Senator Beveridge wrote], the other side must be added, that everywhere throughout Manchuria the Russian railway laborers, officers and troops guarding them, retired in good order protecting and bringing with them, at their own imminent peril, considerable numbers of Chinese converts whom the Russians refused to abandon to the mercy of the military mobs of their fellow-countrymen.

Russians were convinced that their troops acted better than the allies. "The Germans and the English took vengeance on the Chinese for their boorishness. They executed Chinese generals and the mandarin councillors of the Emperor, destroyed the Imperial Palace, broke into the shops of merchants, killed defenseless people and took away their goods and property," Petr Krasnov wrote. "But could Russians do such a thing?!" he asked rhetorically. "Revenge is not a Christian feeling. Christ taught us to forgive those that had trespassed against us."

Condescendingly Krasnov asserted that the Tsar "was sorry for China as one is sorry for a younger brother who has been exceedingly naughty and has done some stupid things." In his "infinite mercy" Nicholas II had forgiven the "cowardly" Emperor of China and his people, "because God had deprived them of reason and 'they knew not what they were doing'!"

When the Boxer upheaval had shaken China, the dispatch of large Russian relief forces had been welcomed by most Westerners. Allied unity in the face of common disaster was brief, however. No sooner had the backbone of the uprising been broken, than international rivalry reasserted itself. Foreign Minister Mikhail Murav'ev had stated in a memorandum in June of 1900 that Russia's position vis-à-vis China was "far from identical with the position of the other powers." The Tsar had seconded this view in a marginal comment, expressing his "deep conviction that the aims of Russia in the East diverge completely from the policy of the European states." The Russians decided to withdraw from the Chinese capital as soon as possible, leaving the onus of pacification in China proper primarily on French, English and German shoulders. They hoped thereby to hasten the restoration of friendly relations between Russia and China, a *sine qua non* for the successful completion and operation of the Manchurian railway and an important element in the security of the Russian frontier. They also wanted to lessen Chinese resistance to Russian demands in Manchuria.

To the British Minister in Peking, Sir Claude MacDonald, Russian evacuation seemed "likely to bring about general chaos, resulting in partition of territory." The German Emperor William II branded the Russian attitude as *"falsch Jalgenholz."* He remarked:

> I don't take it tragically, as I never expected anything
> else from them. Manchuria and their beloved railway
> once *ad saccum*, everything else in China is of abso-
> lutely no interest to them any more. Only in so far
> that is, as they can put the greatest obstacles in the
> way of our eventual success, while they themselves, de-
> spite laying waste and burning and plunder and mur-
> der, as well as "museum-stocking," seek to pose, at
> the expense of the other Europeans, as "friends" of
> the Chinese.

The Manchurian question was not a local issue. It
became entangled in international strategy. "Viewed impartially, Russia cannot be criticized from her stand-point
for her Manchurian policy. Her interests are far beyond
those of any country, excepting Japan," John Barrett
wrote in *Harper's Weekly*. But impartiality is not a
trait of power politics. A look at some of the views about
Russian policy and character reveals as much about the
persons who expressed them as about the Russians, and
shows the extent of mistrust for each other among the
peoples of the world.

When the Russians pressured the Chinese into signing
a secret agreement which granted to Russia various rights
in Manchuria in return for Russia's commitment to
evacuate the region, the United States protested the
terms of the Manchurian agreement to both Peking and
St. Petersburg. "An agreement in which China cedes
to any corporation or company the exclusive right and
privilege of opening mines, establishing railroads, or
in any other way industrially developing Manchuria,

can but be viewed with the gravest concern by the Government of the United States. It constitutes a monopoly, which is a distinct breach of the stipulations of treaties concluded between China and foreign Powers, and thereby seriously affects the rights of American citizens. . . ." The United States feared that other nations would react with similar demands and inevitably wreck the Open Door policy to which Russia had promised to adhere. "It is for these reasons that the Government of the United States, animated now, as in the past, with the sincerest desire of insuring to the whole world the benefits of full and fair intercourse between China and the nations on a footing of equal rights and advantages to all, submits the above to the earnest consideration of the Imperial Governments of China and Russia, confident that they will give due weight to its importance, and adopt such measures as will relieve the just and natural anxiety of the United States."

The American consul in Newchwang had no faith in Russian promises. "Whatever paper agreements Russia may make," he wrote, "I am convinced that she has a deep-seated determination to hold onto Manchuria and by every means in her power, she intends to make Manchuria thoroughly Russian." Though he was sure that "nothing but actual war will ever alter the situation," he warned that "if the political domination of Manchuria falls into the hands of Russia, American interests will be short-lived, and Russia will build here a colony so strong that in a few years the remainder of China will be at her mercy."

President Theodore Roosevelt in a conversation with the German Ambassador to the United States labeled the Russian Ambassador Count Cassini an unabashed liar.

"I can only subscribe to this," Prince Bernhard von Bülow, the German Imperial Chancellor, scribbled on the margin of the dispatch from Baron Hermann Speck von Sternburg. The President had complained that Cassini had given one explanation of Russian policy to the State Department, another one immediately thereafter to the press, and yet another in Paris. "This still surprises Roosevelt!" von Bülow noted. "The Russians act like this always." When he read that the Russians had given the American Government a written guarantee that they would put no obstacles in the way of American wishes, von Bülow remarked *"die pfeifen drauf* [they don't give a hoot],"* and observed that American wishes would never be carried out.

Count Cassini, on the other hand, repeatedly complained to his German colleague, "how difficult it was to discuss questions concerning the Far East with Mr. Hay [the American Secretary of State], as the latter had been so inadequately oriented about them." He was frustrated, furthermore, by the increasingly anti-Russian agitation of the American press, the Republican *Record Herald* by 1903 branding Russian diplomacy as stupid lies. In part American hostility against Russia had been worked up by English, Japanese and German influence. The German Ambassador reported to his government, for example, that in compliance with his instructions, he had "inconspicuously" placed articles about Russian policy in Manchuria in the *New York Times, New York Tribune* and *Washington Times* and that he had succeeded also in his repeated talks with Under Secretary Hill and Secretary of War Root to turn the conversation "inconspicuously" to Russian policy and underline the contradiction between Russian civilian and military administration in Manchuria and Russian professions and the consequences that Russian annexation of Manchuria would entail. In part American hostility to Russia was aroused by the Tsarist Government's persecution of the Jews and by the violent outcry of American Jews (many from Russia) that followed. Count Cassini took the sharp attacks against his country and his own person so much to heart that he fell ill. When he called on the Secretary of State at home to protest the abuse that had been heaped upon his head at a Jewish rally, Hay replied that there was nothing that could be done about it, for the Jews because of their number and wealth were an important political factor in the United States. Cassini's exasperated remark—"It seems to me that I am accredited to Jerusalem and not to Washington"—did not endear him with the administration.

The British were not impressed by the American stance. Walter Townley, the British Chargé d'Affaires in Peking, likened the American Minister Edwin H. Conger to "the American eagle in the *Punch* cartoon, who was ready to flap his wings for all he was worth if the lion and the bear would do the fighting." At the same time the British mistrusted the Russians. King Edward VII talked to Sir Ernest Satow, the British Minister to China, about Russian "duplicity" in China. "Of course we had known all along that they would not evacuate, but why did they promise to do so?" Commenting on the concessions that Russia had obtained from China in the Manchurian agreement, the *Pall Mall Gazette* asserted that "now, as ever, the loving embrace of the Bear is apt to stifle those on whom it is bestowed." But the newspaper deemed it futile "to kick and hammer at a closed door the opening of which is of no vital importance to British interests." "That Russian influence must be paramount in Northern China is a proposition which no one in his senses can dispute," the *Pall Mall Gazette* observed and recommended: "What we have to do is to look to it that neither Russia nor anybody else— especially anybody else—interferes with our sphere of influence, the Yangtsze Valley." The English lion was no more eager for direct involvement than the American eagle. When the Japanese proposed to the British a *démarche* to warn China against the signing of a separate agreement with Russia, the British government went along primarily for fear that otherwise "the Cabinet in Tokyo would undoubtedly be driven into the arms of Russia forever."

The Germans, who told the Russians that they had not the slightest interest in the future of Manchuria yet warned the United States about the perils of Russian occupation, feared that every proposal of the English government was a "trap" designed to set them at odds with Russia. As Count von Bülow scribbled on a telegram from the German Ambassador in London: "I deem it necessary to point out to [Freiherr H. von] Eckardstein [First Secretary of the German Embassy in London], that he does not have to crawl into a mousehole before every English threat. We shall not fall for such clumsy attempts to be pushed against Russia without any guarantee or concession by England. Neither in China or anywhere else do we find ourselves in a critical position, and England is by no means *carte forcée* for us— at least not so long as we do not commit the foolishness of definitely becoming enemies with Russia, without receiving in turn sufficient equivalents." At first the Germans thought of siding with Russia against the British in China, then tried to persuade England to oppose Russian annexation of Manchuria. They sought to prevent an agreement between Russia and Japan, yet wanted to alienate neither. The attitude of the Kaiser is revealed in a number of marginal comments which he made on two memoranda of his Foreign Secretary, Baron Oswald von Richthofen.

Richthofen reported to the Secretary of State that Count Osten-Saken, the Russian Ambassador to Berlin, had informed him in April of 1901 that the Russo-Chinese agreement, which was to regulate the restitution of Manchuria, had been negotiated solely to give proof of Russia's friendly disposition toward China, and that false stories that had been spread about it had greatly embarrassed the Russian government. As a result it would no longer insist on the signing of the agreement and would calmly let events take their course. The Russian Minister stated that it was the view in St. Petersburg that Germany had warned China against signing the agreement as a favor to the British government. He reiterated that Russia would evacuate Manchuria as soon as local conditions and particularly the security of the railway permitted. Next to the assertion that false stories had been spread about Russia, William II scribbled "Oh you innocent angel you!" As to Russia's intention to let events take their course, he commented: "i.e. Manchuria will be retained simply without a treaty and will not be restituted." He dismissed as "nonsense" the idea that the German warning had been designed to please the British. The Russian promise to evacuate he questioned with the words "or keep"; regarding the time when conditions would permit evacuation, he remarked: "this will hardly be the case in the next 20 years." At the end of von Richthofen's memorandum the Kaiser added:

> The Chinese have simply refused [to sign]! [They have] divulged the terms of the agreement to the other Europeans, and now the *ursus asiaticus*[97] cannot get the pot of honey amicably! He is angry that his finely spun little plan has become known, and we must of course bear the blame! Because he will now simply "rob" the honey, an appearance he would have rather avoided. Furthermore, it all costs money.

In the second memorandum Richthofen reported that Count Hatzfeldt, the German Ambassador, had telegraphed from London that the Russians (who had accused the Germans of warning China against them to please England) had informed the British that they had foregone further negotiations in Manchuria as a concession to them and that they wished to work "hand in hand" with them on other outstanding questions. "Aha!" William exclaimed on the margin and wrote "right" when Richthofen pointed out that the Russian communication to England was much friendlier than that to Germany. To explain the difference in attitude, Richthofen included another secret telegram in which Hatzfeldt wired on April 6, 1901:

> The fear of an agreement between England and Germany in the Chinese indemnity question, which could lead to an understanding in other questions as well, appears to have induced the Russo-French diplomacy here in the last few days to intrigue especially hard

[97]Asian bear.

and to sow the seeds of mistrust against the intentions of the imperial [German] government. The main role in these intrigues seems to have been assumed this time by the French Ambassador Cambon.

In which direction these intrigues have moved among other things can be seen from the following: I am assured in *strictest* confidence, that Mr. Arthur Balfour in a conversation with the head of one of the top local financial houses, which has wide contacts with the continent, asked whether he believed it possible that His Majesty the Kaiser had quite suddenly taken a position completely on the side of Russia and against England.

Irate, William II put "Hallunke! [Rascal!]" next to the name of the French Ambassador. He reacted to the suggestion that he had aligned himself completely with the Russians with the oath, "Hell and Damnation! To think that I would do such a thing!" At the bottom of the telegram he scribbled: "I do not understand these Britons! Such lack of character is absolutely shocking. These people are incorrigible!"[98]

The Kaiser did not see the log in his own eye. While decrying British unscrupulousness, William II sought to promote war between Russia and Japan, partly to weaken Russia vis-à-vis Germany in Europe, partly to drive Russia into German arms as an ally against Britain. When the German Ambassador in London, Count Paul Wolff Metternich, reported in August of 1903, that the

[98]It is difficult to render in English the full flavor of the Kaiser's scribbled remarks. He wrote: *"Hölle und Teufel! mir solches zuzutrauen!"* and then: *"Ich begreife die Briten nicht! Eine solche Charakterlosigkeit ist ja geradezu ungeheuerlich. Diese Leute sind ja unverbesserlich!"*

English and French governments each have sufficient grounds to wish that no war break out in the Far East, the German Chancellor von Bülow jotted on the margin: "So much better if it breaks out. Then they will have to show their colors." Next to Wolff Metternich's observation, that a war would confront England and France "with the unpleasant alternative of either giving their allies the cold shoulder or, if they intervened, to kill the young Anglo-French entente," von Bülow noted: "That is the main thing."

The conclusion of a secret agreement between Russia and China aroused popular indignation in Japan. "This Russo-Chinese entente, which would thus put all of North China under Russian domination seems to jeopardize the maintenance of peace in the Far East," Baron Albert d'Anethan, the Belgian Minister to Japan, reported in January of 1901. Two months later he wrote: "In the military world the idea is now expressed loudly and publicly that the present time would be most favorable for making war, and that one must not wait until Russia has built the formidable fleet which she will have in a few years." In May d'Anethan stated that the Japanese people were "firmly in favor of an aggressive policy against Russia." Japanese newspapers felt that assurances that Russia had no territorial designs on Manchuria could not be taken seriously, and viewed repeated Russian declarations merely as a sign of bad conscience.

In March of 1901, Japan approached Germany and England to join with her in "encouraging" Russia to withdraw the draft agreement—the sort of a tripartite intervention that Russia had led half a decade earlier to thwart Japanese ambitions in Manchuria. When

Russia modified her agreement with China, it still proved "most dangerous both on account of its contents and being negotiated behind the back of the powers" from the Japanese point of view, and the Japanese Ambassador in London requested renewed joint pressure for further modification.

In Japan more and more voices demanded war. In June of 1903, a memorial drawn up by seven professors of Tokyo University was published in the newspaper *Jiji*:

> If the Russian diplomats with smooth words want to talk us into proposals which mean only a temporary dropping rather than a solution of the question—such as for example the proposal to exchange Manchurian and Korean interests—we would be stupid, if we let ourselves be trapped [the professors stated]. No, we must understand clearly, that we can be satisfied only with an unconditional return of Manchuria. We must take the question by its root and must show that we are determined, if necessary, to wage war to attain a solution in the sense of our demands.

Meanwhile the Chinese played a double game of their own. They "leaked" facts and falsehoods about the Russian demands in the time-honored effort to set the foreign powers against each other. Forced to negotiate with the Russians and afraid to ally themselves either with Russia or Japan, they secretly appealed to the governments of Great Britain and Germany to bring pressure on Russia to modify her demands and to mediate in the event that Russia resorted to force. But attempts of the Chinese government to disassociate itself from the agreement were unsuccessful. In the words of the German Minister in Peking: "It is self-evident, that the central government was informed of the content of the agreement and gave its approval. It is typically Chinese, however, that in order to save 'face,' the document which seals the establishment of a Russian protectorate over Manchuria is passed off as the result of an agreement between Russian and Chinese local authorities."

Russia rejected all foreign queries on the ground that it would not be compatible with the character of an independent state, when negotiating with another, to communicate to a third party the details of such negotiation. She confined herself to saying that the agreement would in no way infringe on the rights of any third power. Russia felt that the occupation was the result of Chinese aggression and that she could, if she so desired, lay claim to all of Manchuria by right of conquest. That she did not do so and signed an agreement which "regulated" her withdrawal was proof, she contended, of her moderation and goodwill. "There is no doubt that hardly any other state, if it had found itself in the same position as Russia, would have followed such an unselfish policy in China," a Russian newspaper asserted. "Even the eastern population and the military had been convinced that the right bank of the Amur, which was conquered with Russian blood, would henceforth remain Russian."

In 1860 Russia had obtained territory from China after she had promised to induce the English and French forces to withdraw. Her right to build the railway across Manchuria and the Port Arthur lease also had been obtained ostensibly in appreciation for assistance, this time against Japan. In 1900-1901 Russia sought to gain concessions from China in Manchuria by softening Western demands at Peking. To Westerners Russian policy was sheer duplicity. But the Russians, who had not participated in the Opium Wars and had watched the British, French and Japanese also annex portions of the Manchu empire, sincerely believed in their friendship for China. The remarks of von Hedenstrom, the Russian consul in Hakodate, were typical: "The characteristic difference between the conduct of all nations vis-à-vis China and Russia's way of dealing with this state is that the others, particularly Germany, England and Japan, have acted either openly hostile or brusquely and rudely, Russia on the other hand, always friendly."

The Russians regarded the English as no less deceitful than the English regarded them. They resented not only the charges of perfidy that had been levied against them in connection with the Manchurian agreement, but the lack of gratitude that Great Britain had shown them for their sacrifices in China. As Prince Esper Ukhtomskii complained about England:

Our hard, thankless work for Europe, this great mistress of lying and pretending under the mask of Christianity or of enlightened radicalism (depending on which is more advantageous to don in a given case!!) is still capable of accepting as due tribute. But as soon as the moment of payment comes, Schiller's classic dictum resounds from the stage:

> *Der Mohr hat seine Pflicht gethan—*
> *Der Mohr kann gehn.*[99]

[99]The Moor has done his duty—
The Moor may go.

The Russian government had been sincere in its original promise to withdraw from Manchuria. The first stage of the evacuation was duly effected. But by November of 1902, orders and counterorders brought the withdrawal to a halt. In reporting what Russian units had departed, the German military attaché noted that where the Russians remained, they were housed in temporary quarters and that even the barracks and block houses along the railway appeared to be strictly defensive in nature. The officers did not seem to be making preparations for a prolonged stay. In Mukden there was much talk about evacuation in spring and many complained that they did not know whether to make provisions for the winter or not. Yet, as Count Montgelas concluded, all this meant nothing, for the officers, even the highest generals, did not know themselves whether evacuation would or would not take place.

It was not a matter of "security." The Russian government itself was undecided. Opinions changed. For example, Foreign Minister Count Vladimir Lamsdorff, who had argued against the annexation of Manchuria for fear of international complications, found that economic and strategic reasons weighed increasingly against withdrawal. About two thirds of the Chinese Eastern Railway had been destroyed. Could the Chinese be trusted to protect Russian interests in Manchuria, considering the fact that all their previous assurances to this effect had been exploded by the Boxer uprising? The severity of the upheaval and the persistence of unrest as well as the mounting displacement of Russian workers in such places as Harbin by Chinese nationals revived the specter of the Yellow Peril. Some Russians argued that Manchuria should be retained as a buffer against the yellow race; others countered that the acquisition of Manchuria would actually provide a funnel for the inflow of Orientals, though this could be countered by sending in Russian settlers. In July of 1903, the German Ambassador in St. Petersburg reported that "complete perplexity" reigned in the Russian capital concerning the policy to be pursued in Manchuria. "The costs which Russia has had to bear in Manchuria have been so enormous, that they cannot be met forever."

To most Englishmen and Americans Russia was "wrong" in denying equal commercial opportunity in Manchuria to other nationals. To the Russians, on the other hand, this was "right," for Russia could not compete with American and English capital in a free market. By 1900, the United States had already "pretty largely a monopoly of the Manchurian trade." In the words of Professor Wright, who toured Manchuria at the time:

According to the last report of the British consul at Newchwang, two-thirds of the imports into China the year before the war were from America. . . . The Russians themselves were also among the best patrons of American trade, a large part of the material for the construction of the railroad being purchased in America. We rode out of Port Arthur on a train drawn by a Philadelphia locomotive, over rails made in Baltimore, which were laid on ties that came from Oregon. In Harbin almost all the vast stores of railroad material had been imported from America. We counted the names of no less than twelve American firms who had contributed to this stock. This trade is not likely to be affected soon by any regulations which may ensue from Russian control; for she is not yet prepared to supply the new demands which will be created.

Western diplomats in St. Petersburg realized that the contradictions underlying Russian policy and pronouncements were not necessarily intentional.

The most probable explanation in my opinion and I believe also in those of my Japanese and American colleagues [wrote the British Ambassador Sir Charles Scott], is to be found first in the fact that Count Lamsdorff's policy, as approved by the Emperor, in regard to the final evacuation of Manchuria in strict accordance with the terms of the Manchurian Convention and the public Declarations of the Russian Foreign Office, has been adopted in opposition, not only to the Russian military party, to which any withdrawal from a territory once occupied is always extremely distasteful, but also to the aspirations of the Russo-Chinese Bank, and that it is not even heartily approved of by many of Count Lamsdorff's own subordinates in the Foreign Office and Russian Diplomatic Service. . . . I cannot help thinking that the theory of a confusion of authority and of a disagreement of views between different Departments of the Russian Government offers a safer explanation of the contradictions which have mystified everyone concerned. . .than any explanation tending to affix a charge of deliberate deceit and breach of faith on the Emperor and Count Lamsdorff. . . .

The Russians themselves were aware that the contradictions in their system made negotiation difficult. As the Russian press wrote:

The vacillations, inconsistencies, and obscurities so often observed in our policy are to be explained by circumstances sufficiently known to us all, but with which foreign Cabinets are unfamiliar.

Manchuria occupies the attention of three different Departments, each of which has its own views, each of which considers the question of Russian policy from a different standpoint. The Foreign Office is naturally chiefly occupied with the question of avoiding conflicts or misunderstandings with foreign Powers, and is inclined to make pacific assurances even in the cases where it is not in the power of the Department to carry them into effect and in matters wholly outside the diplomatic sphere. The War Office, on the other hand, does not see its way to withdraw its troops from a territory which is still in need of military protection, and is therefore very often compelled by the force of circumstances to resort to measures inconsistent with the assurances given by the Foreign Office. The Ministry of Finance has its attention fixed on the immense material interests involved in the Eastern Railway, and is compelled to insist on the greatest circumspection in the manner of evacuation and on the very gradual withdrawal of our forces. Where three Departments are involved, it is in the highest degree unlikely that unity of purpose or consistency in word and act should mark our policy. . . .

Throughout the history of her expansion in Asia and elsewhere Russia had been plagued by the unauthorized actions of self-styled empire builders. While the Tsarist government was prone to take advantage of some of their "conquests," it often was confronted by unexpected complications and had to disassociate itself from their actions. Thus General Gribskii on August 7, 1900 crossed the Amur River at Blagoveshchensk and after holding a "thanksgiving service" where the Manchu settlement of Sakhalian had once stood declared the region to be Russian territory. In a telegram to the Minister of War, General Grodekov stated: "Fifty years ago [Captain] Nevelskoi raised the Russian flag at the mouth of the Amur on its right bank, and laid the foundation for our possessions on that great river. Now, after hard fighting, we have taken possession of the right bank, thus consolidating the great enterprise of annexing the whole of the Amur to Russia's dominions, and making of that river an internal waterway, and not a frontier stream, whereby free and unmolested navigation of that artery through one of the vastest regions of the Empire has been secured." But while the Tsar was delighted by the "plucky action" of his troops, he eventually decided not to annex any part of Chinese territory in view of the renewal of friendly relations between Russia and China.

Similarly the controversial demands which "Russia" presented to China as condition for evacuation emanated not from the central government but from Grigorii Plancon, the Russian Chargé d'Affaires in Peking, who wanted to make a name for himself while the Russian Minister was away. In presenting the demands he not only exceeded his instructions, but achieved the opposite of what he had desired, for his action provided the powers with the excuse for intervention and gave an unintended boost to Chinese patriotism. The German Minister regarded Plancon's action as "foolish," and reported that the Russian Minister, Pavel Lessar, had been ordered back at once to his post to try to make up for the rashness of his subordinate. In the words of Mumm, Lessar "would no doubt first have to saturate the fat Manchurian morsel thoroughly with spittle, so that the Russian boa constrictor could down it smoothly and digest it without getting a political stomach-ache."

Before the conclusion of the Russo-Chinese agreement, the powers had resigned themselves to Russian domination of Manchuria as a *fait accompli*. Even Japan seemed inclined to accept a "temporary" occupation of Manchuria. As the newspaper *Nichi Nichi Shimbun* noted, Manchuria would be in a state of disorder for years, if the Russians withdrew. Given a choice between the rotten Manchu civilian administration and the strict Russian military administration, Japan would have to favor the latter as the lesser evil, even if the military occupation by Russia should last for a prolonged period of time.

The attempt to legalize Russia's position in Manchuria by a secret agreement with China was a mistake. The Russian Minister in Tokyo, Aleksandr Izvolskii (who later was to become foreign minister) realized this. As he told his German colleague, Russia's position in Manchuria was similar to that of England in Egypt.[100] She could act there as she pleased and command absolute obedience from the Chinese. What was the purpose of an agreement? It could trigger the partition of China and would only create bad blood.[101] It irritated the British, provoked the Japanese and put Germany into a difficult position. "The reason why Russia desired a formal agreement," he said, "lay essentially in a tendency that

[100]Chancellor von Bülow made the marginal comment: "correct."
[101]Bülow's comment: "yes."

prevailed in St. Petersburg and which he could not understand, to spare the Chinese. To be sure, one handled them roughly, but first one put on kid gloves so as not to offend them too much."

The *Japan Weekly Mail* called the Russian agreement with China "a curiously clumsy display of diplomacy." Instead of delaying the evacuation simply on the grounds that the Chinese were unable to protect the foreigners, the Russians bound themselves in their negotiations to evacuate in certain stages at specified dates. Thus it was a "perplexity" to the *Japan Weekly Mail* "to conceive what Russia really contemplates, or to detect any thread of wise continuity running through her whole procedure in Manchuria." The *Japan Weekly Mail* was sympathetic to Russia's expansion across the continent, so far as it had occurred in the 17th and 18th centuries. But it was alarmed by the logic of events: "To what goal her present movement will lead her, constantly expanding and gathering fresh force as it goes, no one can venture to predict. Is there any reason to suppose the Yangtze or the Yalu will stop it since the Amur and the Sungari failed to do so?"

It was the specter of Russia crossing the Yalu, that ultimately was to lead to the Russo-Japanese War, for Manchuria and Korea were linked strategically. Sharing a common frontier with Korea, Russia feared Japanese domination of the peninsula, and would not tolerate Japanese fortification of Korean harbors, lest her communication between Vladivostok and Port Arthur be endangered. "With the annexation of Manchuria the acquisition of Korea would become a geographical necessity. Japan must not have Korea," the Russian consul in Hakodate confided to a European colleague. "The po-

sition of Russia in Manchuria is regarded as a threat
to the independence of Korea. But nearby Korea. . . is
the key to Japan's *Groszmachtpolitik*,"[102] the German
Minister reported from Tokyo. "Should Russia ever
succeed in becoming master of the peninsula, the Land
of the Rising Sun would have to content itself for ever
with its islands." Sir Ernest Satow expressed the "private" view to a Japanese friend that Japan should go to
war with Russia, "for if Russia is left undisturbed in
Manchuria out of which she will never retire willingly,
she will end by taking Corea, and the position of Japan
would then be imperilled."

Russia did not want war. But the course of events
eventually swept her past the point of no return. As
d'Anethan reflected in February of 1904, following the
rupture of diplomatic relations between Japan and Russia: "During the long negotiations conducted between
Japan and Russia, we never thought of a peaceful solu-
tion, knowing that the concessions demanded of Russia
would hardly be given by her and that, on the other
hand, we had too much proof of the stubborn resolution
of Japan."

The Russo-Chinese War had not been wished by
either government. The popular upheaval which had
swept through China had forced the Russians to inter-
vene to protect their citizens and property. The effort to
restore peace and order gradually assumed the propor-
tions of full-scale war. The defeated Chinese armies
could not be left intact. Yet with their disbandment the
ranks of the brigands were swelled at the same time
that the Tartar Generals were deprived of the means of
dealing with them. Continued Russian military expedi-

[102]Policy to attain great power status.

tions became necessary. As the Russian commitment in Manchuria increased, so did the investment in blood and money. To protect her interests Russia took measures which unavoidably clashed with the interests of Japan. Left to themselves, Russia and Japan might have found a modus vivendi. But the other powers welcomed the possibility of war between the two leading Far Eastern powers and promoted it. As Francis Bertie reflected in London: "The yellow danger would be kept in check by Russia and the Russian danger by Japan."

The outbreak of war between Russia and Japan in 1904 was no surprise. Observers of many nations, including Russia, had been expecting it. But the outcome of the war was unforeseen. No one but the Japanese had believed in the defeat of Russian land forces. The over-confidence of the Russians—a factor in their refusal to negotiate seriously and thus one of the causes of the war—was due in part to the ease with which Russian troops had defeated vastly larger forces during the Russo-Chinese War. In the victory of Russia in 1900, there lay the seeds of her defeat in 1904-1905.

If the Japanese were more formidable enemies than the Chinese in those days, the Russians themselves were to be less ardent in 1904-1905 than they had been in 1900. It was to a certain extent a matter of morale. The Russo-Japanese War was the most unpopular war that Russia had ever fought. Officers and men lacked the will to win. It was different in the Russo-Chinese War. The massacres of Christians and the torture and murder of Russians and the bombardment of Russian territory by the Chinese had embued the Russian forces with fighting spirit. This spirit lasted throughout the brief conflict with China. It began to fade during the occupation. By the time the Russo-Japanese War broke out, the Russian troops in the Far East were tired of service in Manchuria. Corruption had set in. An English officer reported in November of 1903, that Russian officials and officers were living beyond their official salaries and in addition were accumulating wealth. "The direct results of this will be very soon felt when defects and deficiencies in stores and ammunition become known, and the effect of it on the campaign may be momentous," he discerned. The victories of Russia over China in 1900 were quickly forgotten, and as hundreds of books were written about the world-shaking defeat of Russia by Japan, the Russo-Chinese War was buried in history.

The Russo-Japanese War began with a surprise attack on Port Arthur and was fought over much of the same terrain as the Russo-Chinese War. Following the conflict, Manchuria was not returned to China, but was dominated by both Russia and Japan. In the 1930's Japan gained control over Manchuria and northern China. In the final stages of World War II the Russians overran Manchuria again, as swiftly as in 1900. They evacuated the region subsequently, but in the 1960's, as relations between China and the West deteriorated anew, the possibility of Manchuria becoming a battleground reasserted itself.

The occurrence of a Russo-Chinese War must not be taken as proof of a particular hatred felt by the Chinese for the Russians. In 1900, as in the 1960's, China was arrayed against most of the world. The fanatic Boxers are remembered in Communist China as "Anti-Imperialist Patriots." The words of the *Japan Weekly Mail*, written in 1900, ring true today:

The fashion at present is to abuse the Chinese, and to talk of treating them as though they had been guilty of some unpardonable crime against the civilized world. But when we sit down quietly and review the events of the past . . . years, we cannot fail to remember that what we have all chiefly wondered at was China's long-suffering, and what we have all habitually sneered at was her apparent pusillanimity and want of patriotism. She has been undergoing a kind of vivisection. Her territories have been seized on ridiculously flimsy pretexts; her ports have been "rented" virtually by force; concessions for building railways and working mines have been wrested from her whether she would or not; she has been divided up into spheres of influence by Western States just as though she were a jelly or a cheese; she has been compelled to open her doors wide to foreigners of all complexions, while foreign nations, on their side, close their doors in the face of her people for reasons which are as insulting as the fact is irksome. We have watched her suffering all this tamely, and timidly; and we have flouted her for cowardice and ridiculed her for helplessness. If, then, her people have at length been goaded to desperation; have at length risen to assert their manhood and their patriotism, have we whose custom is to ridicule their submissiveness any right now to censure their wrath?

But if the Chinese wrath is directed against the White Man in general, Russia in the 1960's as in 1900 is the only Western Power directly subject to invasion by China. The thoughts penned by a Russian resident of Blagoveshchensk in 1900 are shared by some of his countrymen today. "In general this unexpected war, which began and ended so strangely," Kirkhner wrote, "forces one to stop and think what is concealed deep in the soul of our yellow-faced neighbor and what serious enemy he can make, if he be trained and armed European-style and be given good commanders and generals." Kirkhner recalled how the Chinese had prepared for war while professing friendship. "This gives reason to say that one must not rely too much on the peaceful feelings and assurances of the peaceful Chinese and should be more careful."

Bibliography

The story of the Russo-Chinese War has never before been related in detail. While the Spanish-American War was perhaps the best covered war in history, not a single newspaper man accompanied the armies of either side in Manchuria. Nor were the published eyewitness accounts widely known. Most of them were printed in the Russian Far East. Except for one or two, they are not available in any American library.

This account of the Russo-Chinese War has been reconstructed primarily from Russian diaries, memoirs, reports and letters, found in the collections of the Library of the University of Helsinki (once a depository library of the Russian Empire), the M. E. Saltykov-Shchedrin State Public Library and the Library of the Academy of Sciences in Leningrad and the Lenin Public Library in Moscow. Every effort was made to locate corresponding Chinese sources, but all that was found in Chinese proved marginal. Only one Chinese article and one Chinese compilation of documents dealt with the general topic at some length, and even they did not describe the military operations in detail. German, French, Belgian, British and American documents were consulted also, but their accounts of the war in Manchuria were based on Russian reports. Newspapers were scanned for opinions and propaganda. Except for Russian papers, published in Blagoveshchensk, Port Arthur and Khabarovsk, which contained official proclamations and eyewitness accounts, newspapers were not used as sources of factual information. As the German Minister wrote from Peking on July 1, 1903: "East Asia is the most fertile soil for wild rumors, that I have seen so far in my diplomatic career, and the local press is, if possible, even less conscious of its responsibility in the spread of *Tartaren-*

nachrichten [Tartar or false news] than ours in Europe." Foreign
views of the war and of Russian aims have been confined primarily to the chapters on the struggle for Ying-k'ou and the pacification of Manchuria and the epilogue. The sources from which
most information was drawn are marked with an asterisk.

Thanks are due to the Inter-University Committee on Travel
Grants, which enabled the author to pursue his research in the
Soviet Union, the Finnish and Russian librarians and professors
who provided microfilm copies of the desired material, and to
the American Council of Learned Societies, the Social Science
Research Council, and the American Philosophical Society, which
financed their acquisition. The author is indebted also to the
directors and staff of the Zentralbibliothek der Bundeswehr in
Düsseldorf, the Public Record Office in London, the Belgian Foreign Ministry Archives, the Chinese collection of the Hoover
Library on War, Revolution and Peace, and the Chinese Materials and Research Aids Service Center of the Association for
Asian Studies on Taiwan for providing him with copies of
related research material. He is grateful to the Florida State
University Research Council for assisting in the purchase of
some of the sources and to the History Department for providing
him with time to peruse them. He acknowledges the typing
wizardy of his faithful assistant, Mrs. Tony Walker.

Russian names have been romanized according to the Library
of Congress system, Chinese names according to the Wade-Giles
system. Manchurian place names have been rendered in accordance with maps and gazeteers of the United States Army Map
Service and the United States Board on Geographic Names.

Adams, Brooks. "Russia's Interest in China," *Atlantic Monthly*,
  Vol. LXXXVI (September, 1900), pp. 309-17.
*Aip, *Shtabs-kapitan*. *Vozstanie v Kitae i podvigi russkikh
  voisk na Dal'nem Vostoke* (The uprising in China and the
  feats of the Russian forces in the Far East). St. Petersburg,
  1901.
*Akhsharumov, S. *Nashi Geroi na Dal'nem Vostoke, 1900-1901*
  (Our heroes in the Far East). St. Petersburg, 1903.
Amurskii Krai. Blagoveshchensk, 1900-1903.
Asakawa, Kanichi. *The Russo-Japanese War*. Boston, 1904.

Asiaticus. *Die Kämpfe in China* (The battles in China). A series of six pamphlets. Berlin, 1900-1901.

Avraamii, *Ierom.* "Pekinskoe sidenie" (The Peking siege), *Khristianskoe chtenie,* January 1901, pp. 65-112.

B., F. *Voina Kitaia s Khristianskimi narodami 1900 goda* (The war of China with the Christian peoples of 1900). Tver, 1900.

Badmaev, P. A. *Rossiia i Kitai* (Russia and China). St. Petersburg, 1905.

Barrett, John. "Manchuria Bone of International Contention," *Harper's Weekly,* vol. XLV, No. 2313 (April 20, 1901), p. 414.

Belgium, Ministry of Foreign Affairs. "Correspondence Politique. Legations. Japon." Unpublished dispatches.

*Beveridge, Albert J. *The Russian Advance.* New York, 1903.

Bigham, Clive. *A Year in China 1899-1900.* London, 1901.

Brodskii, R. M. *Amerikanskaia ekspansiia v severo-vostochnom Kitae 1898-1905* (American expansion in northeast China 1898-1905). Lvov, 1965.

Buksgevden, A. *Russkii Kitai. Ocherki diplomaticheskikh snoshenii Rossii s Kitaem* (Russian China. Outlines of Russia's relations with China). Port Arthur, 1902.

*C.-M., Major (comp.). *Die Kämpfe der russischen Truppen in der Mandschurei im Jahre 1900* (The battles of the Russian troops in Manchuria in 1900). Leipzig, 1901.

Canera, Carl. *Deutschlands Kämpfe in Ostasien dem deutschen Volke erzählt* (Germany's battles in East Asia narrated to the German people). Munich, 1902.

Casserly, Captain Gordon. *The Land of the Boxers or China under the Allies.* New York, 1903.

Chang, Tao-hsing. *International Controversies over the China Eastern Railway.* Shanghai, 1936.

Cheminon, J. and G. Fauvel-Gallais, *Les Événements Militaires en Chine* (The military events in China). Paris, 1902.

Ch'ing-chi wai-chiao shih-liao (Historical material on the foreign relations of the Ch'ing dynasty), vol. 5. (Peiping, 1932-33).

Ch'ing shih kao (Draft history of the Ch'ing Dynasty), volumes 1 and 2 (Peiping, 1928).

Christie, Dugold. *Thirty Years in Moukden, 1883-1913.* London, 1914.

Clark, Rev. Francis E. "A New Way Around the World," *Harper's Weekly,* March 30, April 1 and April 13, 1901.

Clyde, Paul Hibbert. *International Rivalries in Manchuria, 1689-1922.* Columbus, 1928.

Curey, M. C. "Russie et Chine en 1900 [Russia and China in 1900]," *Revue d'Artillerie,* vol. 57 (Oct. 1900-Mar. 1901) [Paris, 1900], pp. 486-518.

Demchinskii, Boris. *Rossiia v Manchzhurii (po neopublikovannym dokumentam)* (Russia in Manchuria [on the basis of unpublished documents]). St. Petersburg, 1908.

Deutsch, Leo. *Sixteen Years in Siberia. Some Experiences of A Russian Revolutionist.* Translated by Helen Chisholm. London: John Murray, 1903.

Deutschland in China 1900-1901 (Germany in China 1900-1901). Authored by participants of the expedition, illustrated by combat artist Rocholl, with contributions by Adolph Obst and others. Düsseldorf, 1902.

Dillon, E. J. "The Chinese Wolf and the European Lamb," *The Contemporary Review,* vol. LXXIV (January, 1901), pp. 1-31.

——————, "Micawberism in Manchuria," *The Contemporary Review,* vol. LXXIX (May, 1901), pp. 649-65.

Dix, Lieutenant C. C. *The World's Navies in the Boxer Rebellion.* London, 1905.

Dang, Feng Djen. *The Diplomatic Relations between China and Germany since 1898.* Shanghai, 1936.

*Doroguntsev, Petr. "Tiazhelye dni Kharbina [Difficult days of Harbin]," *Priamurskiia Vedomosti* 1900, No. 352, pp. 13-16.

Douglas, Alexis. *Le Siège de Tien-tsin 15 Juin-15 Juillet 1900.* (The siege of Tientsin June 15 to July 15, 1900). Paris, 1903.

Downs, Charles L. "The Russo-Chinese War of 1900 and the Blagoveshchensk Massacre in Periodical Literature," MS, History Seminar paper, The Florida State University, 1964.

Drentel'n, *Shtabs-kapitan.* "Pesnia Amuru [Song to the Amur]," *Priamurskiia Vedomosti* 1901, No. 374, pp. 11-12.

Dukhovetskii, F. A. "Siniaia kniga o Man'chzhurskom dogovore [The Blue Book about the Manchurian treaty]," *Russkii Vestnik,* July 1902, pp. 342-354.

Eckardstein, Hermann, Baron von. *Ten Years at the Court of St. James 1895-1905*. Translated and edited by George Young. New York, 1922.

Efimov, G. "Imperialisticheskaia interventsiia 1900-1901 v Kitae i bokserskoe vosstanie" (Imperialist intervention in China 1900-1901 and the Boxer uprising), *Istoricheskii Zhurnal*, 1938, No. 4 (April), pp. 63-75.

*Elets, Iu. L. *Amurskaia geroinia. Pri osade Blagoveshchenska Kitaitsami* (An Amur heroine. At the siege of Blagoveshchensk by the Chinese). Moscow, 1901.

*――――. *Nasha sila. Podvigi russkikh voinov, grazhdan i zhenshchin v posledniuiu kitaiskuiu voinu* (Our strength. Heroic deeds of Russian warriors, citizens and women in the last Chinese war). 3rd edition, Moscow, 1901.

*――――. *S trupami. Epizod iz pekinskago siden'ia* (With the troops. An episode from the Peking siege). Moscow, 1901.

*――――. *Smert' idet!* (*Osvobozhdenie Russkim otriadom episkopa, 23 sviashchennikov i 3000 khristian Vostochnoi Mongolii v posledniuiu Kitaiskuiu voinu*) (Death marches! [The liberation by a Russian detachment of a bishop, 23 priests and 3000 Christians of Eastern Mongolia in the recent Chinese war]). Moscow, 1901.

Entsiklopedicheskii Slovar' (Encyclopedia). St. Petersburg: F. A. Brockhaus and I. A. Efron, 1890-1907. 82 vols. plus 4 suppl. vols.

*Ermakov, I. "Pis'mo russkomu soldatu na dal'nii vostok, v Kitai, ot ikh tovarishcha iz S.-Peterburga [Letter to the Russian soldier to the Far East, to China, from their comrade from St. Petersburg]," *Priamurskiia Vedomosti* 1902, No. 422.

France, Ministère des Affaires Etrangères. *Documents Diplomatiques Francais, 1871-1914* (French Diplomatic Documents, 1871-1914). 2nd. ser. Paris, 1931.

――――. *Documents Diplomatiques: Chine, 1899-1900* ("Livres Jaunes"). Paris, 1900.

――――, *Documents Diplomatiques: Chine, 1900-1901* ("Livres Jaunes"). Paris, 1901.

Franke, Otto. *Die Groszmächte in Ostasien von 1894 bis 1914* (The great powers in East Asia from 1894 to 1914). Braunschweig, 1923.

Fursenko, A. A. *Bor'ba za razdel Kitaia i Amerikanskaia doktrina otkrytykh dverei 1895-1900* (The struggle for the partition of China and the American open door doctrine 1895-1900). Moscow, 1956.

Germany, Admiralstab der Marine. *Die Kaiserliche Marine während der Wirren in China 1900-1901* (The Imperial Navy during the disturbances in China, 1900-1901). Berlin, 1903.

*Germany, Auswärtiges Amt, Abtheilung A. "Akten betreffend: die Mandschurei [Documents concerning: Manchuria]," China 25. Microfilms of German Archival Materials before 1918 as captured and held at Whaddon Hall, England. London 1954-1957, reels 119-120.

............, "Chinas Verhältnis zu Ruszland" (China's Relations with Russia), reels 74-75; and "Manchuria, Russische Anneigungen" (Manchuria, Russian attraction) reels 119-21.

Germany, Auswärtiges Amt. *Die Chinawirren und die Mächte 1900-1902* (The China disturbances and the Powers 1900-1902) (vol. 16 of *Die Grosse Politik der Europäischen Kabinette 1874-1914* [The great policy of the European cabinets 1871-1914]). Berlin, 1924.

Geroi nashi na Dal'nem Vostoke 1900-1901. Al'bom rissunkov (Our heroes in the Far East 1900-1901. Album of drawings). St. Petersburg, 1903.

Glinskii, B. B. *Prolog russko-iaponskoi voiny* (Prologue of the Russo-Japanese War). St. Petersburg, 1916.

Gorelik, S. B. *Politika SShA v Man'chzhurii v 1898-1903gg. i doktrina "otkrytykh dverei"* (The policy of the United States in Manchuria in 1898-1903 and the Open Door doctrine). Moscow, 1960.

Golovachev, P. *Rossiia na Dal'nem Vostoke* (Russia in the Far East). St. Petersburg, 1904.

*Great Britain, Foreign Office. *Confidential Correspondence and Papers, China* (Confidential Prints), vols. 91-150 . London, 1900-1904.

Grekov, Major General M. I. *Na Dal'nii Vostok. Pokhodnyia pis'ma* (To the Far East. Campaign letters). St. Petersburg, 1901.

Grom russkikh pobed v Kitae. (Razgrom "Bol'shogo Kulaka")

(The thunder of Russian victories in China. [The crushing of the "Big Fist"]), Moscow, 1900.

*Grudzinskii, Sergei. "Vospominaniia o man'chzhurskikh bezporiadkakh [Recollections of the Manchurian disorders]," *Priamurskiia Vedomosti* 1901, Nos. 374-76, 378, 380, 382, 391-92.

Hosie, Alexander. *Manchuria Its People, Resources and Recent History.* New York, 1904.

Hummel, Arthur W. *Eminent Chinese of the Ch'ing Period (1644-1912).* Washington, 1943-44. 2 vols.

*Ianchevetskii, D. "Ot Tunchzhou do Pekina [From Tungchow to Peking]," *Priamurskiia Vedomosti* 1900, No. 350, pp. 16-17.

*—————. "Posledniia izvestiia iz Kitaia [Latest news from China]," *Priamurskiia Vedomosti* 1900, No. 350, pp. 17-18.

—————. *U sten nedvizhnago Kitaia. Dnevnik Korrespondenta "Novago Kraia" na teatre voennykh deistvii v Kitae v 1900 g.* (At the walls of immobile China. Diary of the correspondent of *Novyi Krai* in the theater of operations in China in 1900). St. Petersburg, 1903.

Illustrated London News, vol. CXVII, Sept. 1, 1900. p. 304.

Ivachev, I. P. "Bor'ba s khunkhuzami na man'chzhurskoi granitse [The struggle with the hunghutze [bandits] on the Manchurian border], *Istoricheskii Vestnik* 1900, October, pp. 177-206, Nov., pp. 538-64.

*Ivanov, I. E. *Ocherki pokhodno-boevoi zhizni vo vremia bokserskago vozstaniia v 1900 godu. Iz dnevnika komandira 2-i roty 1-go Vostochno-Sibirskago strelkovago Ego Velichestva polka* (Sketches of the military campaign life during the Boxer Rebellion in 1900. From the diary of the commander of the 2nd Company of the 1st East Siberian Rifle Regiment of His Majesty). Moscow, 1907.

*—————. *Vpechatleniia iz Voenno-Pokhodnoi zhizni za vremia okkupatsii Manchzhurii v 1900-1903 gg.* (Impressions from the military campaign life during the occupation of Manchuria in 1900-1903). St. Petersburg, 1907.

"Iz chastnago pis'ma ob osade bokserami posol'stv v Pekine [From a private letter about the siege of the Legations in

Peking by the Boxers]," *Priamurskiia Vedomosti* 1900, No. 354, pp. 18-19.

*"Izvlechenie iz telegramm o deistviiakh nashikh voisk v Man'- chzhurii vo 2-i polovine marta i nachale aprelia 1901 goda [Excerpts from telegrams about the actions of our forces in Manchuria in the second half of March (old style) and the beginning of April (old style) 1901],"*Priamurskiia Vedomosti* 1901, No. 382, pp. 2-4.

Japan, Gaimusho. *Nihon gaiko monjo* (Diplomatic documents of Japan), vol. 33 (40-42) (*Hokushin jihen* [North China in- cident]). Tokyo, 1956-57.

The Japan Weekly Mail, 1900-1903.

*K. K. (Konstantin Kushakov ?). "Deistvie iuzhnago otriada okhrannoi strazhy [Action of the southern detachment of the (railway) guard]," *Novyi Krai* 1900, Nos. 89-135.

Kent, Percy Horace. *Railway Enterprise in China.* London, 1907.

Khvostov, A. "Russkii Kitai, nasha pervaia Koloniia na Dal'nem Vostoke [Russian China, our first colony in the Far East]," *Vestnik Evropy,* vol. XXXVII, No. 5 (September-October 1902), pp. 653-696.

Khvostov, V. M. *Istoriia diplomatii* (History of diplomacy), vol. II (1871-1914). Moscow, 1963.

*Kirkhner, A. V. *Osada Blagoveshchenska i vziatie Aiguna* (The siege of Blagoveshchensk and the taking of Aigun). Blagoveshchensk, 1900.

Kitaiskaia Vostochnaia zheleznaia doroga. *Severnaia Man'- chzhuriia i Kitaiskaia Vostochnaia zheleznaia doroga* (North Manchuria and the Chinese Eastern Railway). Harbin, 1922.

*Korostovets, I. Ia. *Rossiia na Dal'nem Vostoke* (Russia in the Far East). Peking, 1922.

Korsakov, V. V. *Pekinskiia sobytiia. Lichnyia vospominaniia uchastnika ob osade v Pekine, mai-avgust 1900 goda* (Peking events. Personal reminiscences of a participant in the siege of Peking, May-August 1900). St. Petersburg, 1901.

Kosaka, Masataka. "Ch'ing Policy over Manchuria (1900-1903)," *Papers on China* (East Asian Research Center, Harvard Uni- versity), vol. 16 (1962), pp. 126-53.

*Krasnov, Petr Nikolaevich. *Bor'ba s Kitaem. Populiarnyi ocherk stolknoveniia Rossi s Kitaem v 1901 godu* (The struggle with China. A popular account of the clash of Russia with China in 1901). St. Petersburg, 1901.

Krausse, Alexis. *China in Decay.* London, 1900.

Kropotkin, Petr Alekseevich. "Russian Interest in China," *Forum,* vol. 31 (May, 1901).

*Kushakov, Captain Konstantin. *Iuzhno-manchzhurskie bezporiadki v 1900 godu* (The South Manchurian disorders in 1900). Askhabad, 1902.

Kutuzov, Count Petr Arkad'evich. *Zhelatel'nyia osnovy russko-kitaiskago soglasheniia* (Desirable bases for a Russo-Chinese agreement). St. Petersburg, 1900.

*Kuznetsov, Pavel. *Man'chzhurskoe vozstanie v 1900 godu. (Dnevnik ochevidtsa)* (The Manchurian uprising in 1900. [Diary of an eyewitness]). St. Petersburg, 1901.

*L., M. "Iz st. Stretenskoi v Blagoveshchensk. (Iz putevykh vpechatlenii) [From Stretenskaia Station to Blagoveshchensk. (Travel impressions)]," *Priamurskiia Vedomosti* 1900, No. 352.

Langer, William L. *The Diplomacy of Imperialism, 1890-1902.* New York, 1935. 2 vols.

*Lavretskii, M. "Otryvok iz vospominanii sotennago komandira [Excerpt from the memoirs of a sotnia commander]," *Priamurskiia vedomosti* 1900, No. 356, pp. 12-51.

Legras, Jules. "La Mandchourie russe [Russian Manchuria]," *Revue des Deux Mondes,* vol. X (1902), pp. 115-158.

Lensen, George Alexander (ed.). *Korea and Manchuria between Russia and Japan 1895-1904. The Observations of Sir Ernest Satow, British Minister Plenipotentiary to Japan (1895-1900) and China (1900-1906).* Tallahasee, 1966.

_____ (ed.). *Russia's Eastward Expansion.* Englewood Cliffs, N. J., 1964.

Levi, Werner. *Modern China's Foreign Policy.* Minneapolis, 1953.

*"Liao-ian [Liao-yang]," *Novyi Krai,* July 18 (5), 1900.

Lopez, Gerald Arthur. "The Russians in Newchwang," MS, History Seminar Paper, The Florida State University, 1964.

Lung, Chang. *La Chine a l'aube du XXe, siècle. Les relations diplomatiques de la Chine avec les puissances depuis la guerre sino-japonaise jusqu'à la guerre russo-japonaise* (China at the dawn of the twentieth century. The diplomatic relations of China with the powers from the Sino-Japanese War to the Russo-Japanese War). Paris, 1962.

Malozemoff, Andrew. *Russian Far Eastern Policy 1881-1904. With Special Emphasis on the Causes of the Russo-Japanese War.* Berkeley, 1958.

Mamola, Clara Zebroski. "Newchwang and the Powers, 1858-1906," MS, MA thesis, The Florida State University, August, 1965.

*Manaev, Colonel. "Kopiia raporta komandira 6-go vostochno-sibirskago strelkovago polka, polkovnika Manaeva, koman-duiushchemu voiskami priamurskago voennago okruga, ot 8-go sentiabria 1901 g. No. 48 [Copy of the report of the commander of the 6th East Siberian rifle regiment, Colonel Manaev, to the commander of the forces of the Priamur Military District, of September 8 (21), 1901, No. 48]," *Priamurskiia Vedomosti,* 1901, No. 403, pp. 17-20.

McCarthy, Michael J. F. *The Coming Power. A Contemporary History of the Far East 1898-1905.* London, 1905.

*Merzhanov, L. "Pis'ma iz Man'chzhurii [Letters from Manchuria]," *Priamurskiia Vedomosti* 1901, Nos. 383, 386, 393.

Morse, H. B. *The International Relations of the Chinese Empire,* vol. 3 *(The Period of Subjection 1894-1911).* Shanghai, 1918.

Müller, Alfred von. *Die Wirren in China und die Kämpfe der verbündeten Truppen* (The disturbances in China and the battles of the allied troops). Berlin, 1902. 2 vols.

*Murzhak, M. "Napadenie kitaiskago otriada na pristan' San'-sin, razgrom i sozhzhenie eia, otstuplenie russkikh na barzhu *Chibis* i dal'neishee otstuplenie vniz po r. Sungari" (Attack of a Chinese detachment on the San-hsing dock, its defeat and burning, the withdrawal of the Russians onto the barge *Chibis* and further withdrawal down the Sungari river), *Priamurskiia Vedomosti* 1900, No. 350, pp. 14-16.

Myshlaevskii, A. *Voennyia deistviia v Kitae 1900-1901* (Military action in China 1900-1901), St. Petersburg, 1905.

The New York Times, 1900-1903.

Nish, I. H. "Japan's Indecision During the Boxer Disturbances," *The Journal of Asian Studies,* vol. XX, No. 4 (August, 1961), pp. 449-61.

Northend, Benjamin. "Russia in the East," *Munsey,* vol. XXV (1901), pp. 364-75.

Novye russkie vladeniia na Krainem Vostoke. (Kvantunskaia oblast') (The new Russian possessions in the Far East. [The Kwantung region]). St. Petersburg, 1902.

Novyi Krai. Port Arthur, 1900-1903.

Orlov, General Nikolai A. "Srazhenie pri Iakshi" (The battle near Iakshi), *Istoricheskii Vestnik,* vol. LXXXIV (May, 1901), pp. 603-627.

――――――. "Srazhenie pri Onguni [The battle near Ongun]," *Istoricheskii Vestnik,* vol. LXXXIV (April, 1901) pp. 137-162.

――――――. Zabaikal'tsy v Manchzhurii v 1900 godu. Ocherki iz pokhoda Khailarskago Otriada Generala N. A. Orlova v Kitae v 1900 g. (Transbaikal Cossacks in Manchuria in 1900. Sketches from the campaign of the Khailar Detachment of General N. A. Orlov in China in 1900). St. Petersburg, 1901.

――――――. "Zaniatie Hailara v 1900 g. [The Occupation of Hailar in 1900]," *Istoricheskii Vestnik,* vol. LXXXV (October, 1901), pp. 98-139.

Pavolodin, P. L. *Kitai i sovremennaia kitaisko-evropeiskaia bor'ba* (China and the contemporary Chinese-Europeon conflict). Moscow, 1900.

"Pis'ma iz Pechiliiskago otriada [Letters from the Pechihli detachment]," *Priamurskiia Vedomosti* 1900, No. 348, pp. 12-15 and No. 371, pp. 16-18.

Playfair, G. M. H. *The Cities and Towns of China. A Geographical Dictionary.* Second edition. Shanghai, 1910.

Podrobnyia izvestiia (s pechal'nymi telegrammami) o voine Rossii s Kitaem (Detailed news [with sad telegrams] about the war of Russia with China). Moscow, 1911.

Pokotilov, D. D. Dnevnik s 2-go po 31-oe avgusta 1900 goda (Diary from August 2 [15] to 31 [September 13] 1900). St. Petersburg, 1900.

Popov, A. (ed.). "Bokserskoe vosstanie [The Boxer uprising]," *Krasnyi Arkiv,* 1926, vol. I (14), pp. 1-49.

Pozdneev, D. M. "Bokserskoe dvizhenie kak etap osvoboditel'-noi borby v Kitae [The Boxer Movement as a stage in the Chinese liberation movement]," *Zvezda,* vol. X (1925), No. 4, pp. 156-172.

Pozdneev, Dimitrii. *56 dnei pekinskago siden'ia, v sviazi s bli-zhaishimi k nemu sobytiiami pekinskoi zhizni. Razskaz ochevidtsa* (56 days of Peking siege, in connection with closely related events of Peking life. The account of an eyewitness). St. Petersburg, 1901.

Priamurskiia Vedomosti. Khabarovsk, 1900-1903.

Purcell, Victor. *The Boxer Uprising. A Background Study.* Cambridge, 1963.

Pyn Min (P'eng, Ming). *Istoriia Kitaisko-sovetskoi druzhby* (The History of Chinese-Soviet friendship). Translated from the Chinese by A. F. Katova. Moscow, 1959.

Ramband, Alfred. "Expansion of Russia," *International Quarterly,* September, 1900, pp. 212-251; October, 1900, pp. 342-61.

"Rasprostranenie kitaiskago miatezha ot Telina k Kharbinu (Razkaz ochevidtsa) [Spread of the Chinese uprising from T'ieh-ling to Harbin (The account of an eyewitness)]," *Priamurskiia Vedomosti* 1900, No. 346, pp. 9-20.

Rauch, Fedor von. *Mit Graf Waldersee in China. Tagebuchaufzeichnungen* (With Count Waldersee in China. Diary entries). Berlin, 1907.

Read, Sheridan P. "Russia in North China," *The Independent,* vol. LIII, No. 2726 (February 28, 1901), pp. 486-89.

*Reeves, Captain James H. "Report of Present Conditions in Manchuria," MS, dated U. S. Legation, Peking, China, January 2, 1902.

Rich, Norman. *Friedrich von Holstein. Politics and Diplomacy in the Era of Bismarck and Wilhelm II.* Cambridge, 1965. 2 vols.

Rich, Norman and M. H. Fisher. *The Holstein Papers. The Memoirs, Diaries and Correspondence of Friedrich von Holstein.* Cambridge, 1955-63. 4 vols.

Rockhill, William W. *Report of William W. Rockhill, Late Commissioner to China, with Accompanying Documents.* Washington, 1901.

*Rodinov, Podporuchik. "Iz zhurnala voennykh deistvii 3-i

sotni argunskago polka zabaikal'skago kazach'iago voiska [From the journal of military action of the 3rd sotnia of the Argun regiment of the Transbaikal Cossack forces]," *Priamurskiia Vedomosti* 1901, No. 379, pp. 17-18.

Romanov, B. A. *Rossiia v Man'chzhurii (1892-1906)* (Russia in Manchuria [1892-1906]). Leningrad, 1928.

Rosen, Oscar. "German-Japanese Relations, 1894-1902: A Study of European Imperialism in the Far East," Microfilm of doctoral dissertation, University of Wisconsin, 1956.

Rudakov, A. V. *Obshchestvo I-kho-tuan i ego znachenie v poslednikh sobytiiakh no Dal'nem Vostoke* (The I-ho-t'uan Society and its meaning in the latest events in the Far East). Vladivostok, 1901.

Runich, Sergei. *V Man'chzhurii* (In Manchuria). St. Petersburg, 1904.

Russia, Army, Glavnoe upravlenie General'nago shtaba. *Sbornik materialov po Kitaiu i bor'be s miatezhnym dvizheniem "Bol'shikh Kulakov" 1898-1900 g.g.* (Collection of materials concerning China and the struggle with the insurgent movement of the "Large Fists" [Boxers] 1898-1900). St. Petersburg, 1900.

_____, Glavnyi shtab. *Sobranie materialov o voennykh deistviiakh i politicheskom polozhenii zagranitsei* (Collection of materials about military actions and political conditions abroad). St. Petersburg, 1900-1902.

*_____, Voenno-uchennyi Arkhiv. *Materialy dlia opisaniia voennykh deistvii v Kitae v 1900-1901 g.g.* (Material for description of military action in China in 1900-1901), "Confidential," part I (Reports of the Minister of War to the Emperor), St. Petersburg, 1902-1908. 8 vols.

Russia. Ministerstvo Inostrannykh Del. *Sbornik dogovorov i diplomaticheskikh dokumentov po delam Dal'niago Vostoka 1895-1905 g.g.* (Collection of treaties and diplomatic documents regarding the Far East 1895-1905). St. Petersburg, 1906.

Russia, Ministry of Ways of Communication. *Guide to the Great Siberian Railway.* Edited by A. I. Dmitriev-Mamonov and A. F. Zdiarski, English translation by Miss L. Kukol-Yasnopolsky, revised by John Marshall. St. Petersburg, 1900.

Russia, Voenno-Morskoe Ministerstvo Soiuza SSSR. *Morskoi Atlas* (Naval Atlas). Moscow, 1950. 3 vols.

A Russian Publicist. "Russia and the 'Open Door,'" *The Contemporary Review,* vol. 79 (February, 1901), pp. 184-194.

Russkie geroi v Kitae (Russian heroes in China). Moscow 1900. Reprinted from *Moskovskie Vedomosti,* No. 164, June 16 [29], 1900.

Sakharov, Lieutenant General. *Polozhenie russkikh voisk, naznachennykh dlia podavleniia bezporiadkov v Kitae* (k 10 noiabria 1900 goda) (Position of the Russian forces, assigned for the suppression of the disorders in China [on November 10, 1900]). No place, no date.

Sakharov, Secretary (transl.). "Perevod nadpisi na pamiatnike-kamne, postavlennom v gorode Ningute v chest' zaslug g. voennago gubernatora Primorskoi oblasti general-leitenanta Chichagova [Translation of the inscription on the monument erected in the city of Ninguta in honor of the services of Lieutenant-General Chichagov, military governor of the Maritime Province]" *Priamurskiia Vedomosti,* 1910, No. 381, insert after p. 6.

Sbornik Gazety "Amurskii Krai." Stat'i o voennykh sobytiiakh na Amure, pomeschchennyia v gazete s 1-go iulia po 1-e avgusta 1900 goda (Collection of the newspaper "Amurskii Krai" [Amur Region]. Articles about military happenings on the Amur, published in the newspaper from July 1 [14], to August 1 [14], 1900). Blagoveshchensk, 1900.

Scheibert, Major J. *Der Krieg in China 1900-1901 nebst einer Beschreibung der Sitten, Gebräuche und Geschichte des Landes* (The war in China 1900-1901 together with a description of the customs, habits and history of the land). Berlin, 1901. 2 vols.

Seltzer, Leon E. (ed.). *The Columbia Lippincott Gazetteer of the World.* New York, 1962.

Shteinfel'd, Nikolai. *Russkoe delo v Man'chzhurii s 17 veka do nashikh dnei* (The Russian enterprise in Manchuria from the 17th century to our days). Harbin, 1910.

*Sil'nitskii, A. (ed.). "Rasprostranenie kitaiskago miatezha ot Telina k Kharbinu. (Razskaz ochevidtsa) [The spread of the Chinese rebellion from T'ieh-ling to Harbin. (Account of an eyewitness)]," *Priamurskiia Vedomosti* 1900, No. 346, pp. 9-20.

Skachkov, P. E. and V. S. Miasnikov (eds.). *Russko-kitaiskie otnosheniia 1869-1916. Ofitsial'nye dokumenty* (Russo-Chinese relations 1689-1916. Official documents). Moscow, 1958.

Sokolova, A. "Vospominanie o pogrome v Man'chzhurii po linii KVZHD v. 1898 g." (Recollections about the pogrom in Manchuria along the line of the Chinese Eastern Railway in 1898). *Istoricheskii Vestnik* 1906, October, pp. 81-106; November, pp. 424-446; December, pp. 810-828.

Stepanov, N. I. *Vosem' mesiatsev v pokhode. (Ocherki minuvshei kitaiskoi ekspeditsii)* (Eight months in the field. [Sketches of the bygone Chinese expedition]). Harbin, 1907.

Strelok [rifleman]. "Pokhod v Man'chzhuriiu. Vospominaniia strelka 19-go vostochno-sibirskago strelkovago polka [The campaign to Manchuria. Recollections of a rifleman of the 19th East Siberian rifle regiment]," *Priamurskiia Vedomosti* 1901, Nos. 381, 395, 396, 399.

Suvirov, N. I. *Mandzhuriia. Eia naselenie, bogatstvo i rol' v sobytiiakh na Dal'nem Vostoke, predshestvovavshikh Russko-Iaponskoi voine* (Manchuria. Her population, riches and role in Far Eastern events, preceding the Russo-Japanese War). St. Petersburg, 1904.

Tan, Chester C. *The Boxer Catastrophe.* New York, 1955.

Teplov, V. "Problemy Dal'nego Vostoka [Problems of the Far East]," *Russkii Vestnik,* November, 1903, pp. 382-433 and January, 1904, pp. 414-455.

Tien, H. C., Ronald Hsia and Peter Penn. *Gazetteer of China.* Hong Kong, 1961.

The *Times,* London, 1900-1903.

Treat, Payson J. *Diplomatic Relations between the United States and Japan 1895-1905.* Stanford, 1938.

Ukhtomskii, Prince Esper. *Iz Kitaiskikh pisem* (From Chinese letters). St. Petersburg, 1901.

Ular, Alexander. "Russia, Manchuria, and Mongolia," *Contemporary Review,* vol. LXXXIV, August 1903, pp. 189-208.

Bibliography

Ular, Alexandre. *A Russo-Chinese Empire*. Westminster, 1904.

United States, Corps of Engineers, Army Map Service. *Gazetteer to AMS 1:250,000 Maps of Manchuria* (AMS Series L 542). Washington, 1955.

United States, Department of the Interior. *China. Official Standard Names approved by the United States Board on Geographic Names*. Washington, D. C.: 1956. 2 vols.

*United States, Department of State (National Archives microfilms). "Consular Despatches, Newchwang," 1900-1903.

..............., "Diplomatic Despatches, China," 1900-1903.

..............., "Diplomatic Despatches, Russia," 1900-1903.

United States, House of Representatives, Papers Relating to the Foreign Relations of the United States, with the Annual Message of the President transmitted to Congress December 2, 1902. Washington, 1903.

United States War Department, Adjutant General's Office. *Notes on China*. (Publication No. XXX.) Washington, 1900.

..............., *Reports on Military Operations in South Africa and China*. (Publication No. XXXIII.) Washington, 1901.

*V. "Blagoveshchenskaia 'utopiia.' (Rasprava s kitaitsami v Blagoveshchenske v 1900 g.) [The Blagoveshchensk 'utopia' (drowning). (Massacre of the Chinese in Blagoveshchensk in 1900)]," *Vestnik Evropy*, vol. XLV, No. 7 (July, 1910), pp. 231-241.

Vereshchagin, A. V. *Na voine. Razskazy ochevidtsev 1900-1901 g.* (In the war. Stories of eyewitnesses of 1900 to 1901.) St. Petersburg, 1902.

..............., *Russkiie v Man'chzhurii. Razskazy o poslednem Kitaiskom pokhode v 1900 g.* (Russians in Manchuria. Accounts of the last Chinese campaign in 1900). St. Petersburg, 1904.

"Vesti iz Portartura [News from Port Arthur]," *Priamurskiia Vedomosti* 1900, No. 338, pp. 13-14. Reprinted from *Novyi Krai*, No. 58.

*Vetlitsin, P. "V tylu iuzhno-man'chzhurskago otriada [In the rear of the South Manchurian Detachment]," *Priamurskiia Vedomosti* 1901, Nos. 402 and 404.

Vitte, Count S. Iu. *Vospominaniia* (Memoirs). Moscow, 1860. 3 vols.

*Vrublevskii, Lieutenant Colonel. "Vziatie kitaiskago piketa i sileniia Koushen na pravom beregu reki Amura, protiv kazach'ei stanitsy Radde, 11 iulia 1900 g. [The taking of the Chinese picket and the settlement Koushen on the right bank of the Amur River, opposite the Cossack village of Radde, July 11 (24), 1900]," *Priamurskiia Vedomosti* 1901, No. 375. *Vsepoddaneishyi doklad po povodu sobytii, proiskhodivshikh v 1900 godu v Kitae* (Most devoted report about the events occurring in China in 1900).

*Waite, Carleton Frederick. *Some elements of international military cooperation in the suppression of the 1900 anti-foreign rising in China with special reference to the forces of the United States.* (The University of Southern California School of Research Studies No. 12) Los Angeles, 1935.

Waldersee, Alfred, Count von. *A Field-Marshal's Memoirs: From the Diary, Correspondence, and Reminiscences of Alfred Count von Waldersee.* Condensed and translated by Frederic Whyte. London, 1924.

Weale, B. L. Putnam. *Manchu and Muscovite. Being Letters from Manchuria Written during the Autumn of 1903.* New York, 1904.

Webster, J. "The Sifting Time in Manchuria," *Chinese Recorder and Missionary Journal,* vol. XXXII, No. 9 (September, 1901), pp. 423-35.

Weigh, Ken Shen. *Russo-Chinese Diplomacy.* Shanghai, 1928.

White, John Albert. *The Diplomacy of the Russo-Japanese War.* Princeton, 1964.

Winterhalder, Theodore Ritter von. *Eine Darstellung der Wirren und der Betheiligung von Österreich-Ungarns Seemacht an ihrer Niederwerfung in den Jahren 1900-1901* (An account of the disturbances and the participation of the sea power of Austria-Hungary in their suppression in the year 1900-1902). Vienna, 1902.

*Wright, G. Frederick. "The Breach Between Russia and China," *The Nation,* vol. 71, No. 1839 (September 27, 1900), p. 247.

──────────, "The Irrepressible Conflict in the East," *The Nation,* vol. 74, No. 1914 (March 6, 1902), pp. 187-88.

_____, "Russian Rights in Manchuria," *The Nation*, vol. 76, No. 1977 (May 21, 1903), pp. 411-13.

_____, "The Russian Problem in Manchuria," *The American Monthly Review of Reviews*, vol. XXIV, No. 1 (July, 1901), pp. 60-67.

Wrochem, Hans v. *Erinnerungen eines "Chinesen"* (Recollections of a "Chinese"). Gr. Lichterfelde, Berlin, 1910.

Wu, Hsiang-hsiang. *O ti ch'in-lüeh chung-kuo shih* (The history of Russian encroachment on China), Taipeh, 1953.

Yang, Ju. *Chung O hui shang chiao shou tung san sheng tien pao hui ch'ao* (Copies of telegrams regarding the Russo-Chinese negotiations on the return of the Three Eastern Provinces). Peking, 1935.

*Yang, Shao-chên. "Kêng-tzu nien Chung-O tsai Tung-san-shêng chih ch'ung-t'u chi ch'i chieh-kuo [Sino-Russian hostilities in the Three Eastern Provinces in 1900 and their aftermath]." *Ch'ing-hua hsüeh-pao*, vol. IX (1934), pp. 69-126.

Zabel, Rudolf. *Deutschland in China* (Germany in China). Leipzig, 1902.

Zabriskie, Edward Henry. *American-Russian Rivalry in the Far East. A Study in Diplomacy and Power Politics, 1895-1914.* Philadelphia, 1946.

Zhukov, E. M. (ed.). *Mezhdunarodnye otnosheniia na dal'nem vostoke 1870-1945 gg.* (International relations in the Far East 1870-1945). Moscow, 1951.

Index